Hamburger!!!

GEGE AKUTAMI published a few short works before starting *Jujutsu Kaisen*, which began serialization in *Weekly Shonen Jump* in 2018.

JUJUTSU KAISEN

VOLUME 14
SHONEN JUMP MANGA EDITION

BY GEGE AKUTAMI

TRANSLATION Stefan Koza
TOUCH-UP ART & LETTERING Snir Aharon
DESIGN Joy Zhang
EDITOR John Bae
CONSULTING EDITOR Erika Onabe

Printed in Italy

Published by VIZ Media, LLC
P.O. Box 77010
San Francisco, CA 94107

10 9 8 7 6 5
First printing, February 2022
Fifth printing, August 2024

viz.com

JUJUTSU KAISEN

14

THE SHIBUYA INCIDENT —RIGHT AND WRONG—

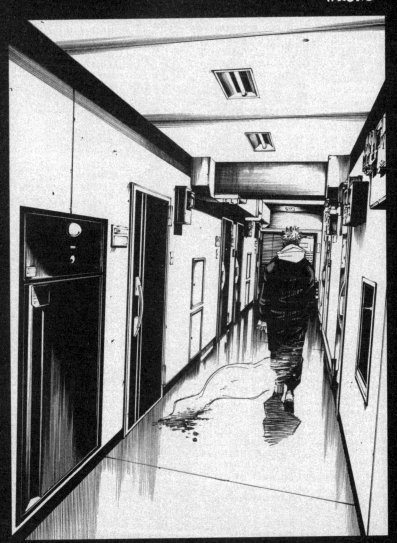

STORY AND ART BY GEGE AKUTAMI

JUJUTSU KAISEN
CAST OF CHARACTERS

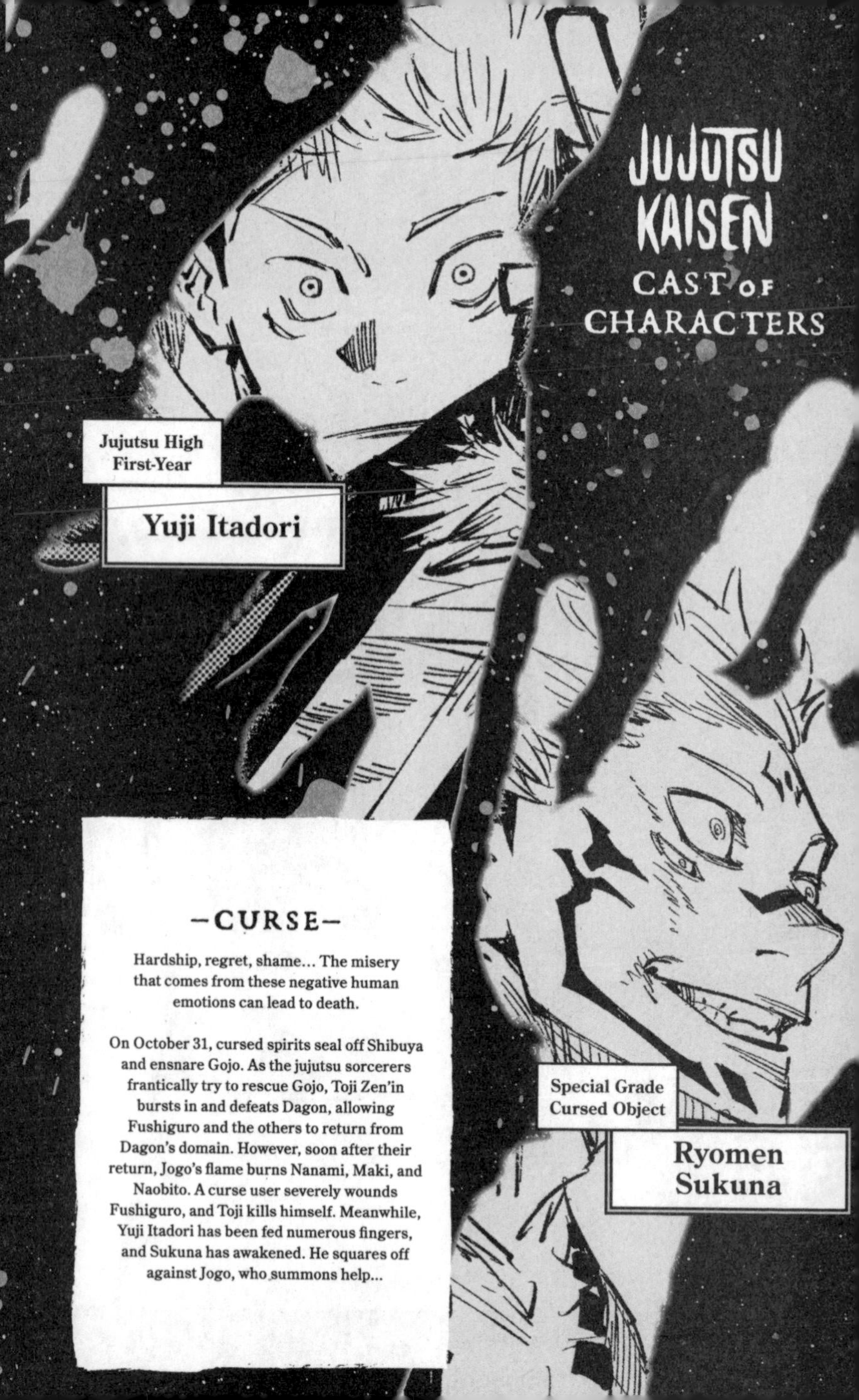
Jujutsu High First-Year
Yuji Itadori
Special Grade Cursed Object
Ryomen Sukuna

—CURSE—

Hardship, regret, shame... The misery that comes from these negative human emotions can lead to death.

On October 31, cursed spirits seal off Shibuya and ensnare Gojo. As the jujutsu sorcerers frantically try to rescue Gojo, Toji Zen'in bursts in and defeats Dagon, allowing Fushiguro and the others to return from Dagon's domain. However, soon after their return, Jogo's flame burns Nanami, Maki, and Naobito. A curse user severely wounds Fushiguro, and Toji kills himself. Meanwhile, Yuji Itadori has been fed numerous fingers, and Sukuna has awakened. He squares off against Jogo, who summons help...

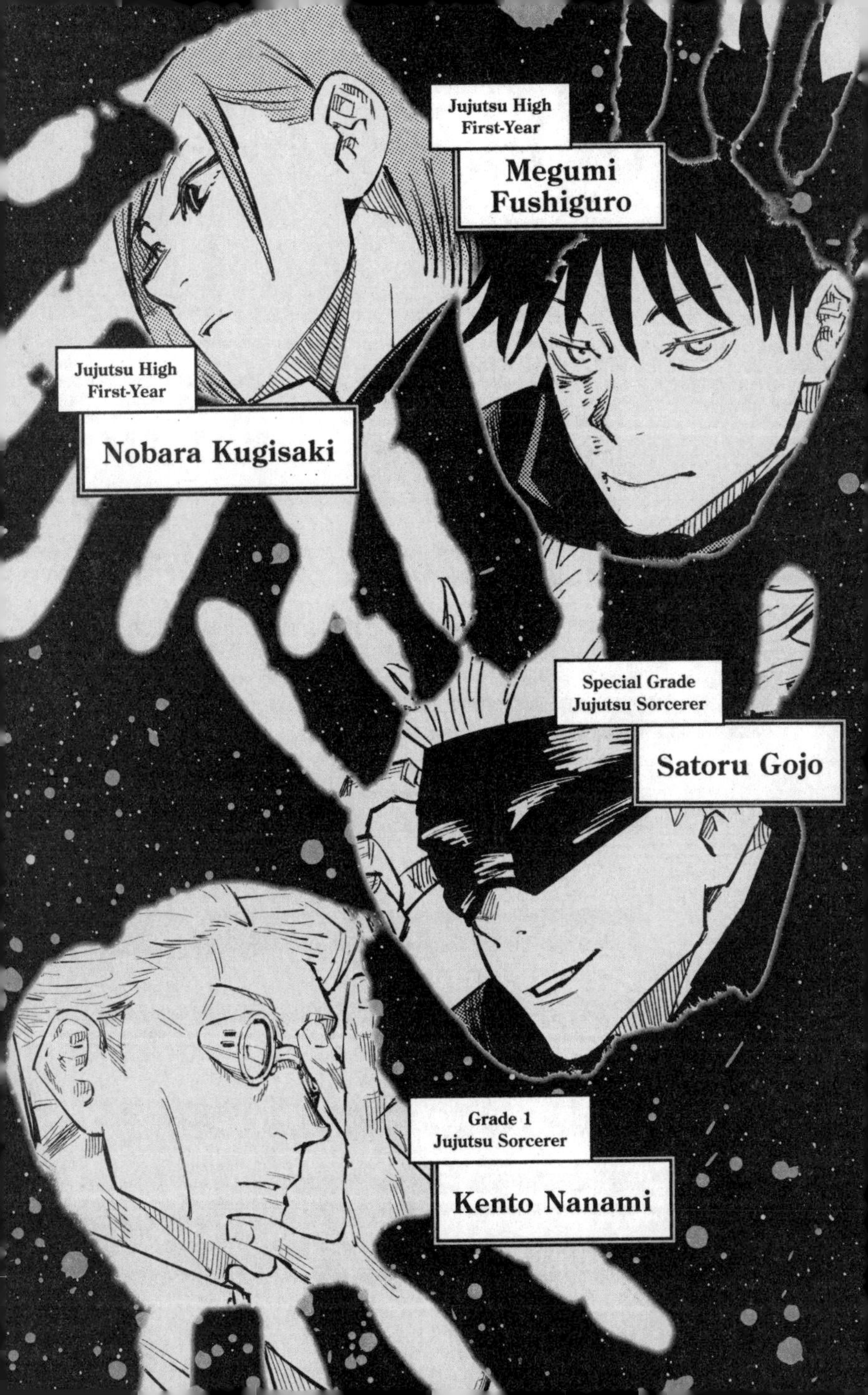
Jujutsu High
First-Year
Megumi
Fushiguro
Jujutsu High
First-Year
Nobara Kugisaki
Special Grade
Jujutsu Sorcerer
Satoru Gojo
Grade 1
Jujutsu Sorcerer
Kento Nanami

JUJUTSU KAISEN

14

THE SHIBUYA INCIDENT —RIGHT AND WRONG—

CHAPTER 116: THE SHIBUYA INCIDENT, PART 34

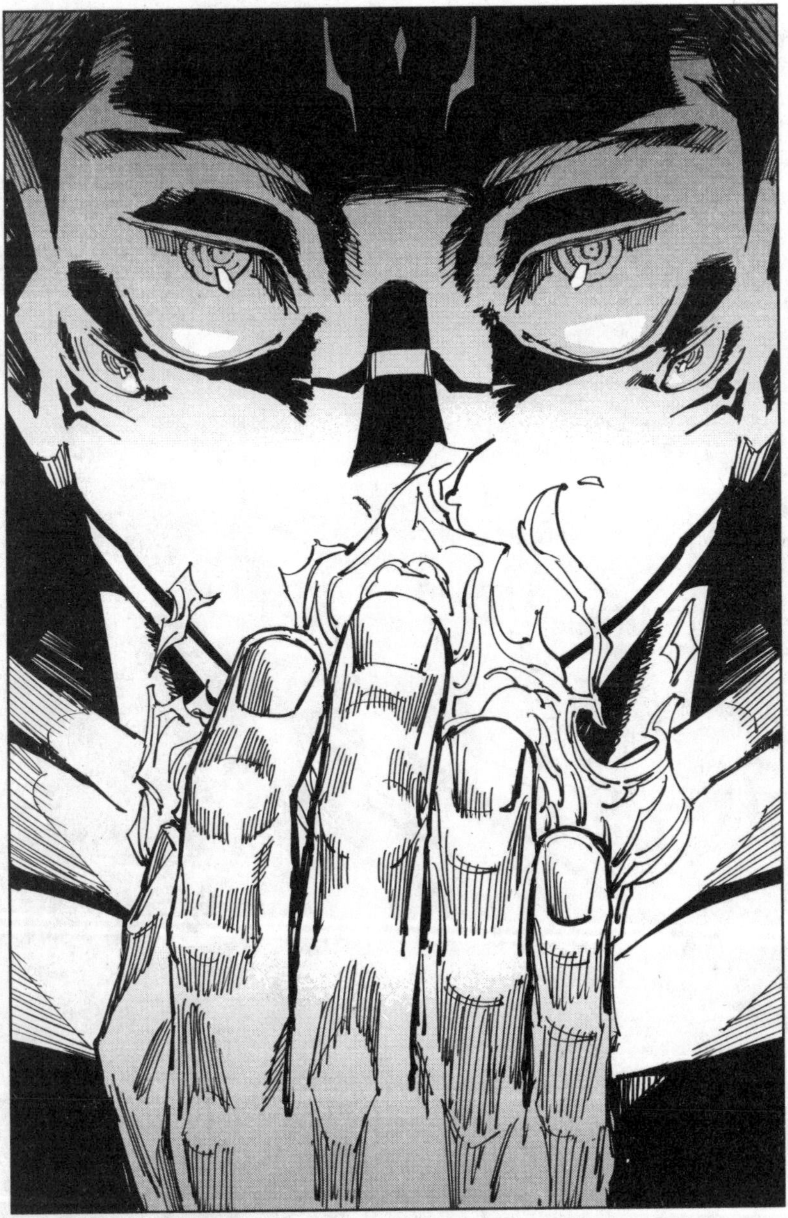

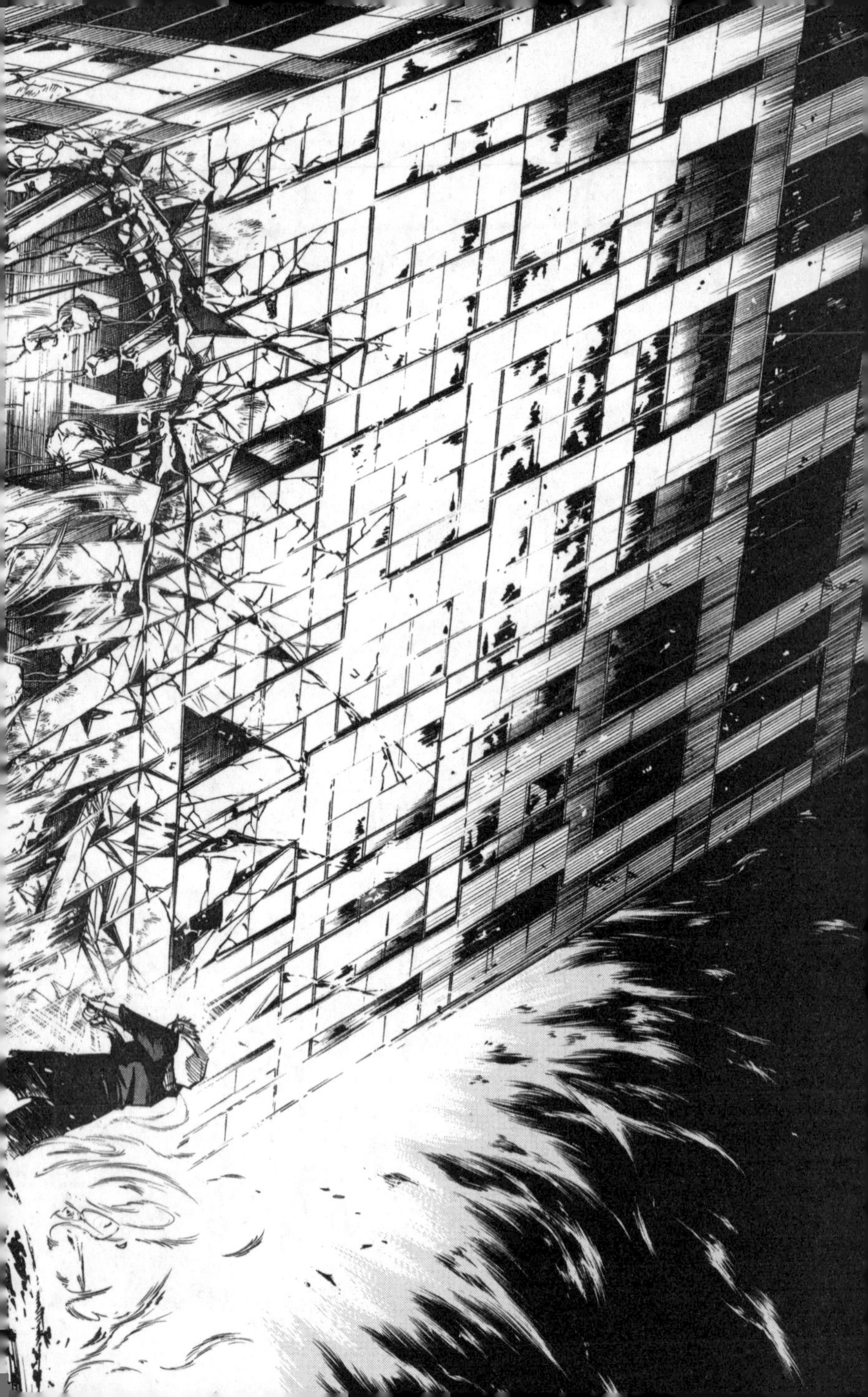

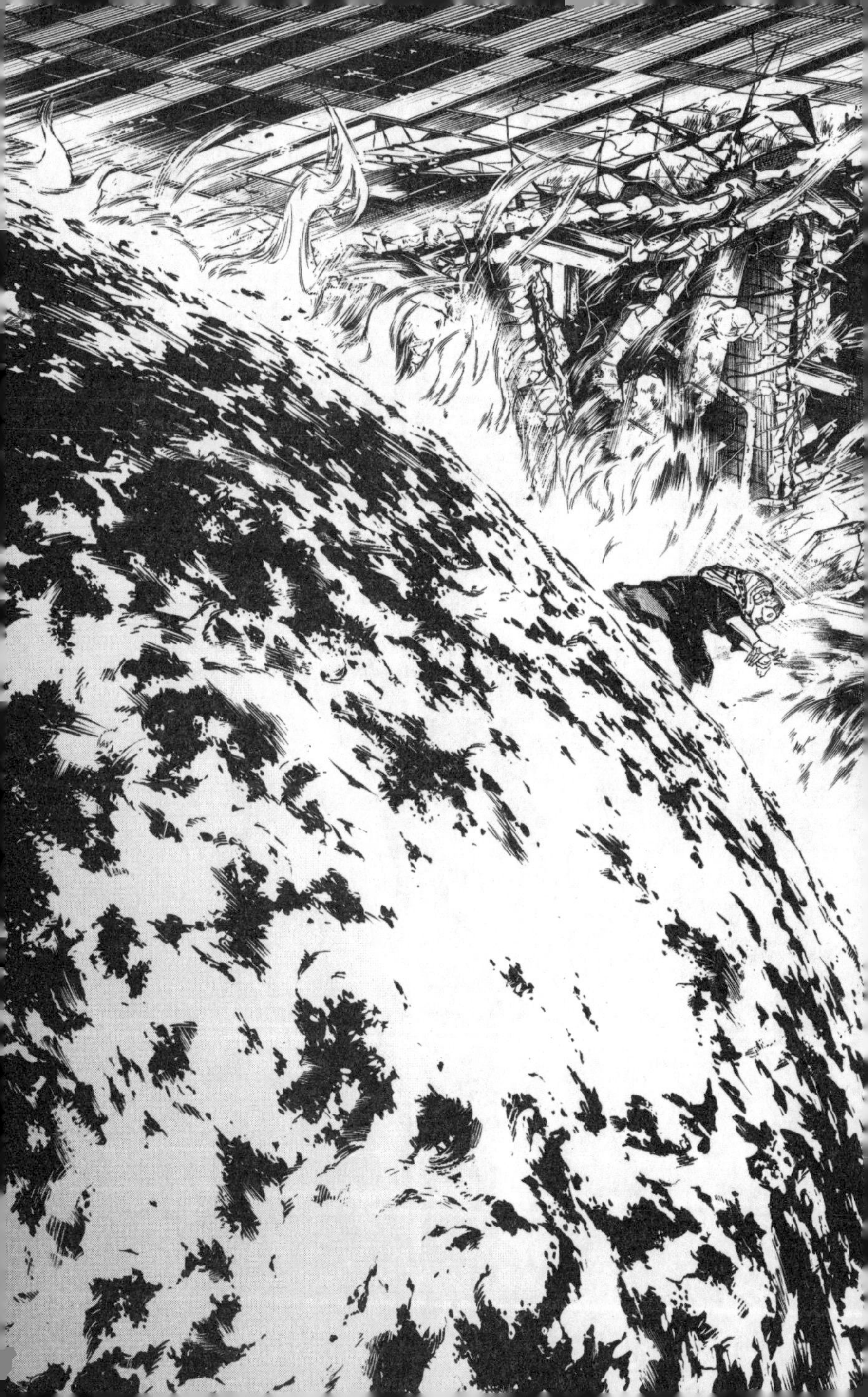

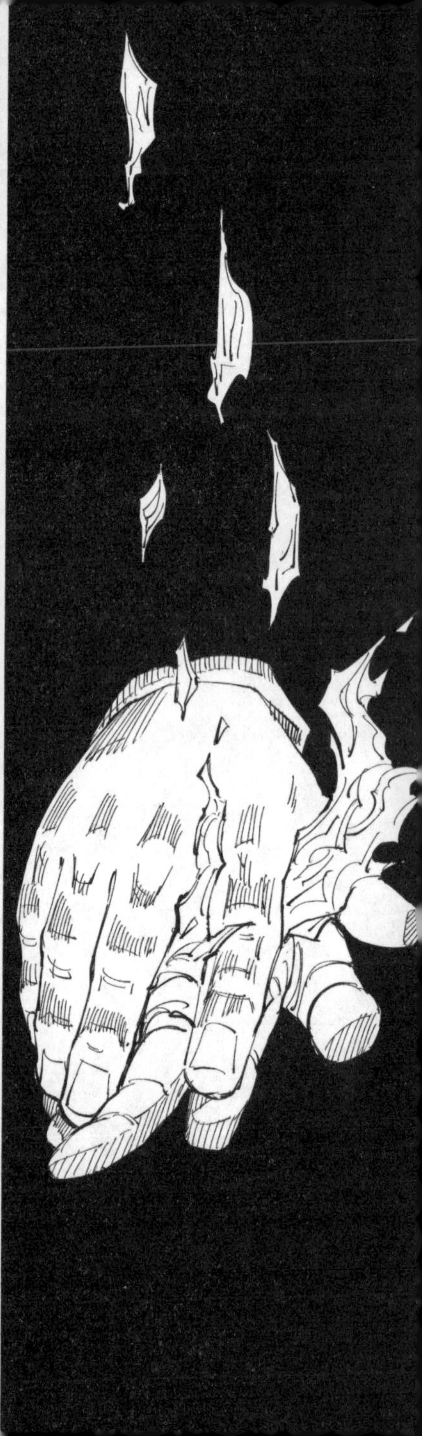
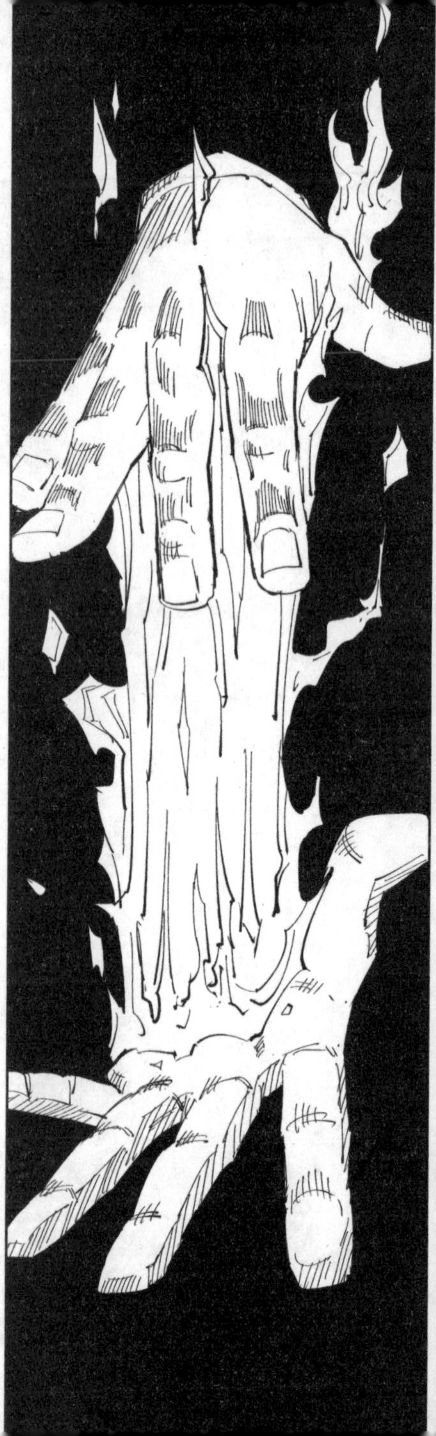

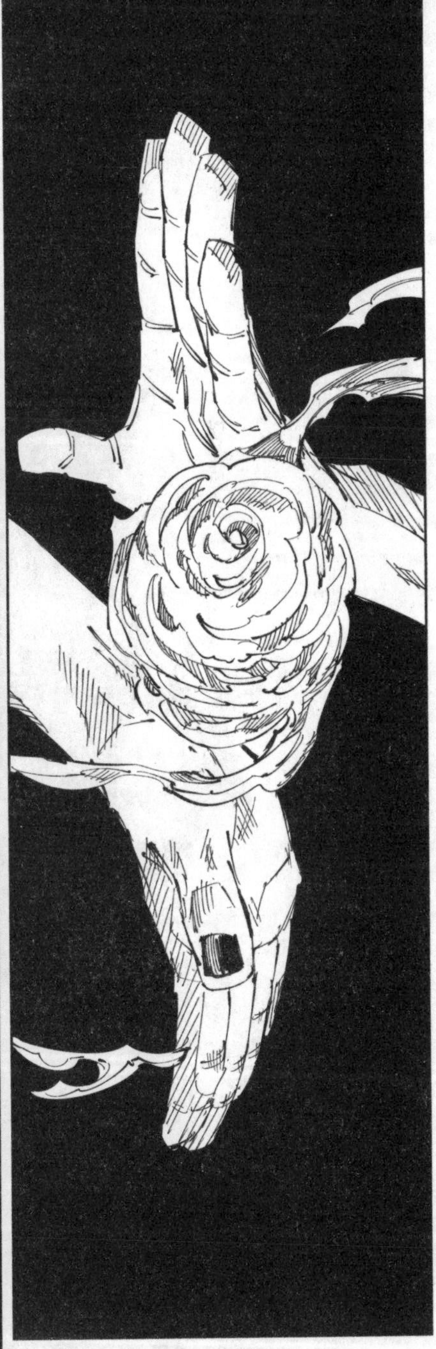
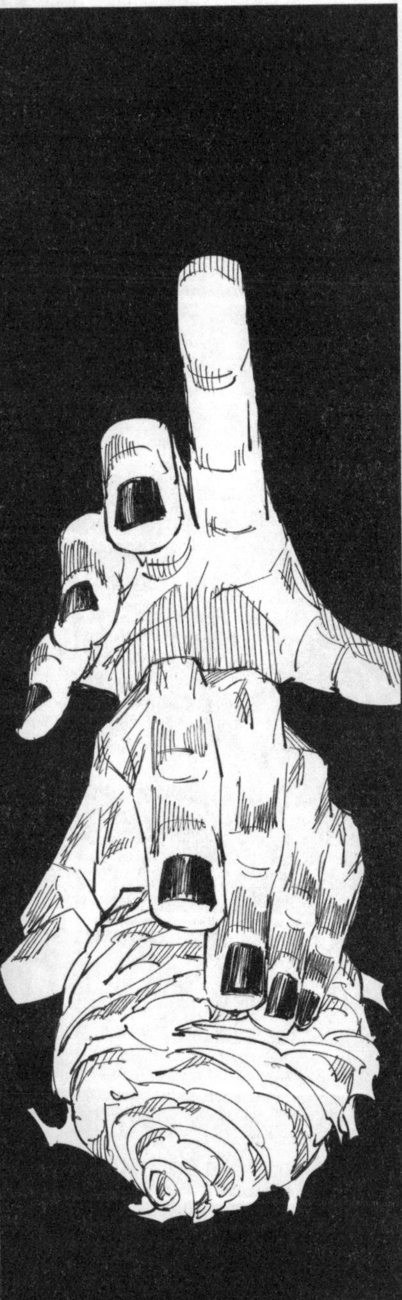

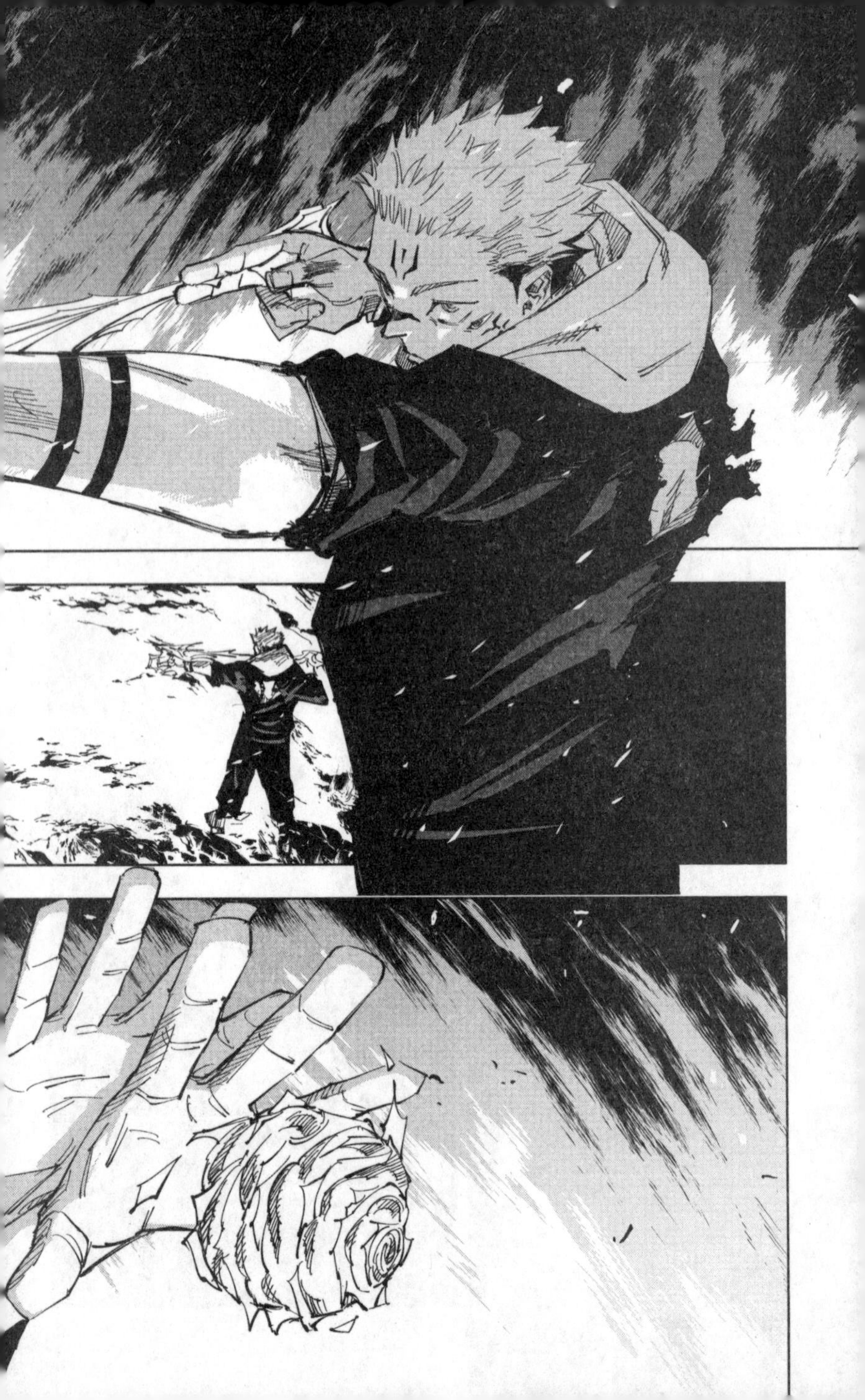

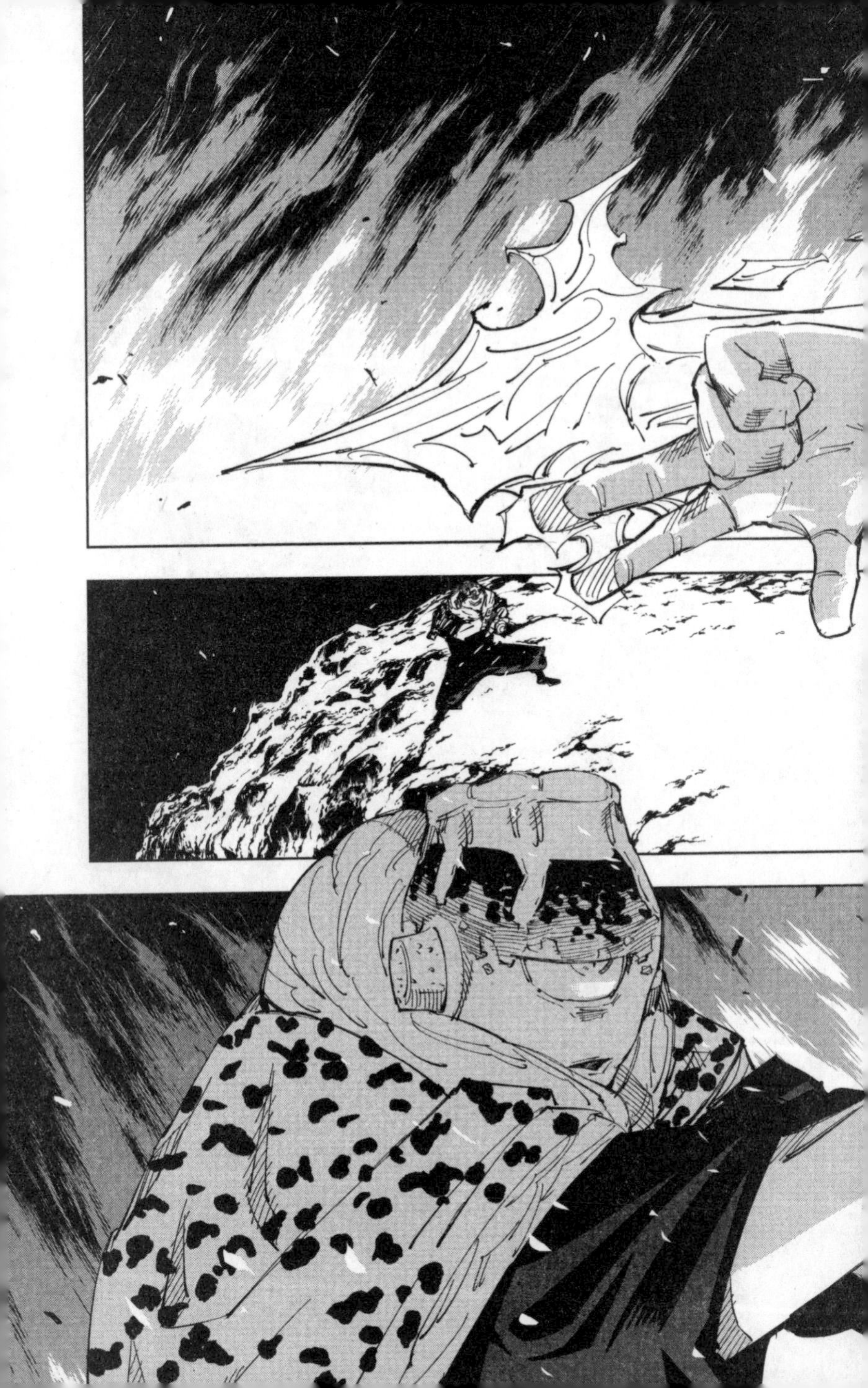

HANAMI.

DAGON.

SORRY.

B WOO...

...IS STILL ALIVE.

MAHITO...

DEATH IS SOMETHING *HUMANS* FEAR AND DETEST.

HOWEVER, *HUMANS* LINGER BEYOND IT AS WELL.

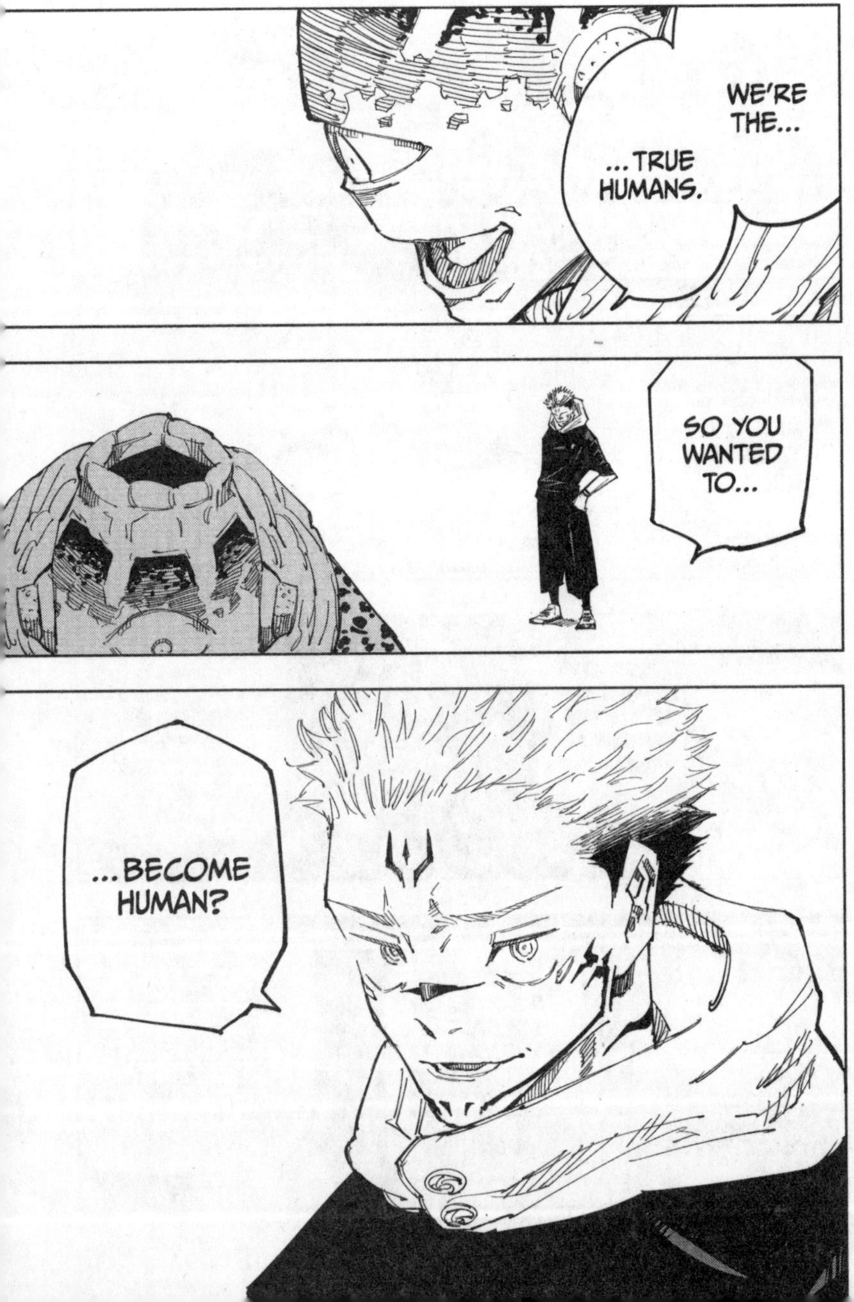
WE'RE THE...
...TRUE HUMANS.
SO YOU WANTED TO...
...BECOME HUMAN?

NOT BECOMING A HUMAN *LITERALLY.* MORE LIKE TAKING THEIR PLACE, RIGHT?

YEAH, YEAH... I KNOW WHAT YOU MEAN.

...IT MAKES IT ALL THE MORE FOOLISH.

THAT SAID...

COMPARING THEMSELVES TO THOSE AROUND THEM...

...LEADS TO WEAKNESS AND STUNTS THEIR GROWTH.

HUMANS FLOCKING TOGETHER. CURSES FLOCKING TOGETHER.

BUT YOU LACKED THE *HUNGER* TO TAKE HOLD OF YOUR DESIRES.

TO REACH THE HEIGHTS OF SATORU GOJO AND NOT WORRY ABOUT YOUR FUTURE OR IDENTITY.

YOU SHOULD HAVE BURNT EVERYTHING YOU DESIRED TO A CINDER.

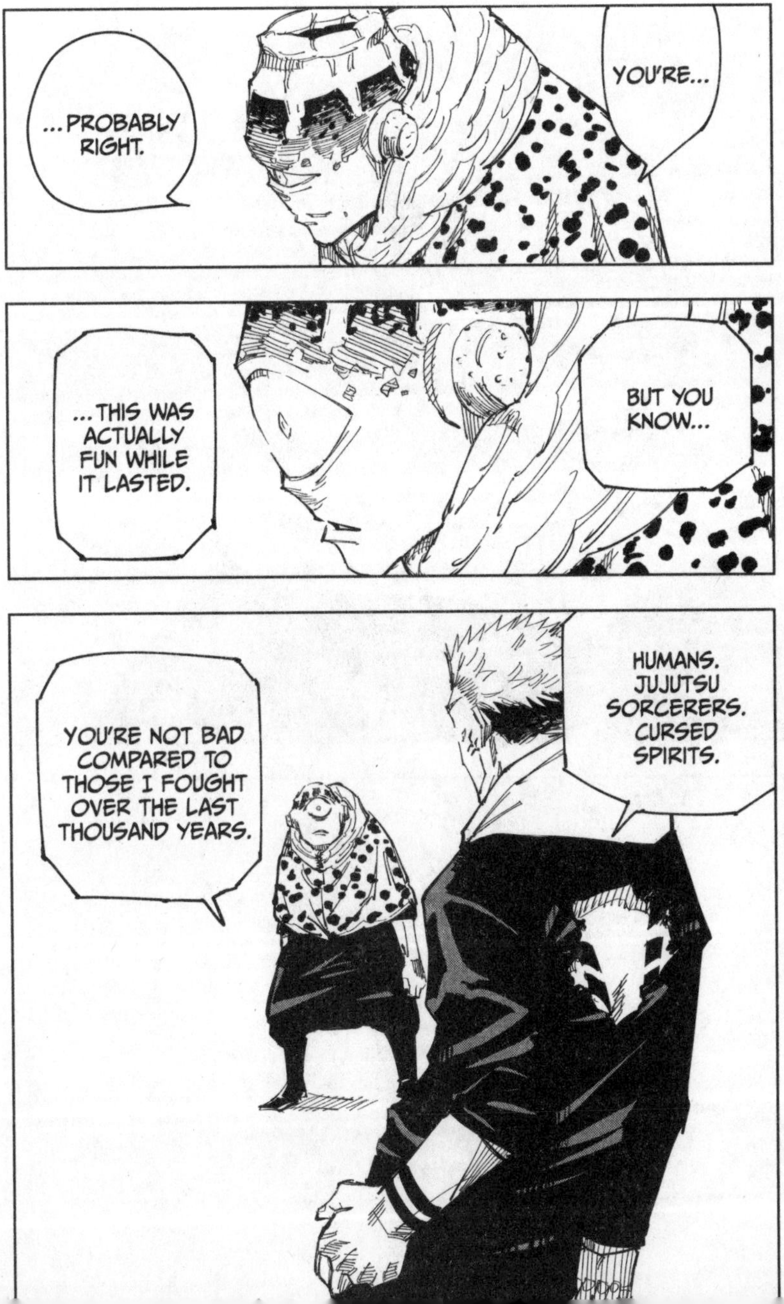
YOU'RE...
...PROBABLY RIGHT.
BUT YOU KNOW...
...THIS WAS ACTUALLY FUN WHILE IT LASTED.
HUMANS. JUJUTSU SORCERERS. CURSED SPIRITS.
YOU'RE NOT BAD COMPARED TO THOSE I FOUGHT OVER THE LAST THOUSAND YEARS.

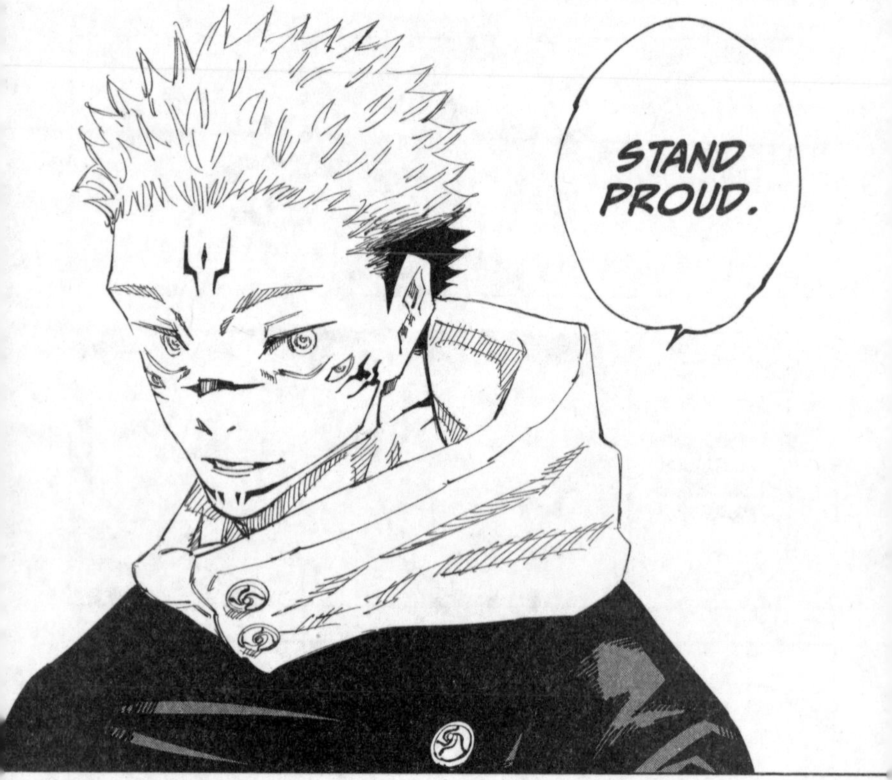
STAND PROUD.
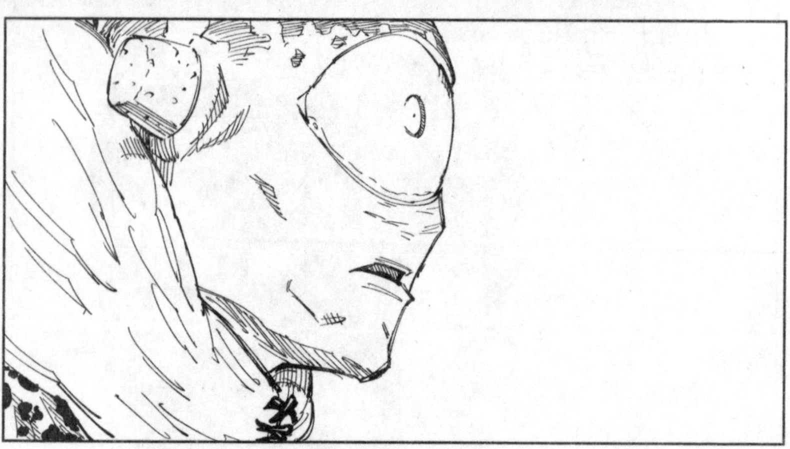

DON'T ASK ME.

I DON'T KNOW WHAT THAT IS EITHER.

THMP

MASTER SUKUNA.

I'VE COME TO ESCORT YOU.

KKAKL
KKAKL

WHO ARE YOU?

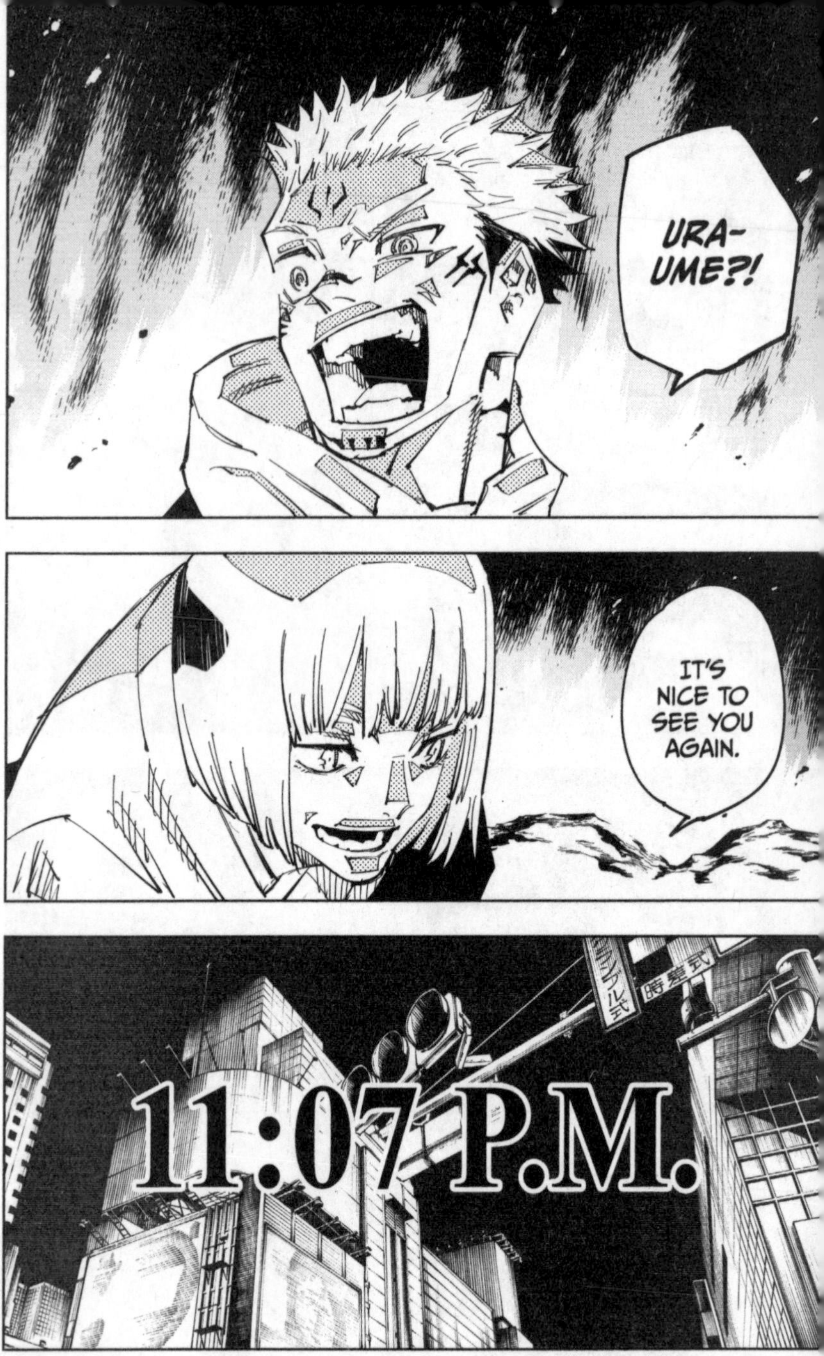
URA-UME?!
IT'S NICE TO SEE YOU AGAIN.
時差式
11:07 P.M.

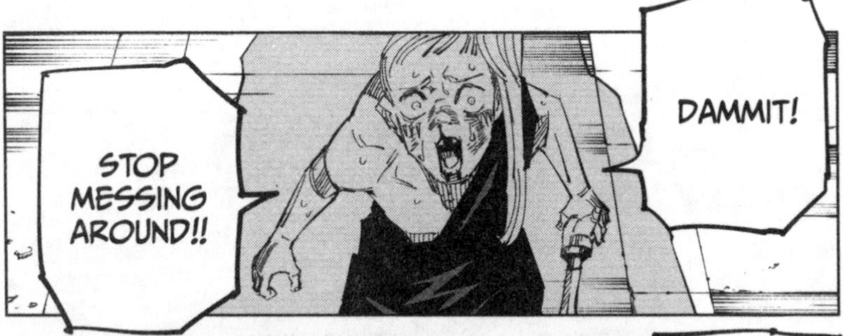
DAMMIT!
STOP MESSING AROUND!!
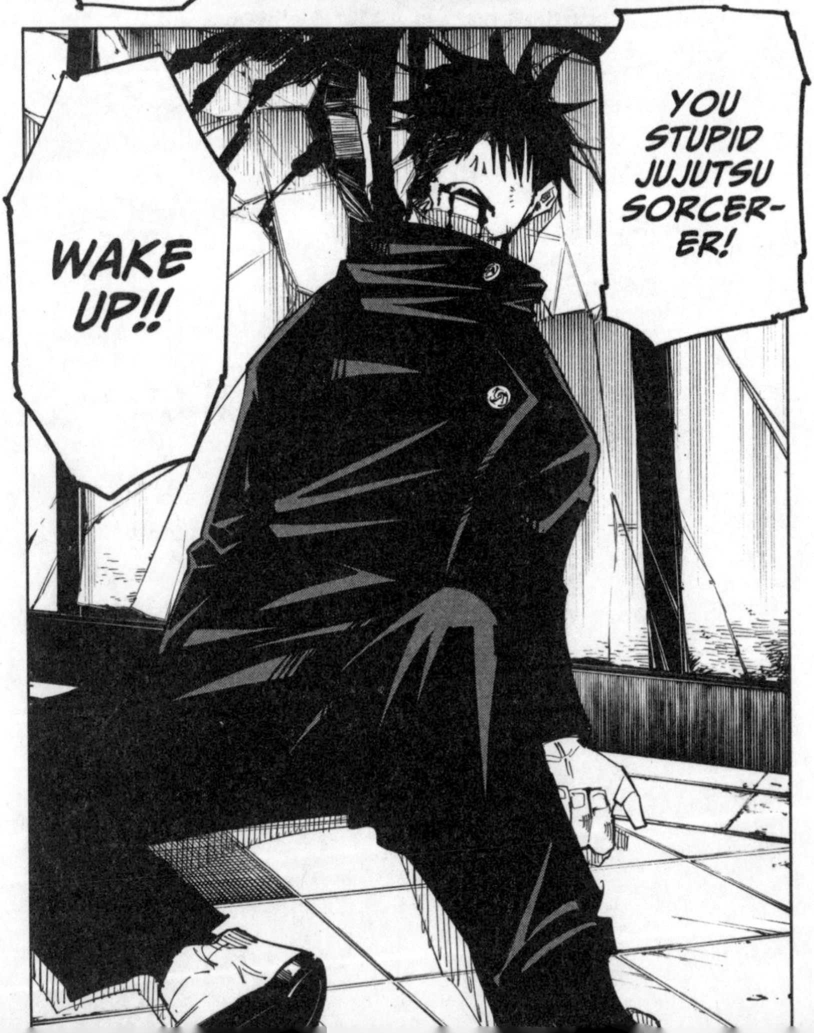
YOU STUPID JUJUTSU SORCERER-ER!
WAKE UP!!

THE 2020 VALENTINES RANKINGS THAT I SERIOUSLY ALMOST FORGOT

PROBABLY RIGHT AROUND WHEN THE PAST ARC ENDED.

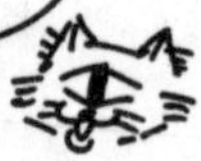

RANKINGS (VALENTINES RECEIVED)	CHARACTER	AKUTAMI'S COMMENT
1 (54)	GOJO	OKAY, I GET IT ALREADY...
2 (30)	GETO	NOT TOO BAD.
3 (23)	FUSHIGURO	YOU NEED TO TRY A LITTLE HARDER.
4 (22)	ITADORI	SQUEAKING BY AS THE MAIN CHARACTER.

Chapter 117: The Shibuya Incident, Part 35

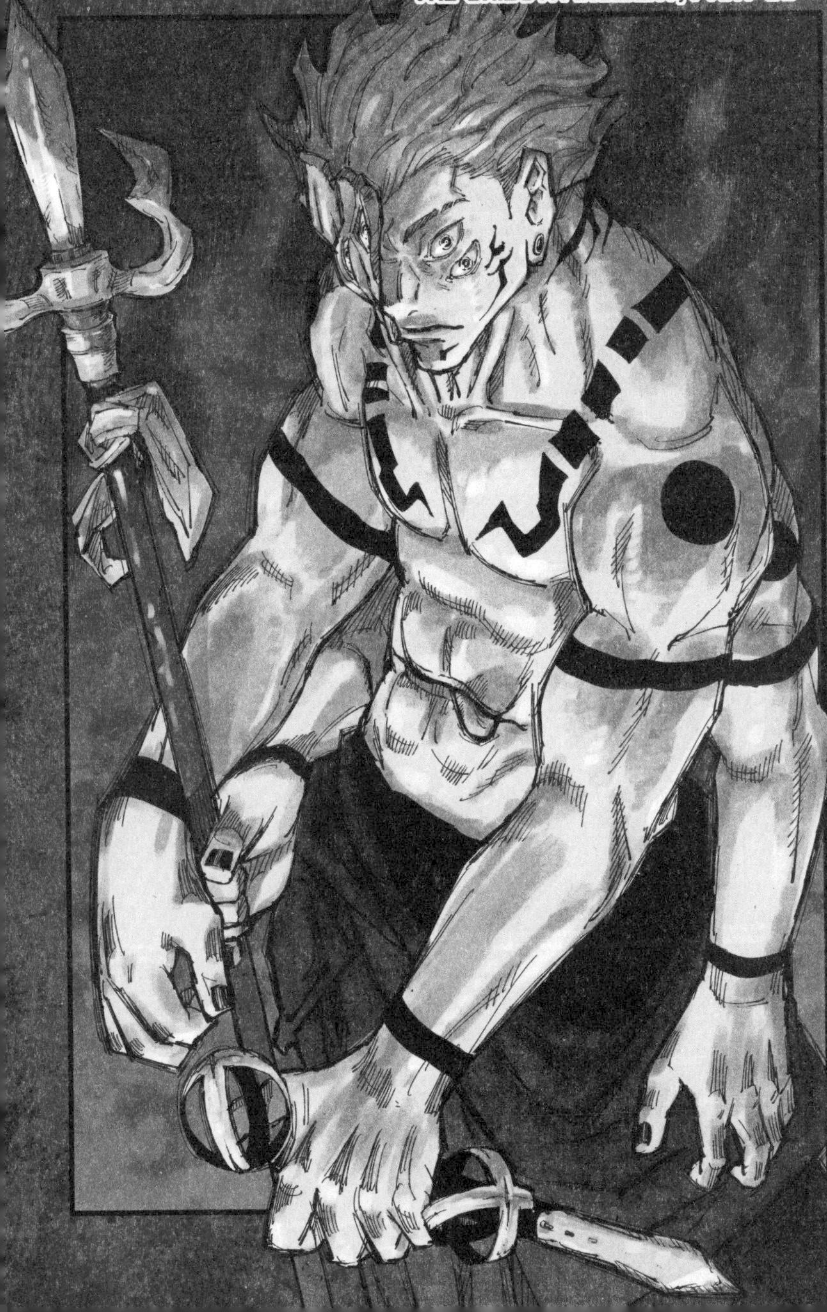

JUJUTSU KAISEN

THE *TEN SHADOWS TECHNIQUE* BEGINS WHEN...

...A SORCERER RECEIVES TWO DIVINE DOGS.

...THE SORCERER AND THEIR DIVINE DOGS MUST EXORCISE THEM TOGETHER.

IN ORDER TO USE OTHER SHIKIGAMI...

...TO EXORCISE AND AMASS EVEN MORE SHIKIGAMI. UP TO TEN.

THEN THE SORCERER GAINS MORE SHIKIGAMI, WHICH THEY CAN UTILIZE...

...

ARE YOU FINISHED YET?

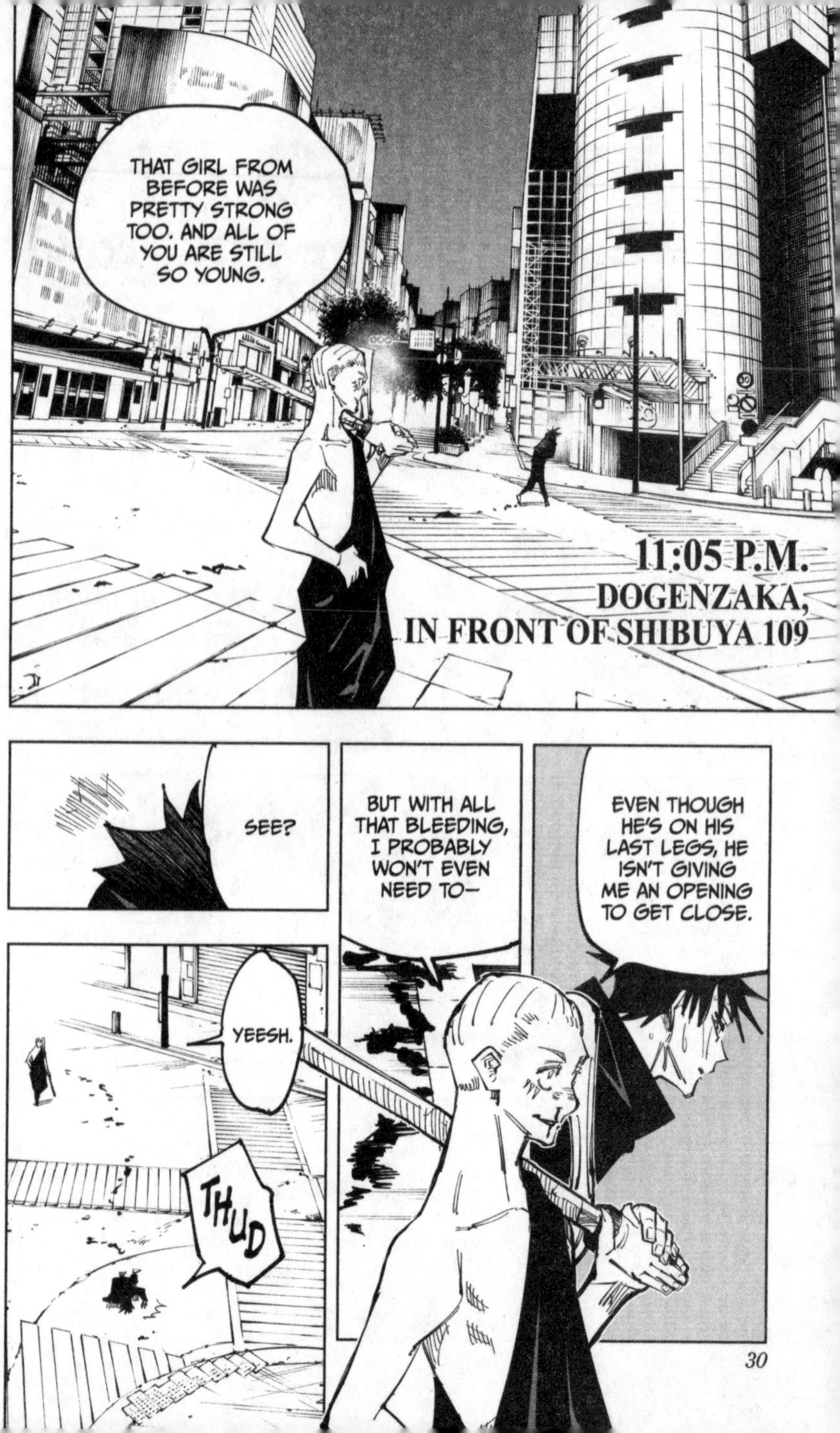

THAT GIRL FROM BEFORE WAS PRETTY STRONG TOO. AND ALL OF YOU ARE STILL SO YOUNG.
11:05 P.M.
DOGENZAKA, IN FRONT OF SHIBUYA 109
EVEN THOUGH HE'S ON HIS LAST LEGS, HE ISN'T GIVING ME AN OPENING TO GET CLOSE.
BUT WITH ALL THAT BLEEDING, I PROBABLY WON'T EVEN NEED TO—
SEE?
YEESH.
THUD

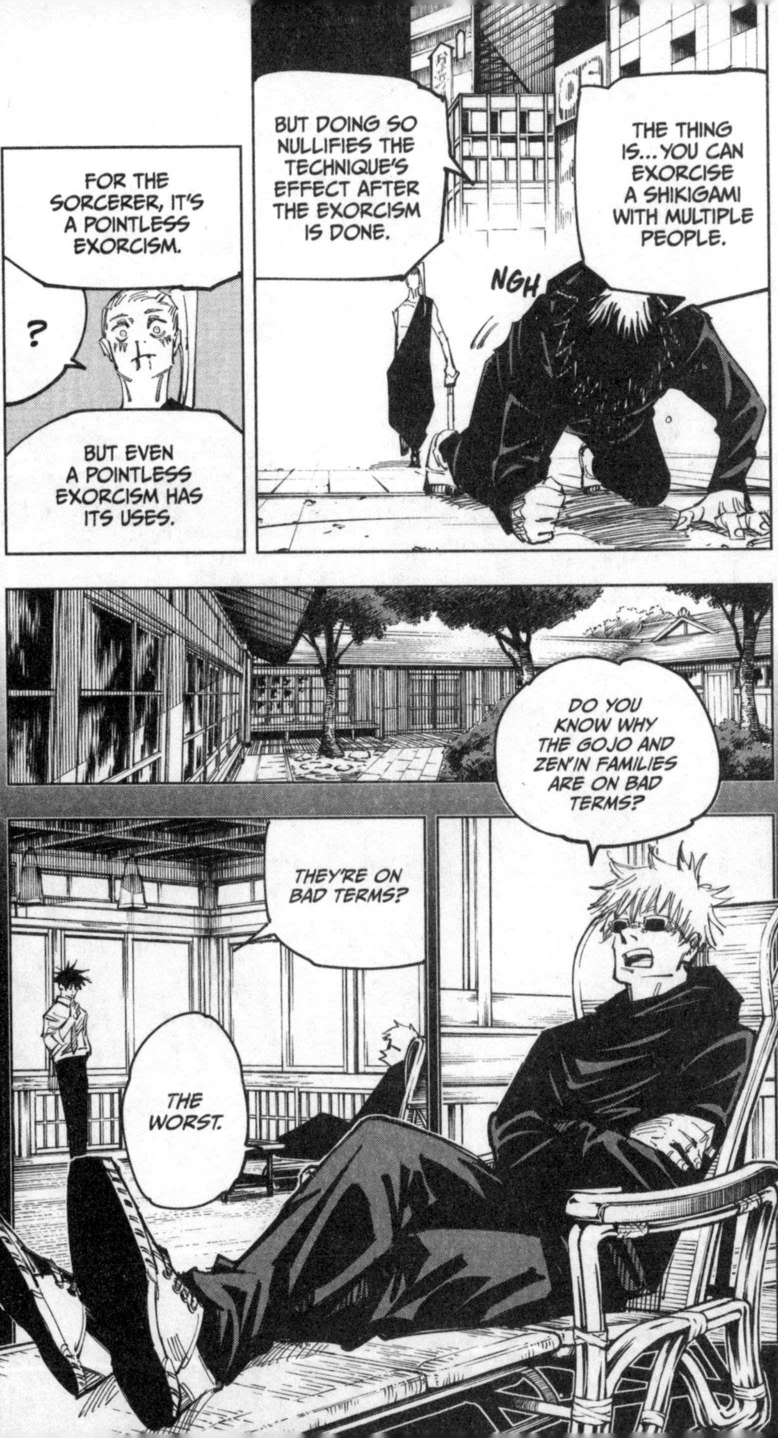
THE THING IS...YOU CAN EXORCISE A SHIKIGAMI WITH MULTIPLE PEOPLE.
BUT DOING SO NULLIFIES THE TECHNIQUE'S EFFECT AFTER THE EXORCISM IS DONE.
NGH
FOR THE SORCERER, IT'S A POINTLESS EXORCISM.
?
BUT EVEN A POINTLESS EXORCISM HAS ITS USES.
DO YOU KNOW WHY THE GOJO AND ZEN'IN FAMILIES ARE ON BAD TERMS?
THEY'RE ON BAD TERMS?
THE WORST.

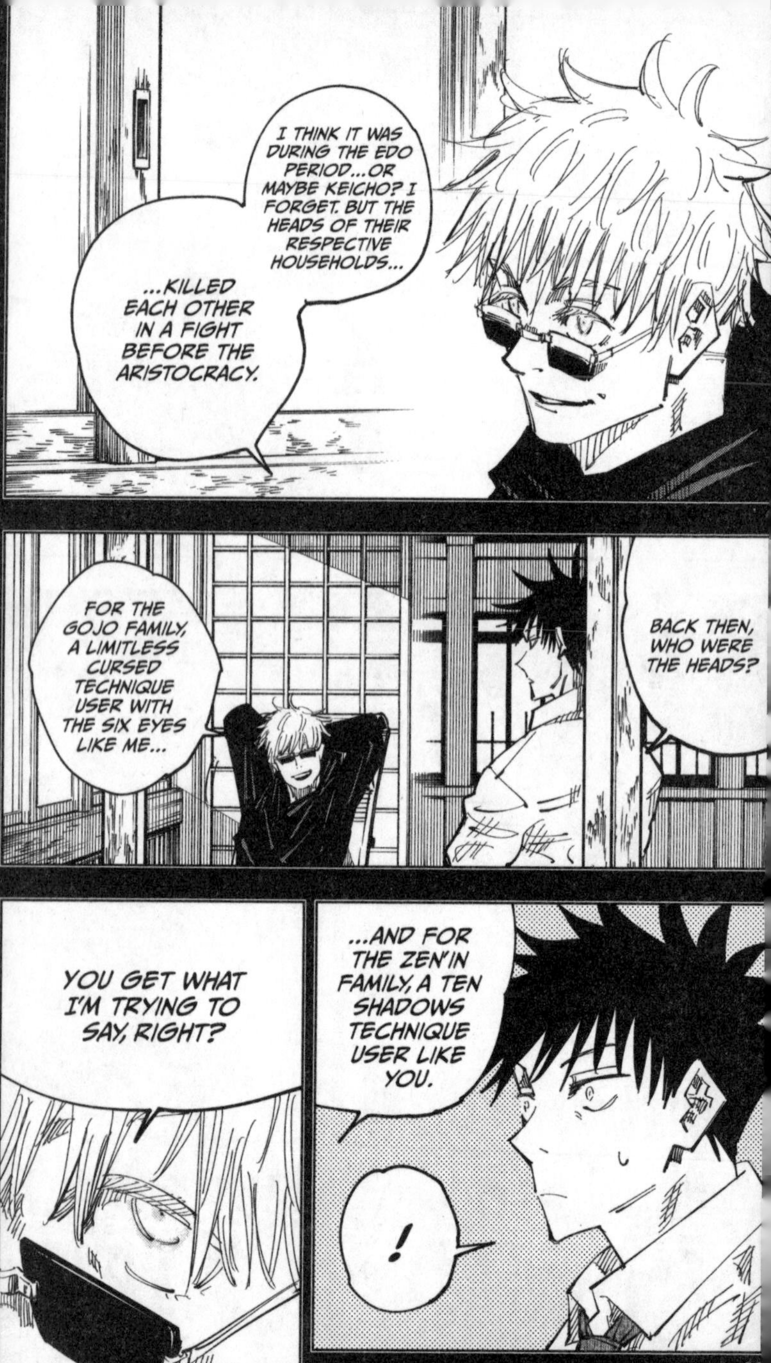
I THINK IT WAS DURING THE EDO PERIOD...OR MAYBE KEICHO? I FORGET. BUT THE HEADS OF THEIR RESPECTIVE HOUSEHOLDS...
...KILLED EACH OTHER IN A FIGHT BEFORE THE ARISTOCRACY.
BACK THEN, WHO WERE THE HEADS?
FOR THE GOJO FAMILY, A LIMITLESS CURSED TECHNIQUE USER WITH THE SIX EYES LIKE ME...
...AND FOR THE ZEN'IN FAMILY, A TEN SHADOWS TECHNIQUE USER LIKE YOU.
!
YOU GET WHAT I'M TRYING TO SAY, RIGHT?

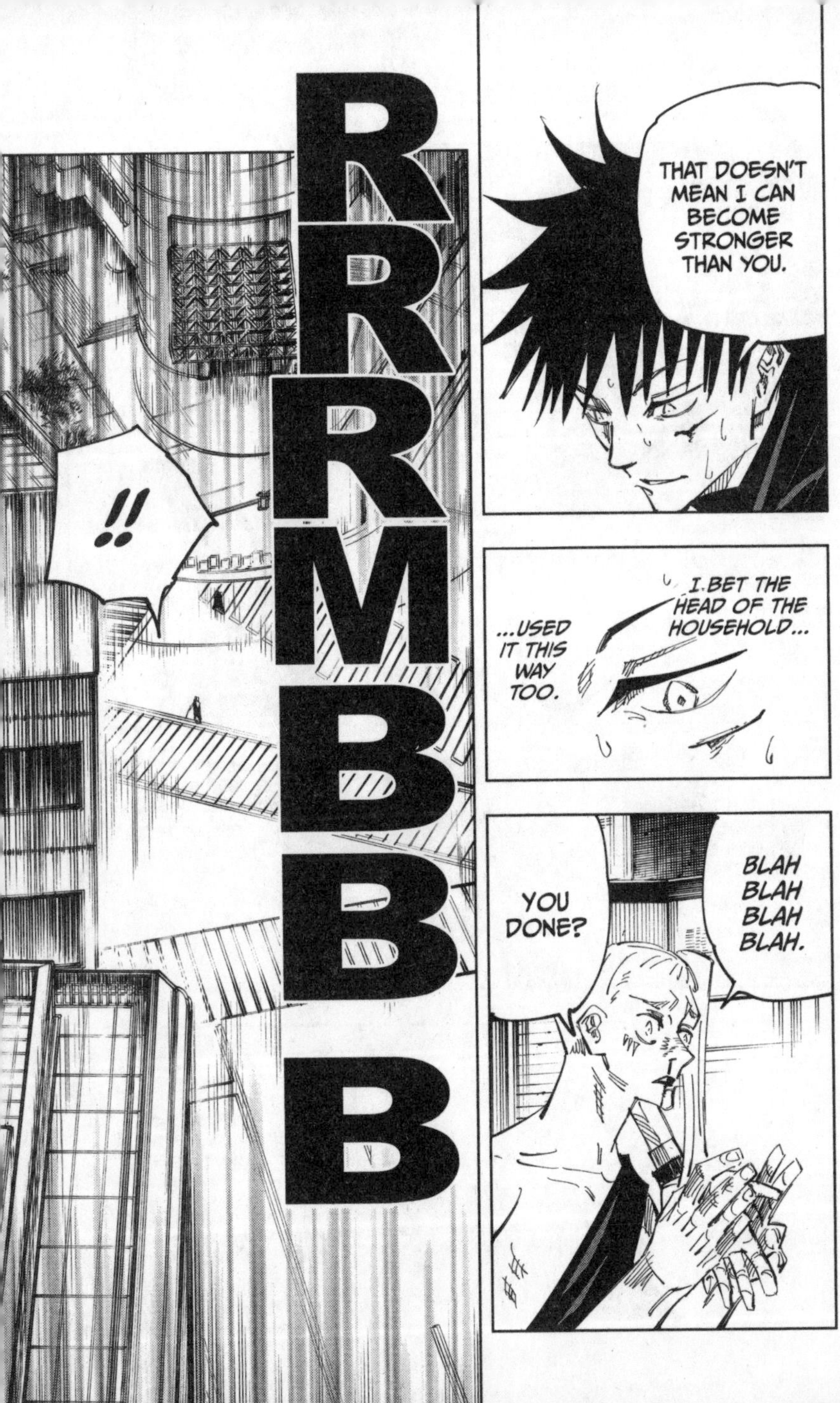
THAT DOESN'T MEAN I CAN BECOME STRONGER THAN YOU.
I BET THE HEAD OF THE HOUSEHOLD...
...USED IT THIS WAY TOO.
BLAH BLAH BLAH BLAH.
YOU DONE?
!!
RRMBB

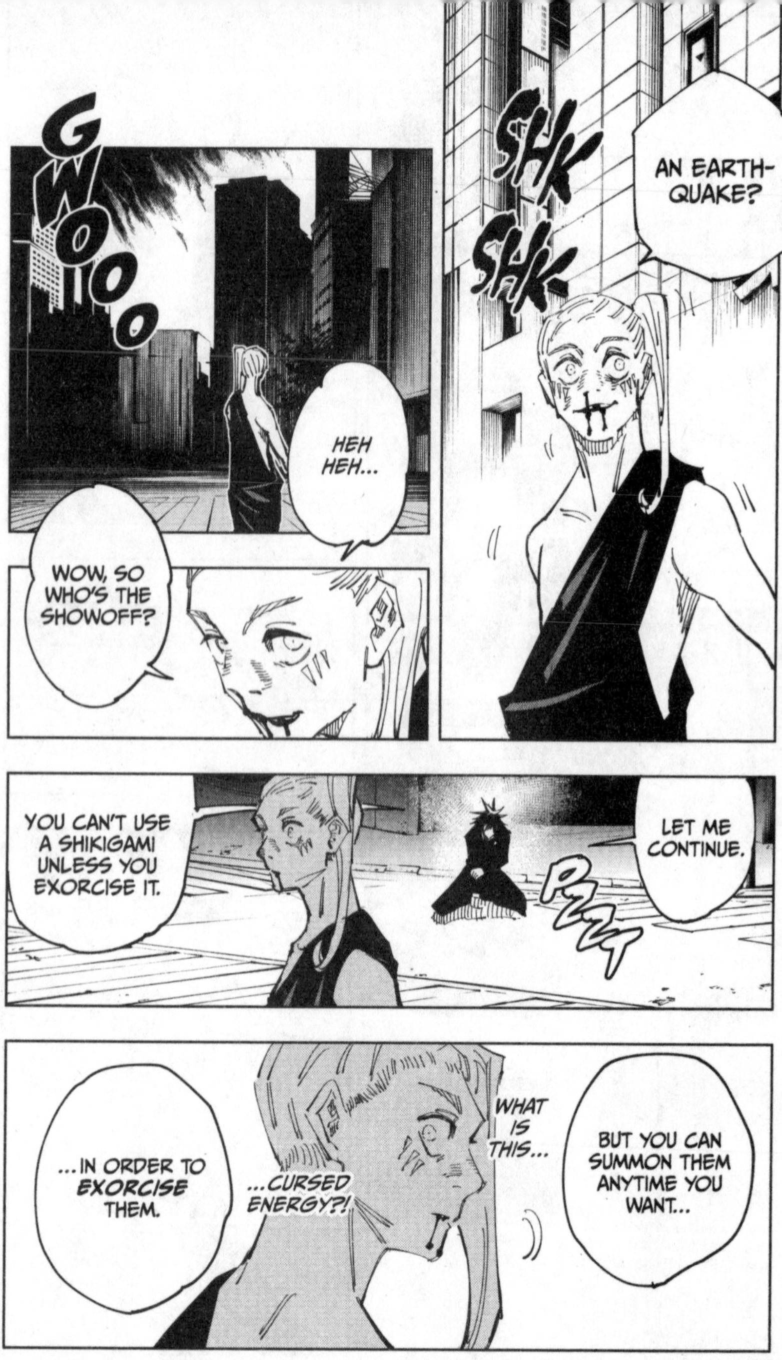
SHK
SHK
AN EARTH-QUAKE?
GWOOO
HEH HEH...
WOW, SO WHO'S THE SHOWOFF?
LET ME CONTINUE.
PZZT
YOU CAN'T USE A SHIKIGAMI UNLESS YOU EXORCISE IT.
BUT YOU CAN SUMMON THEM ANYTIME YOU WANT...
WHAT IS THIS...
...CURSED ENERGY?!
...IN ORDER TO **EXORCISE** THEM.

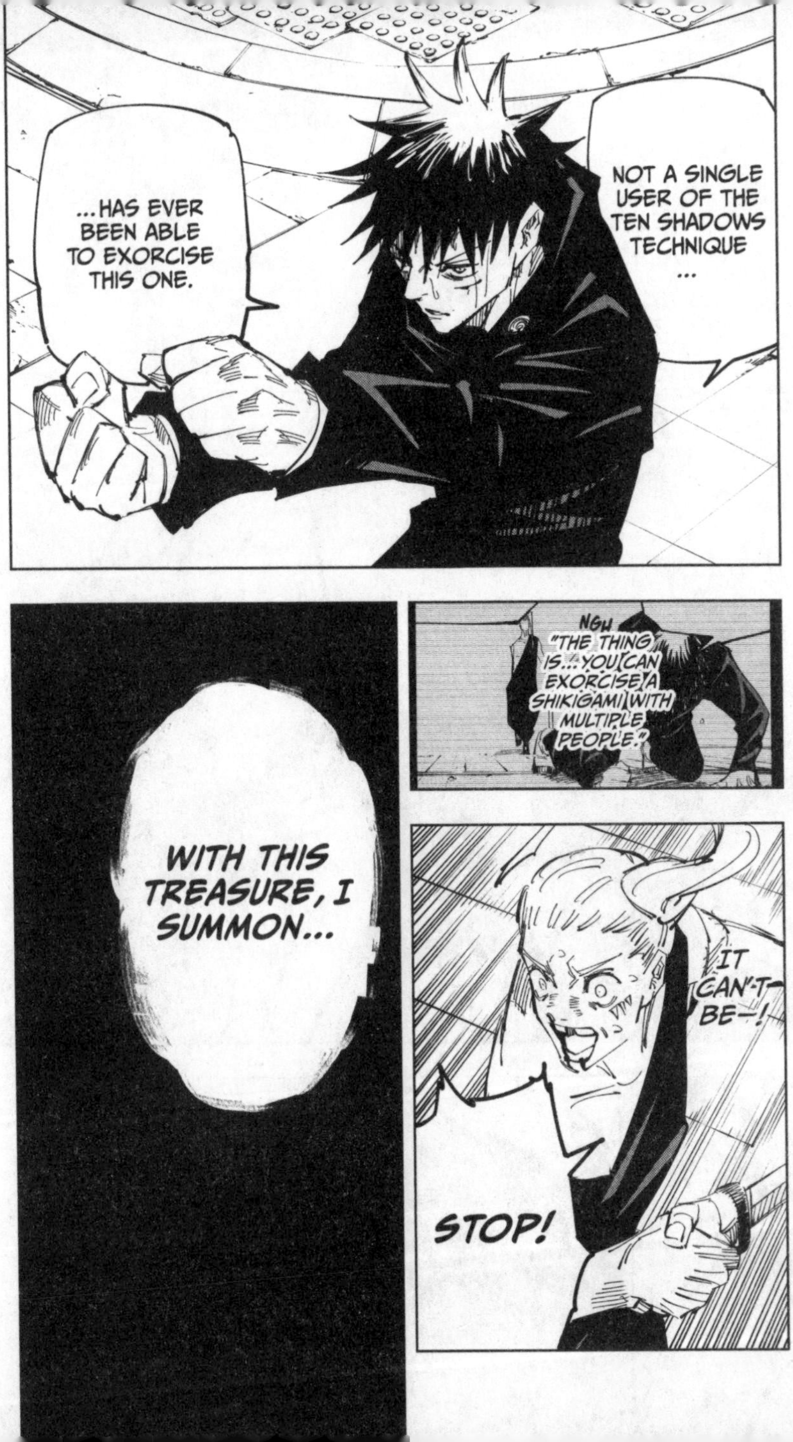
NOT A SINGLE USER OF THE TEN SHADOWS TECHNIQUE ...
...HAS EVER BEEN ABLE TO EXORCISE THIS ONE.
NGH
"THE THING IS... YOU CAN EXORCISE A SHIKIGAMI WITH MULTIPLE PEOPLE."
IT CAN'T BE—!
STOP!
WITH THIS TREASURE, I SUMMON...

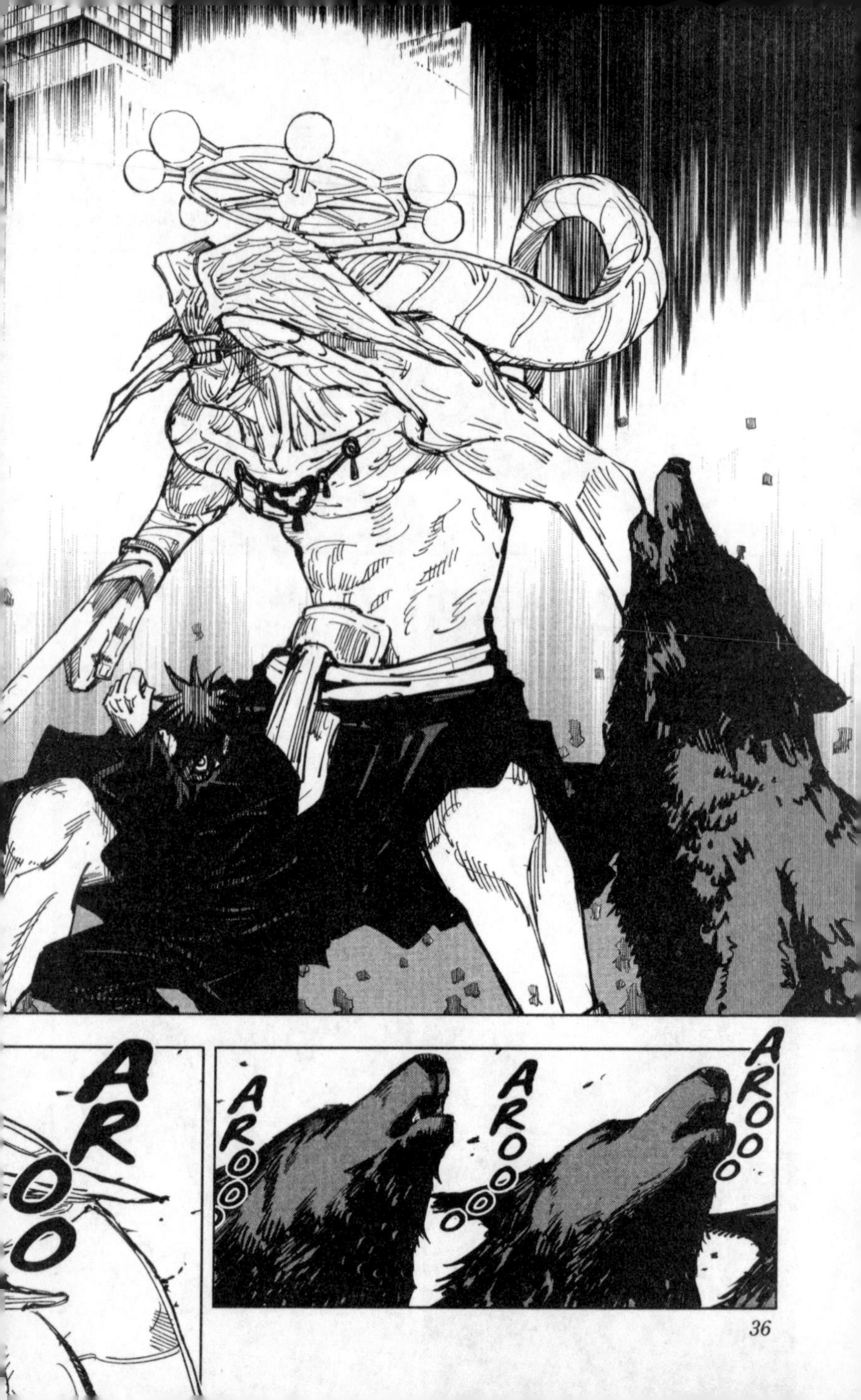
AROOOO
AROOOO
AROOOO
AROO

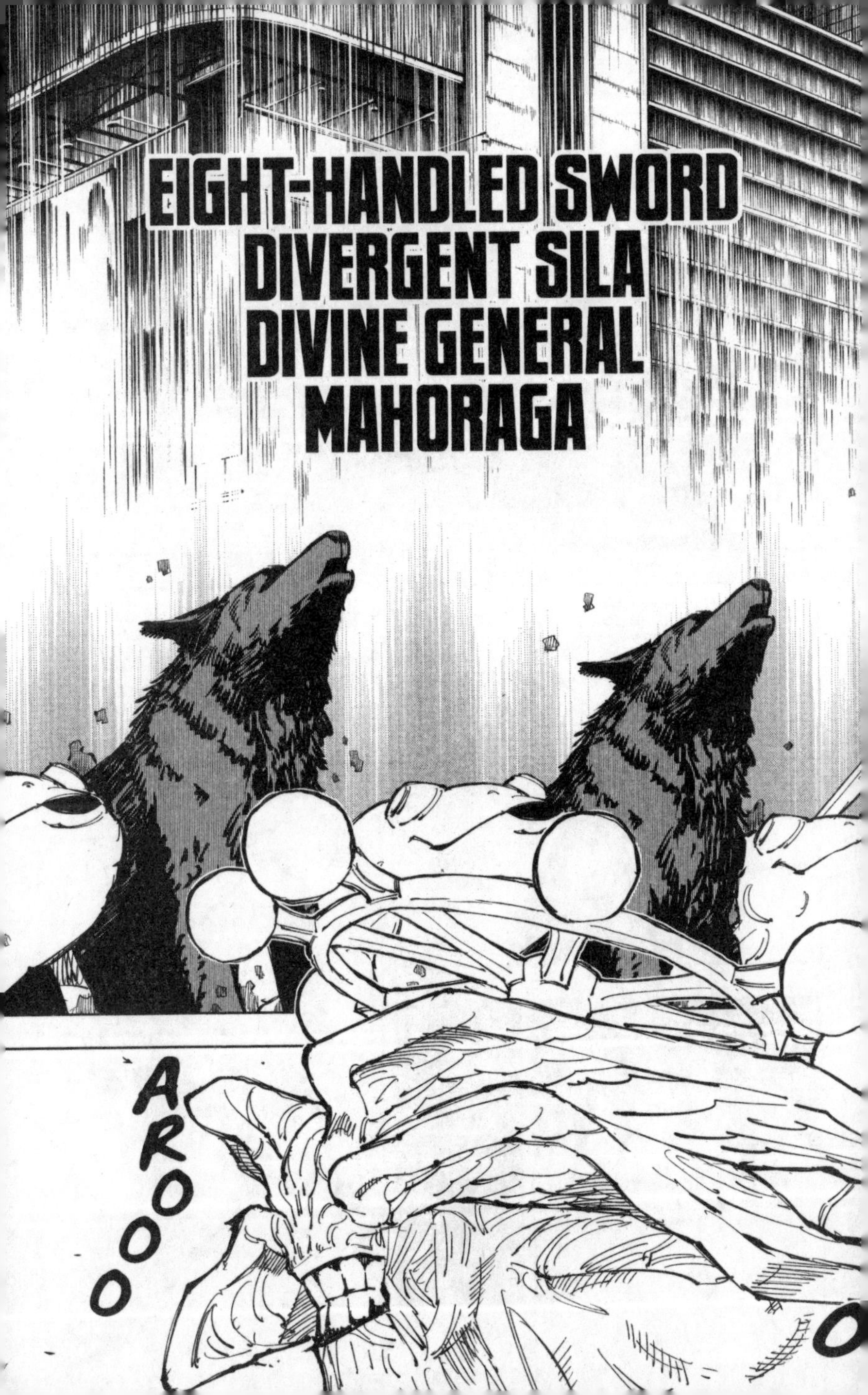
EIGHT-HANDLED SWORD
DIVERGENT SILA
DIVINE GENERAL
MAHORAGA
AROOOO

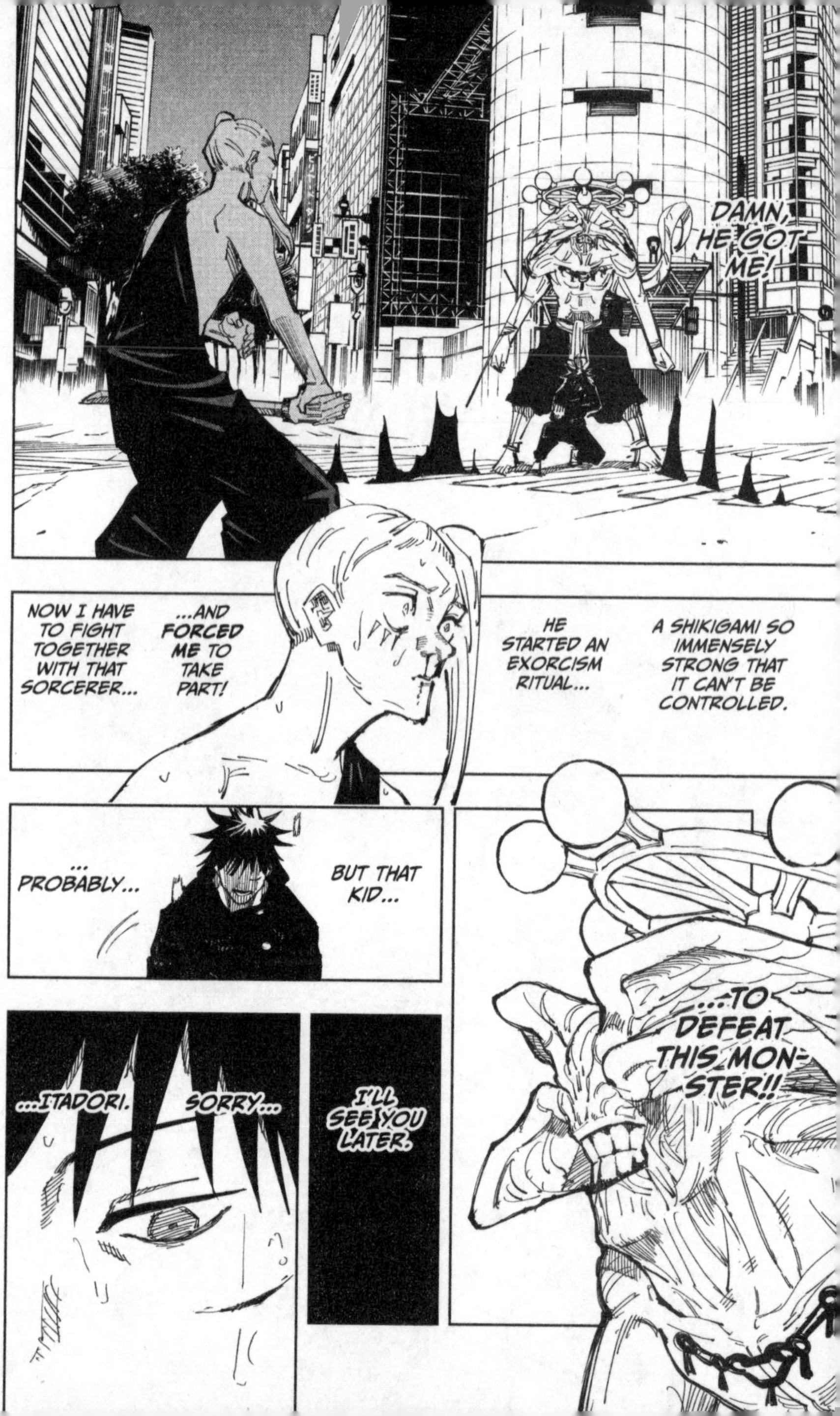
DAMN, HE GOT ME!
A SHIKIGAMI SO IMMENSELY STRONG THAT IT CAN'T BE CONTROLLED.
HE STARTED AN EXORCISM RITUAL...
...AND FORCED ME TO TAKE PART!
NOW I HAVE TO FIGHT TOGETHER WITH THAT SORCERER...
BUT THAT KID...
...PROBABLY...
...TO DEFEAT THIS MONSTER!!
SORRY...
...ITADORI.
I'LL SEE YOU LATER.

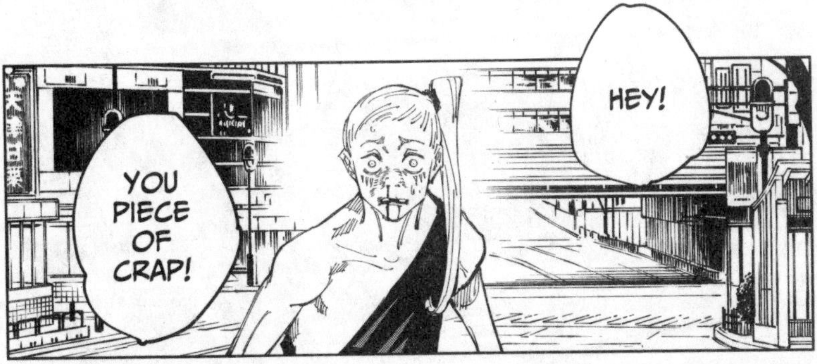
HEY!
YOU PIECE OF CRAP!
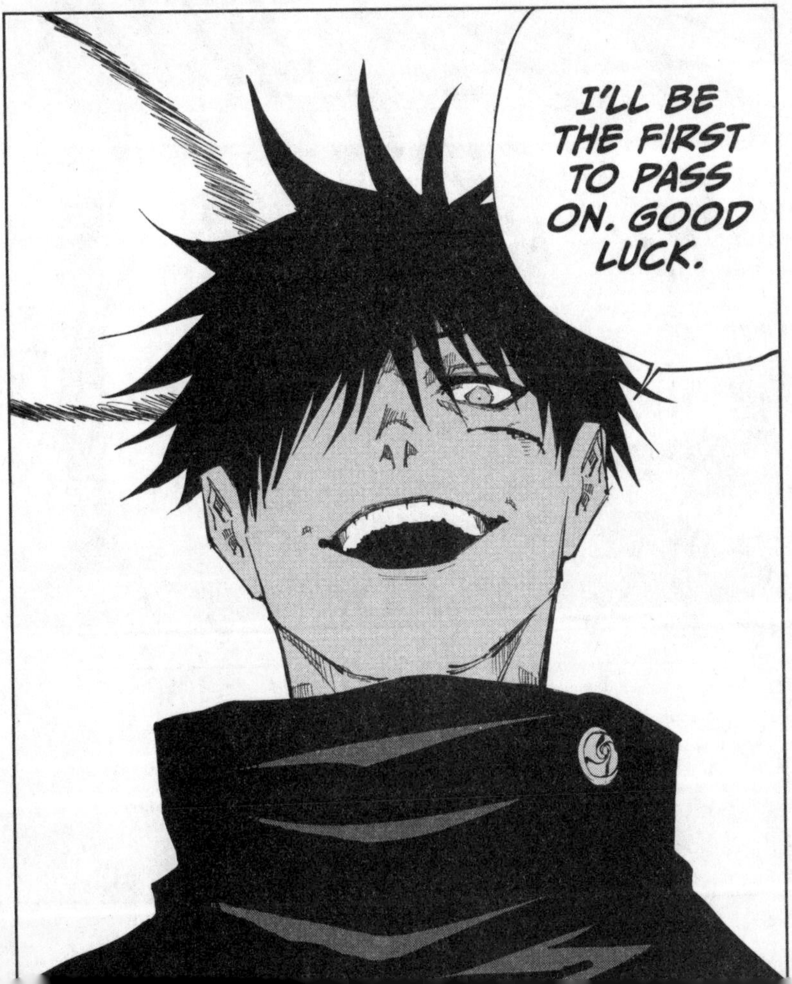
I'LL BE THE FIRST TO PASS ON. GOOD LUCK.

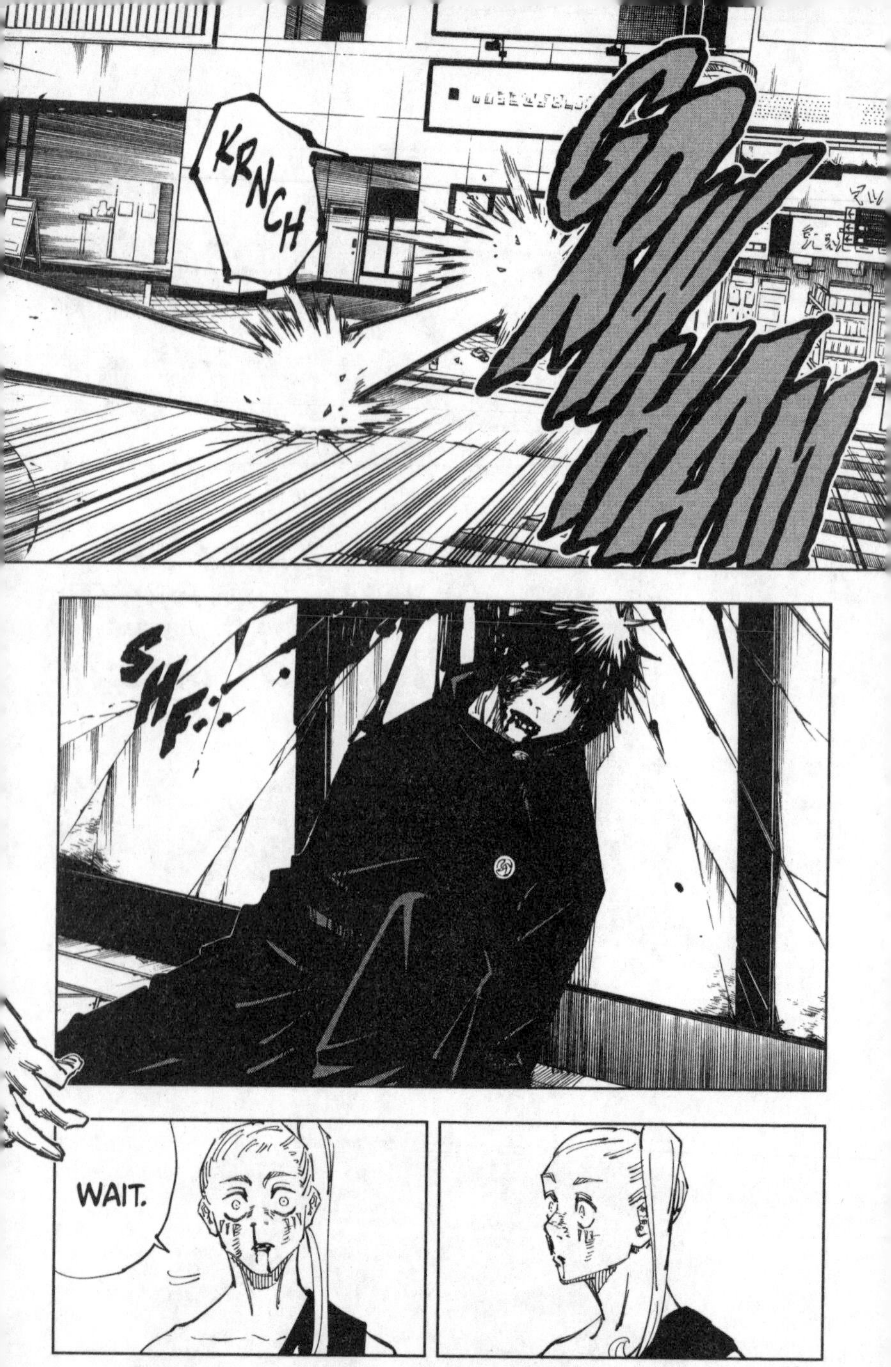
KRNCH
SHF...
WAIT.

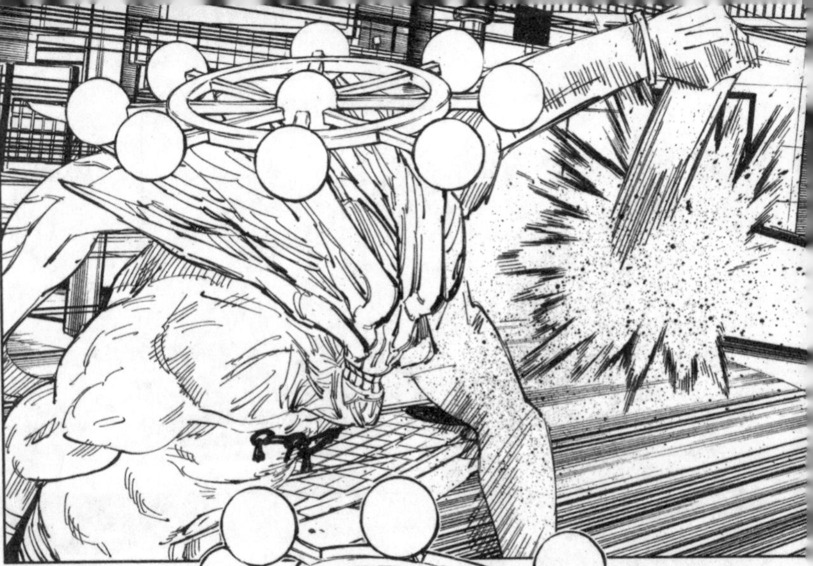
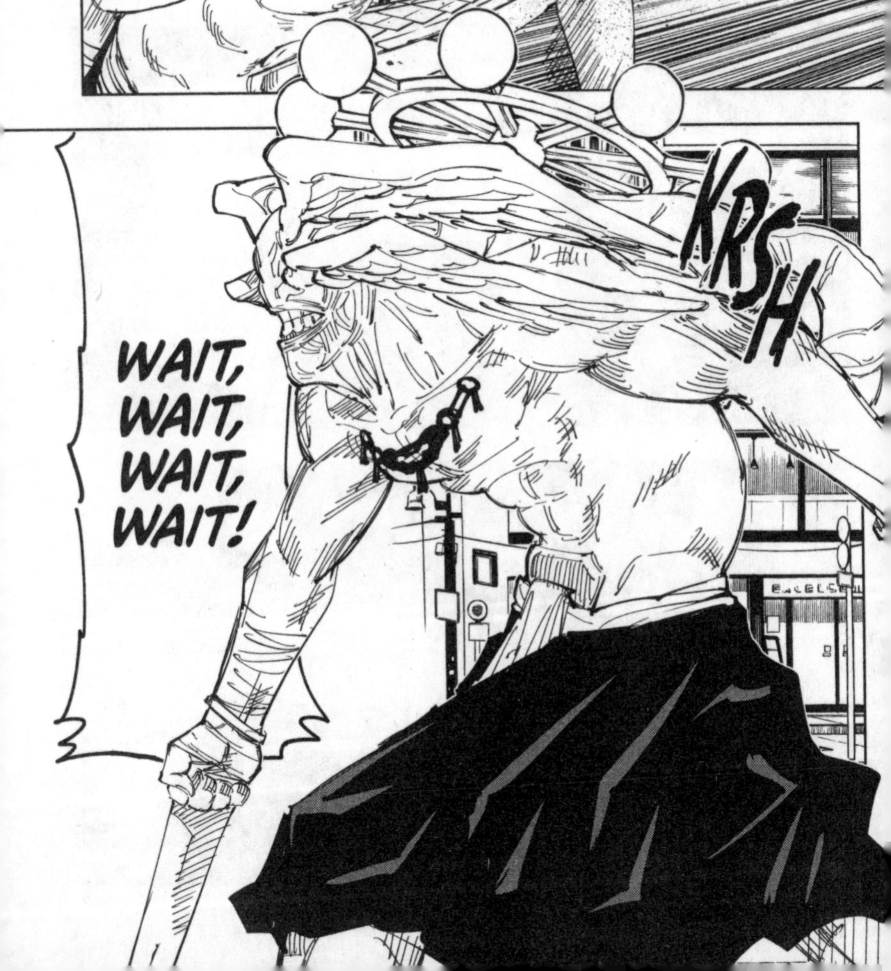
KRSH
WAIT, WAIT, WAIT, WAIT!

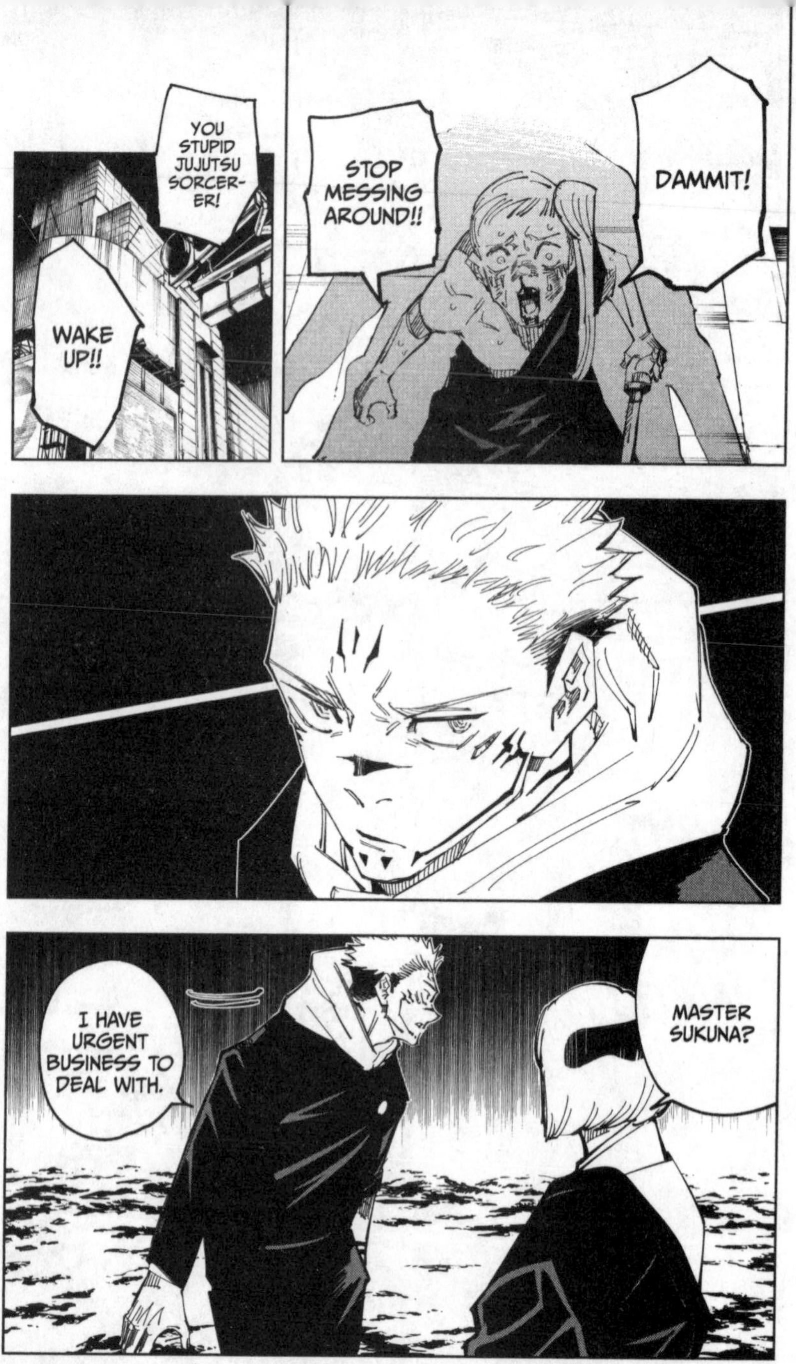
DAMMIT!
STOP MESSING AROUND!!
YOU STUPID JUJUTSU SORCERER-ER!
WAKE UP!!
MASTER SUKUNA?
I HAVE URGENT BUSINESS TO DEAL WITH.

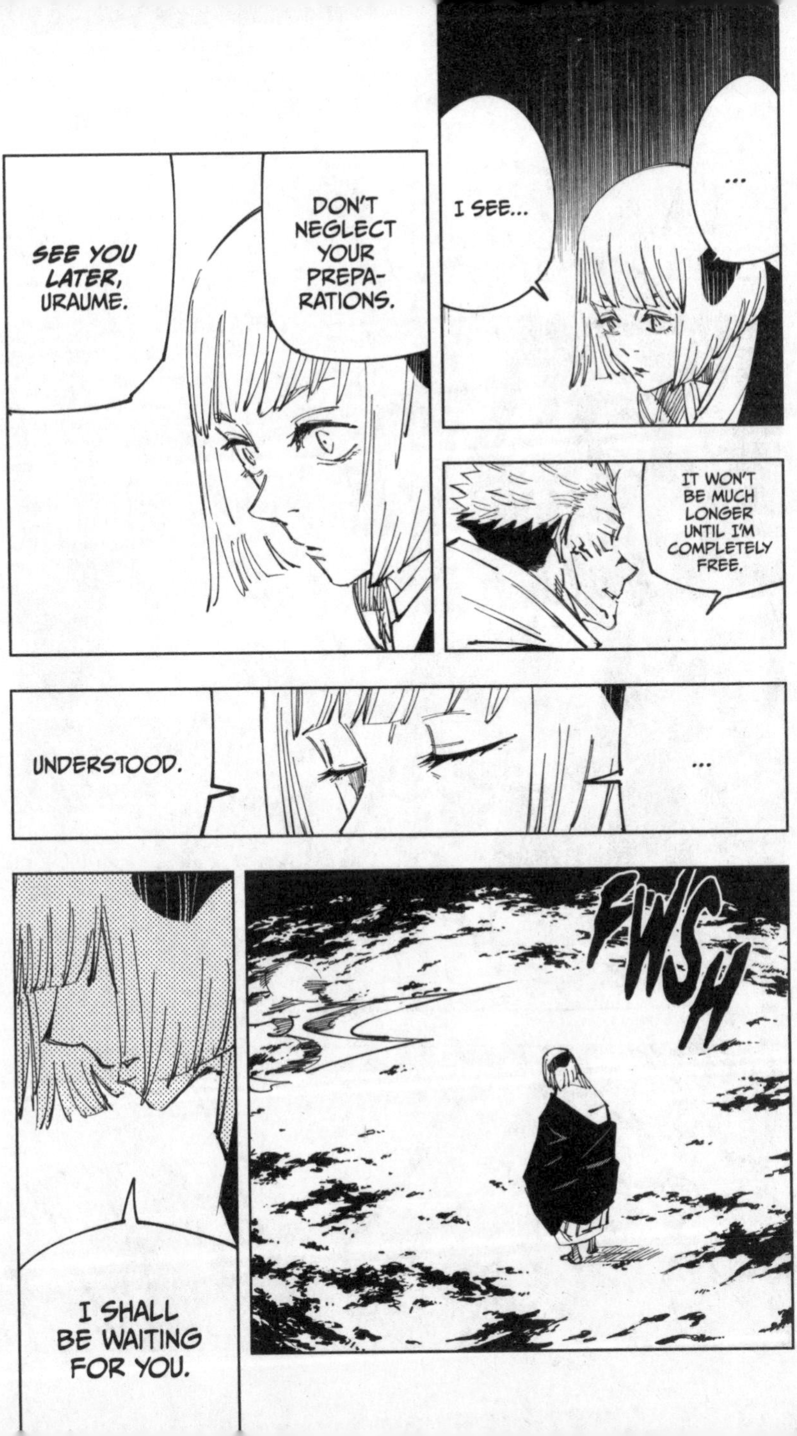
...
I SEE...
IT WON'T BE MUCH LONGER UNTIL I'M COMPLETELY FREE.
DON'T NEGLECT YOUR PREPARATIONS.
SEE YOU LATER, URAUME.
...
UNDERSTOOD.
FWSH
I SHALL BE WAITING FOR YOU.

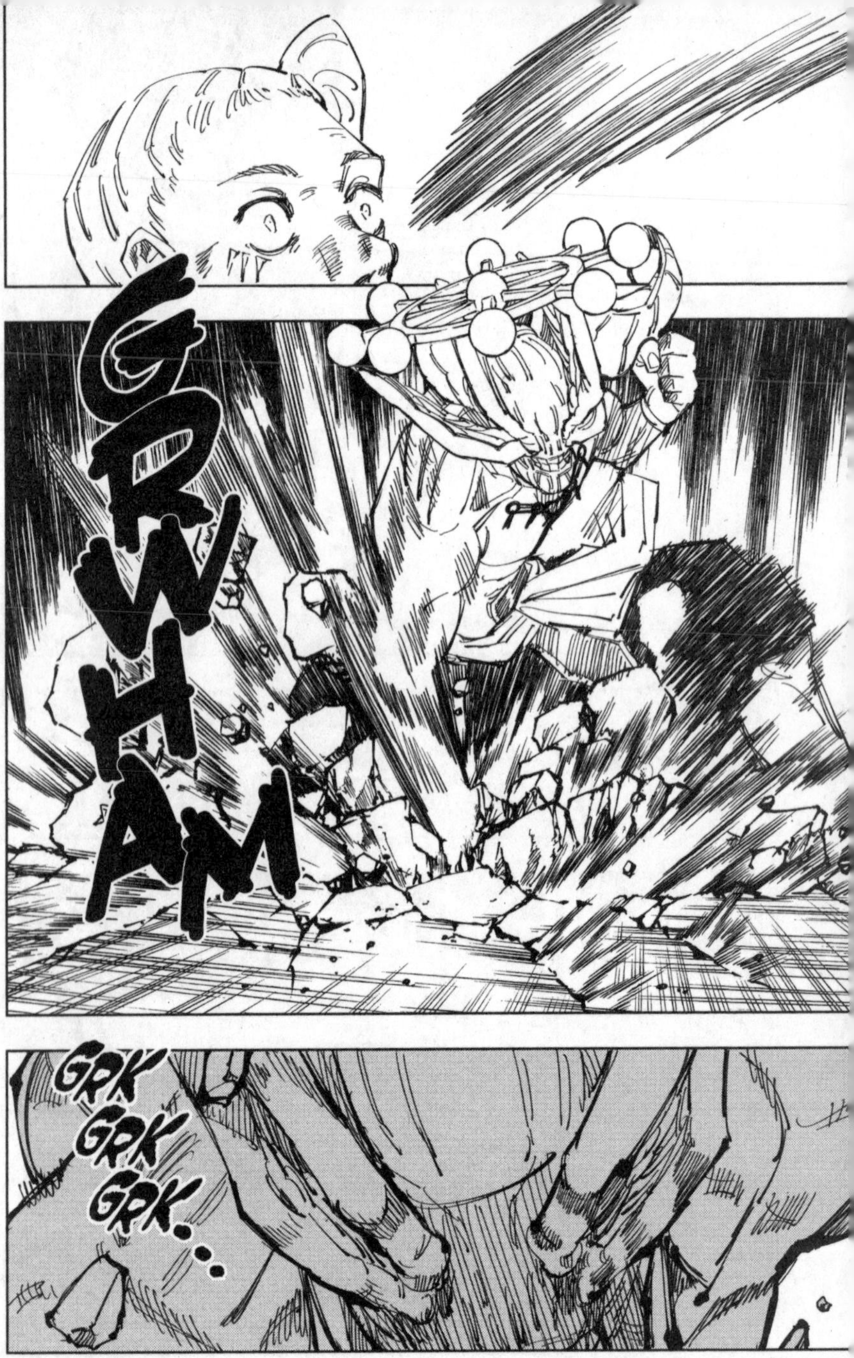
GRWHAM
GRK GRK GRK...

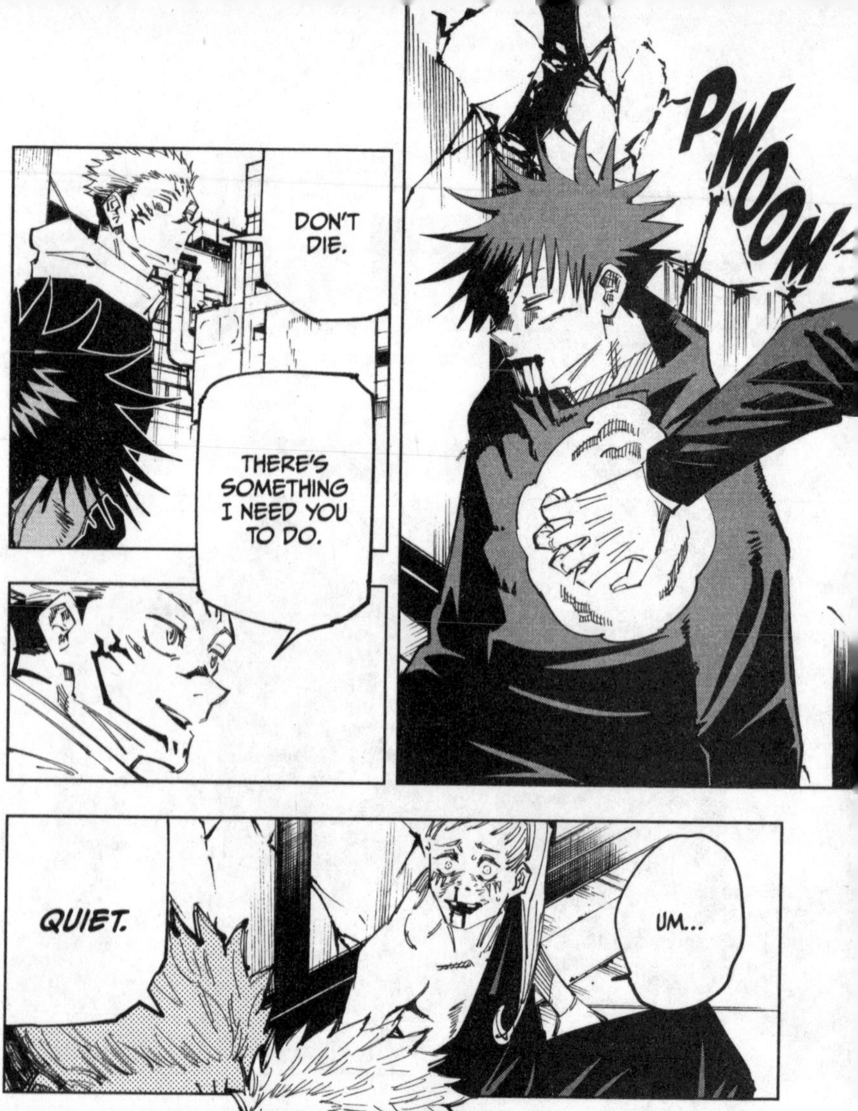
PWOOM
DON'T DIE.
THERE'S SOMETHING I NEED YOU TO DO.
UM...
QUIET.
JUST STAY THERE.
IN ORDER TO KEEP FUSHIGURO ALIVE...
...I NEED TO DEFEAT THE SHIKIGAMI EVEN THOUGH I'M AN OUTSIDER.

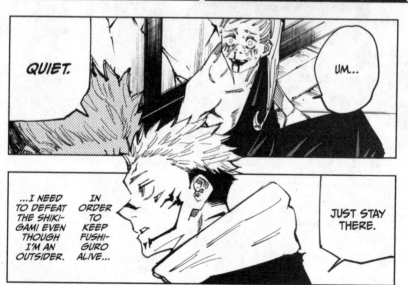

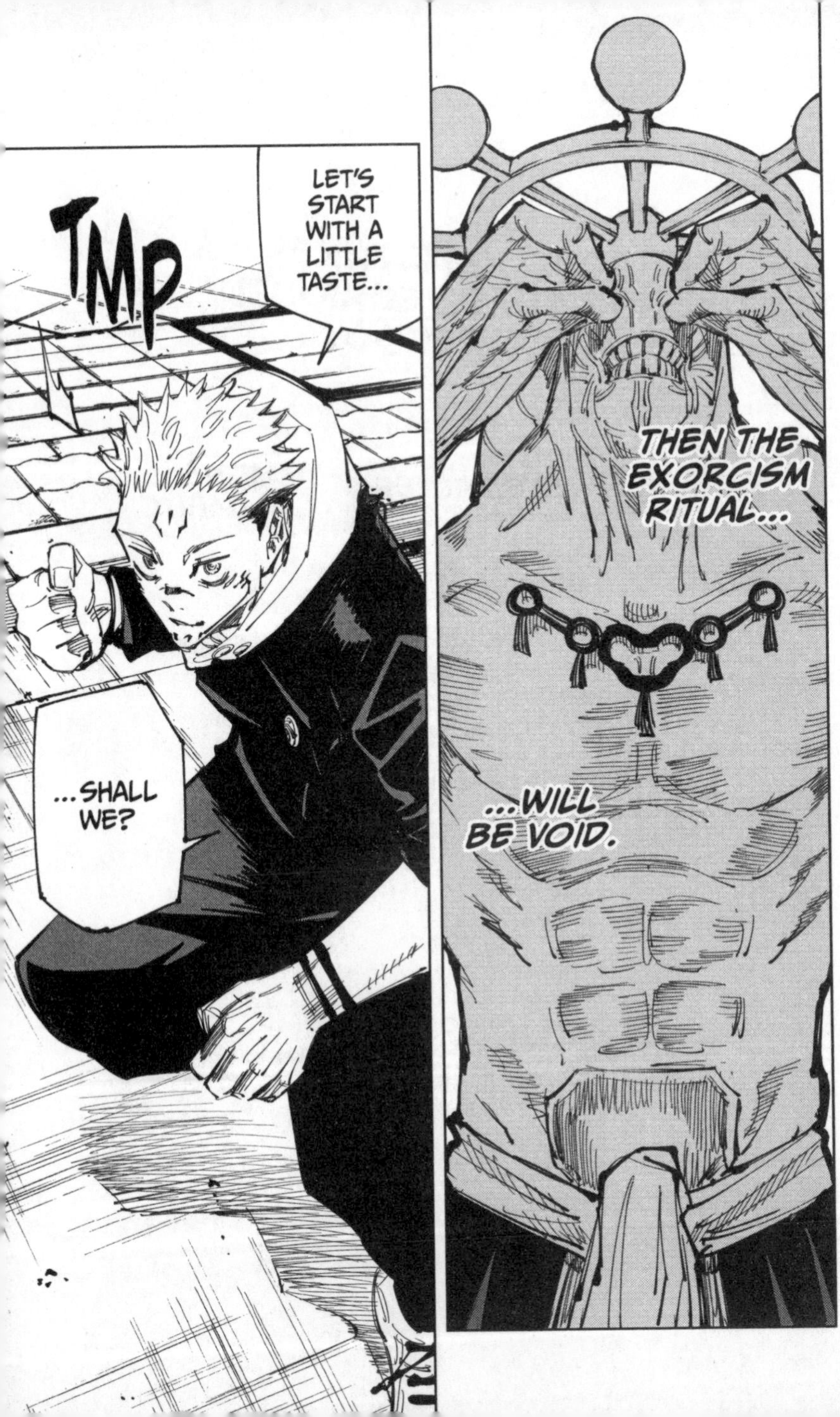
THEN THE EXORCISM RITUAL...
...WILL BE VOID.
LET'S START WITH A LITTLE TASTE...
TMP
...SHALL WE?

THE 2020 VALENTINES RANKINGS THAT I SERIOUSLY ALMOST FORGOT

RANKINGS (VALENTINES RECEIVED)	CHARACTER	AKUTAMI'S COMMENT
5 (19)	NANAMI	FIFTH IS FIRST.
6 (13)	KUGISAKI	NICE!
7 (7)	CHOSO	HE HASN'T BEEN SHOWING UP MUCH, HAS HE?
8 (6)	INUMAKI	EVEN THOUGH I'VE BARELY EXPLORED HIM...
9 (5)	MAKI	MAYBE I'LL CHANGE HER HAIRSTYLE...

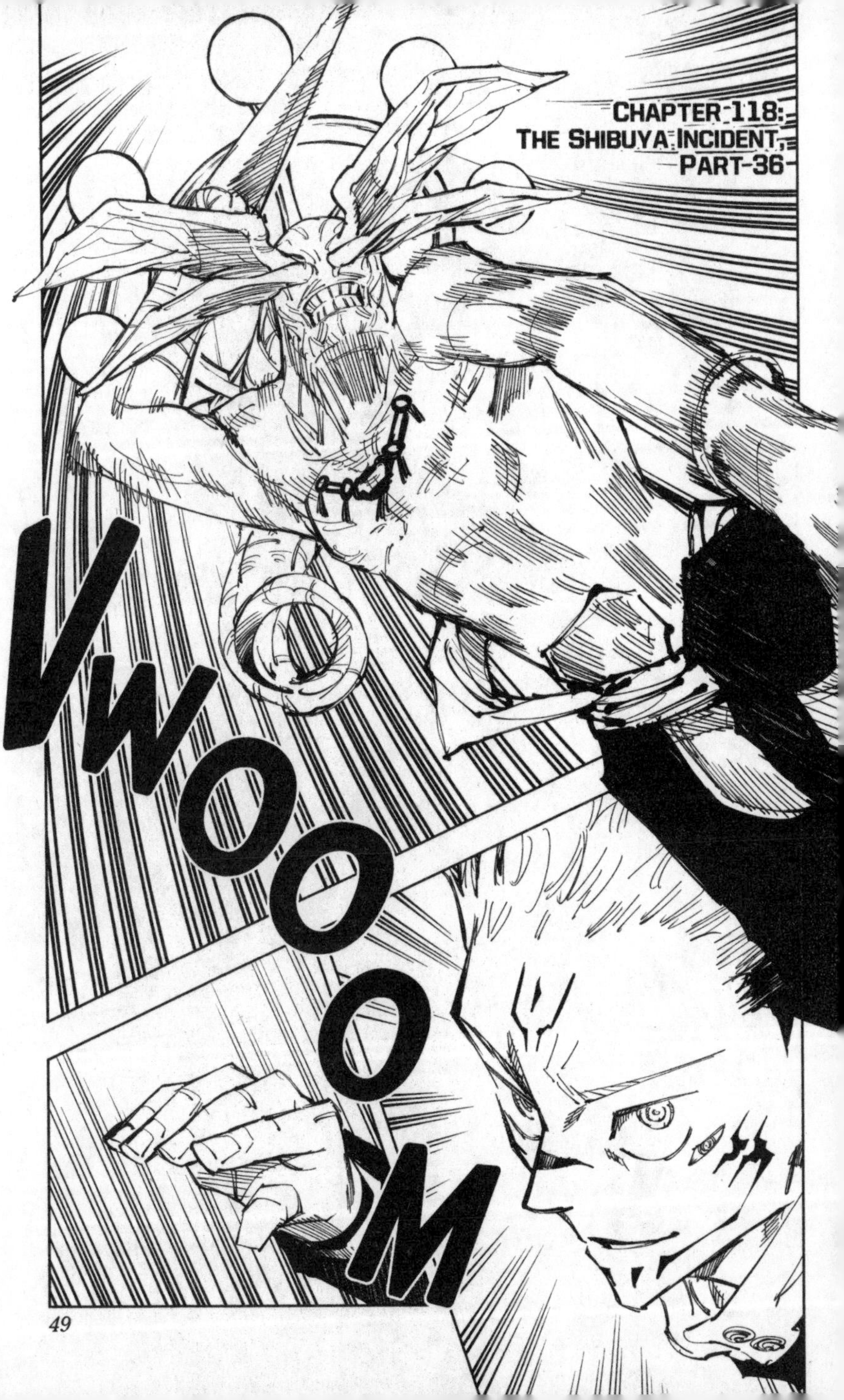
CHAPTER 118:
THE SHIBUYA INCIDENT,
PART 36
VWOOOOM

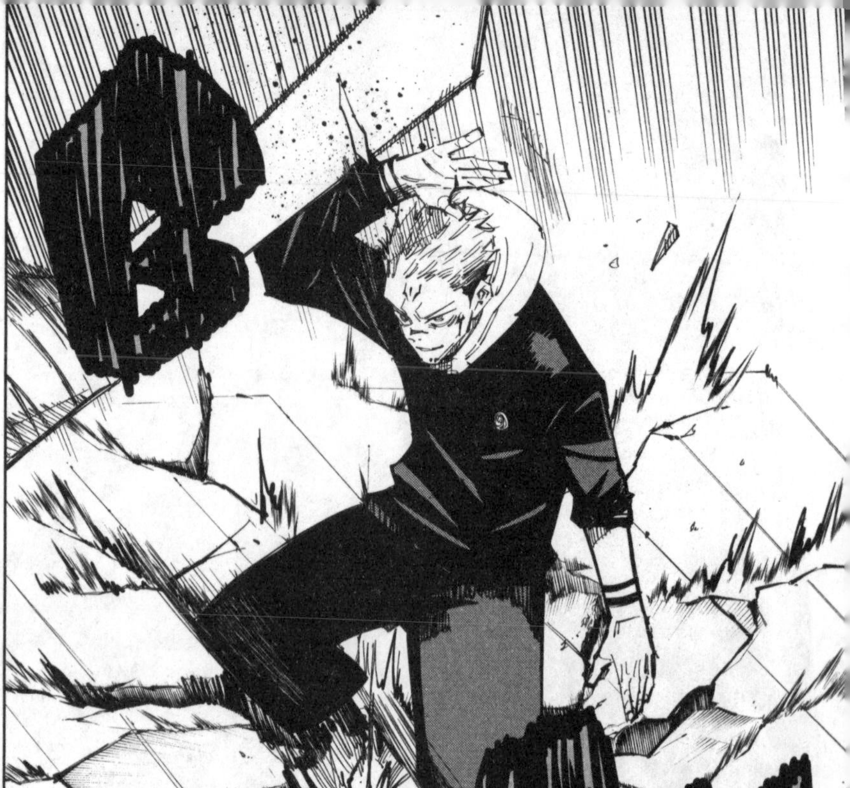
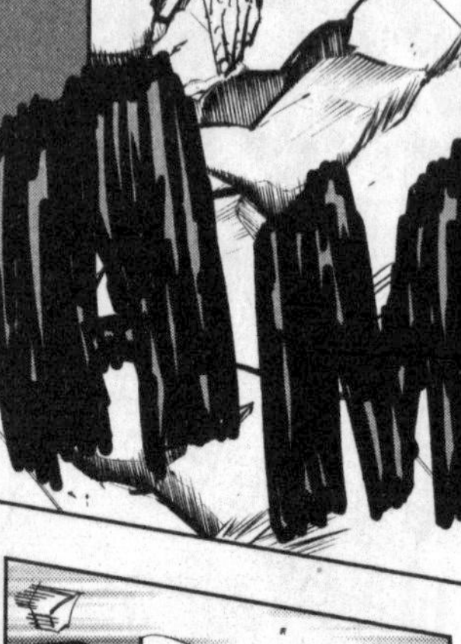
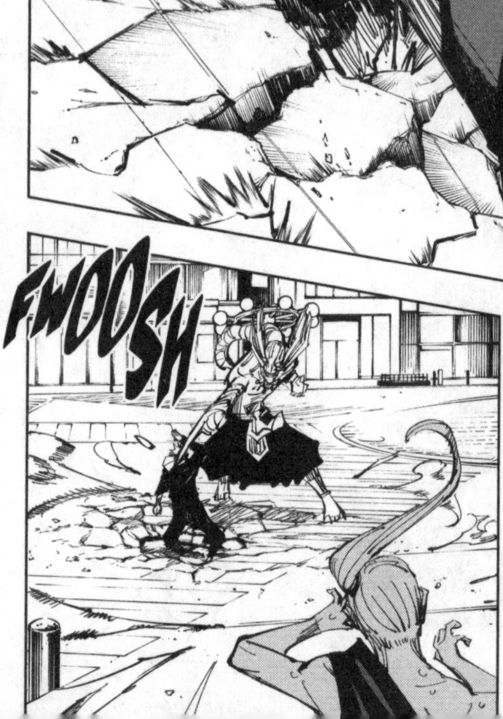
FWOOSH

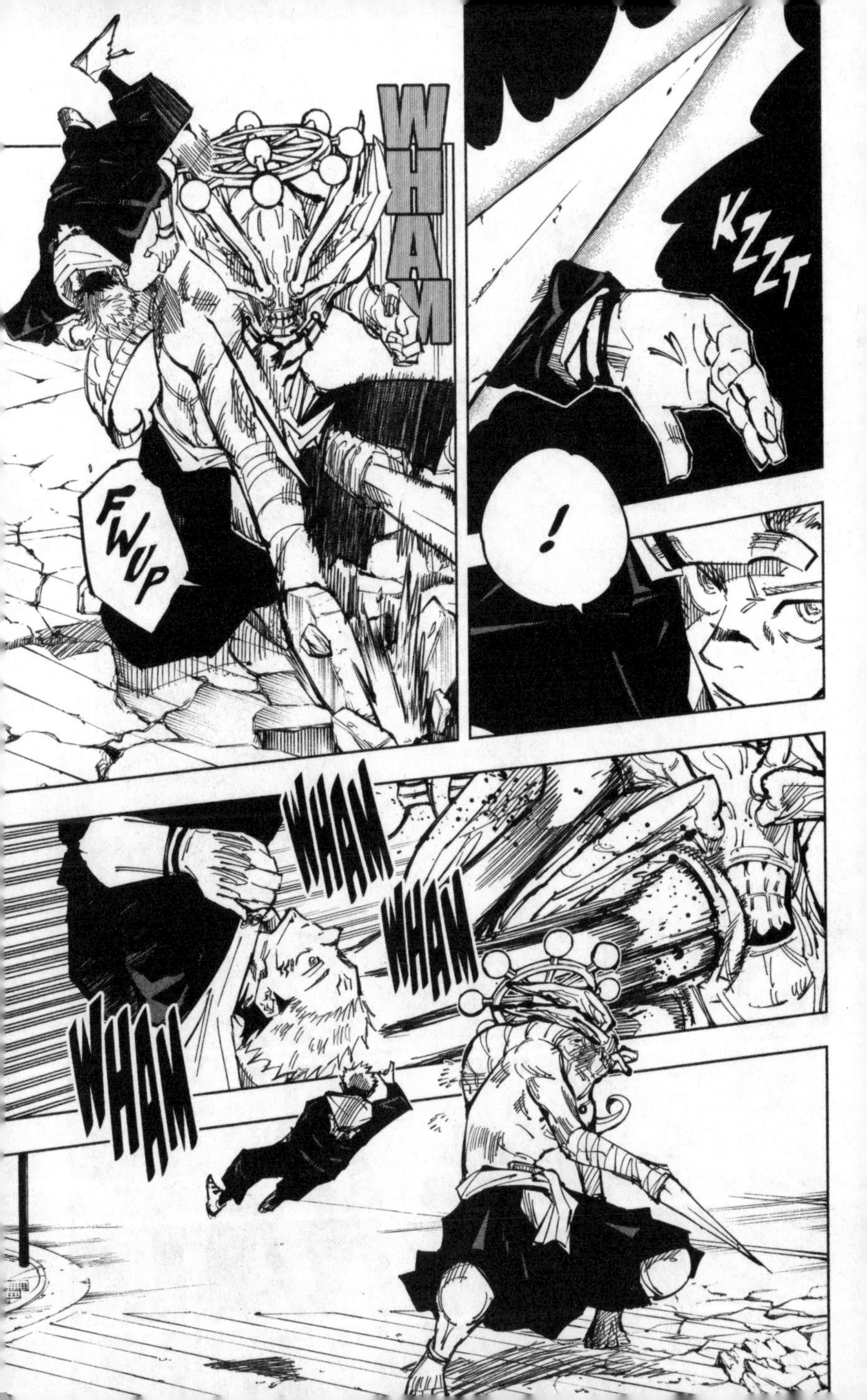
KZZT
!
WHAM
FWUP
WHAM
WHAM
WHAM

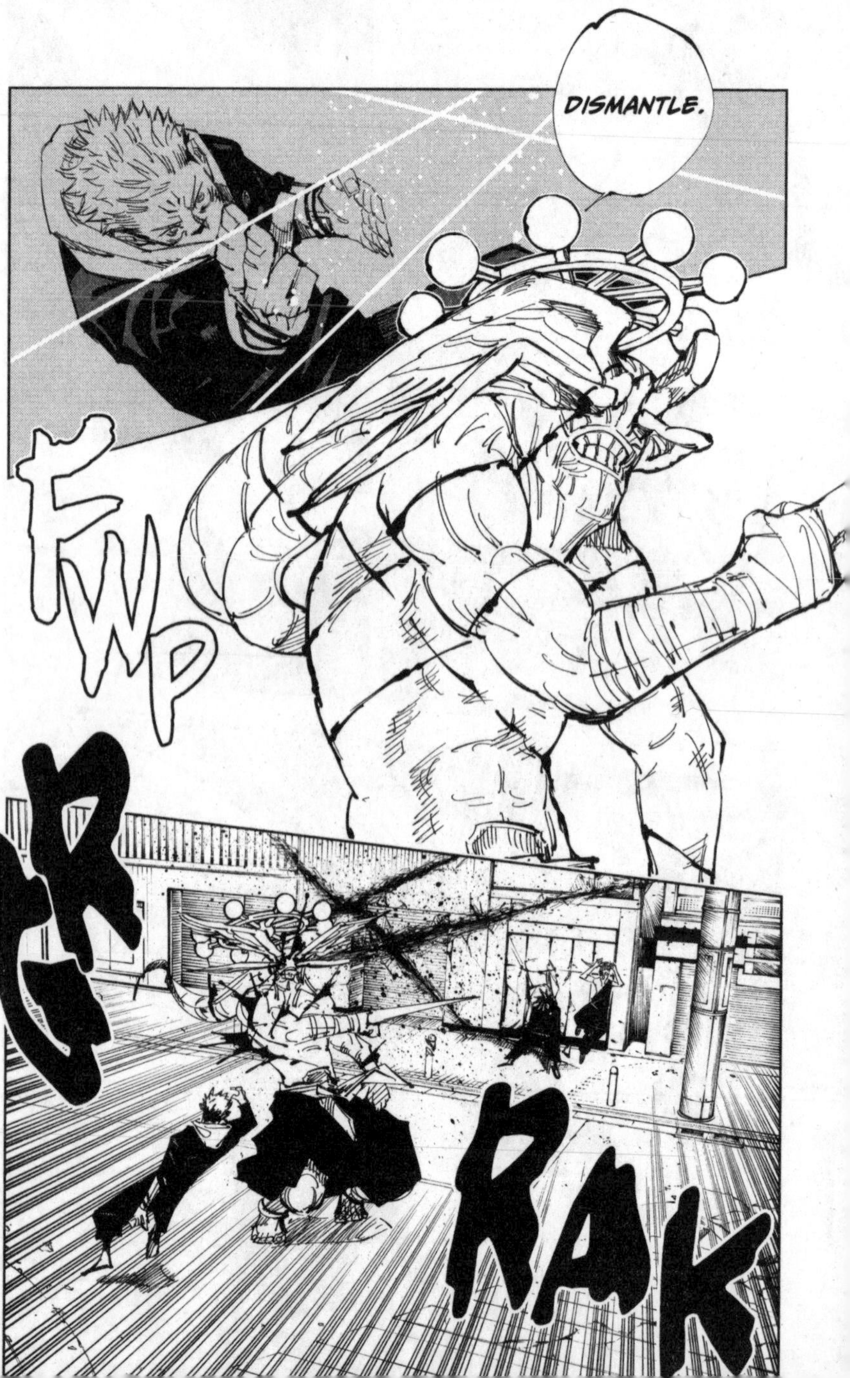
DISMANTLE.
FWP
CRAK

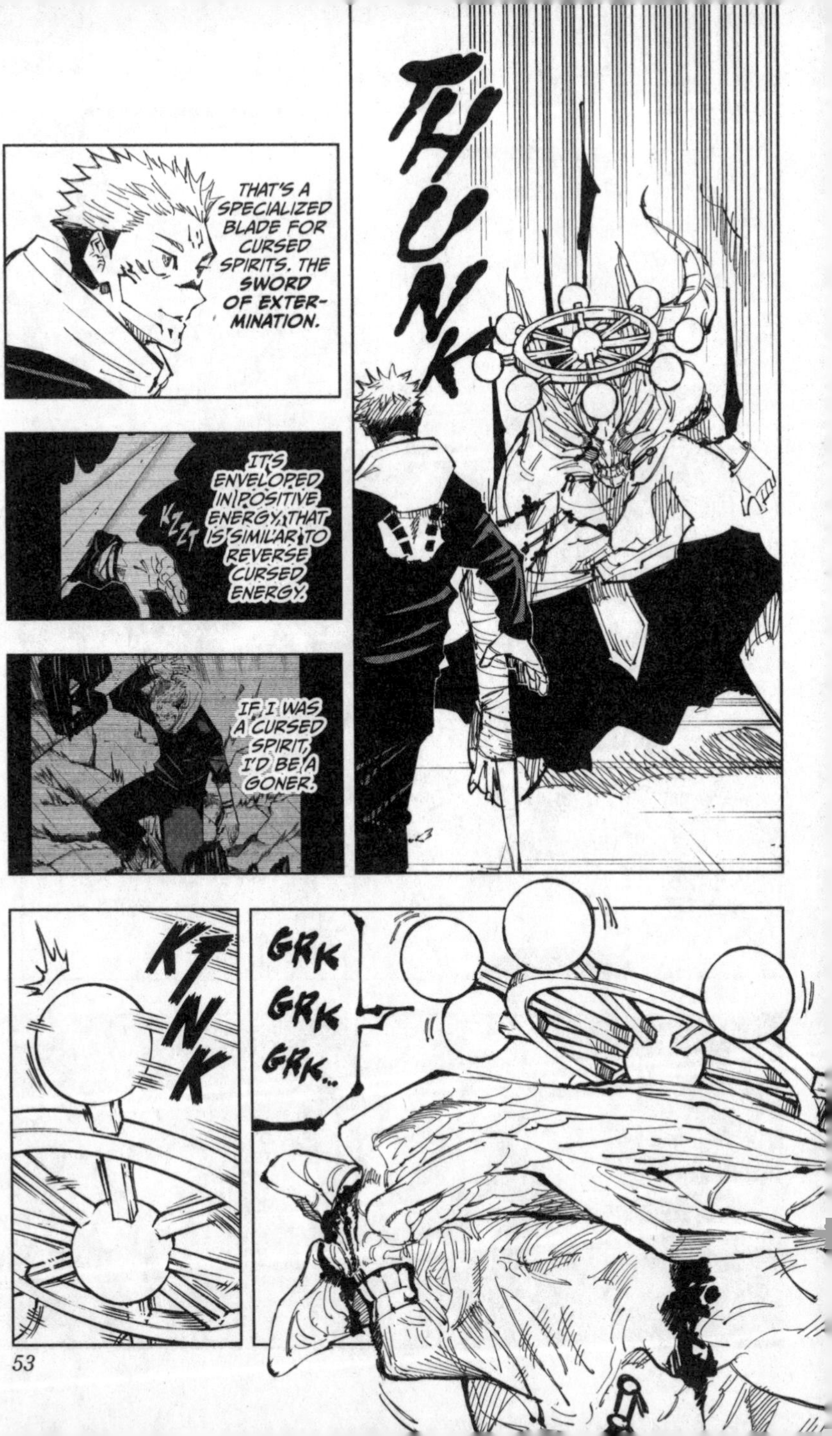
THUNK
THAT'S A SPECIALIZED BLADE FOR CURSED SPIRITS. THE SWORD OF EXTERMINATION.
IT'S ENVELOPED IN POSITIVE ENERGY THAT IS SIMILAR TO REVERSE CURSED ENERGY.
KZZT
IF I WAS A CURSED SPIRIT, I'D BE A GONER.
GRK GRK GRK...
KTINK

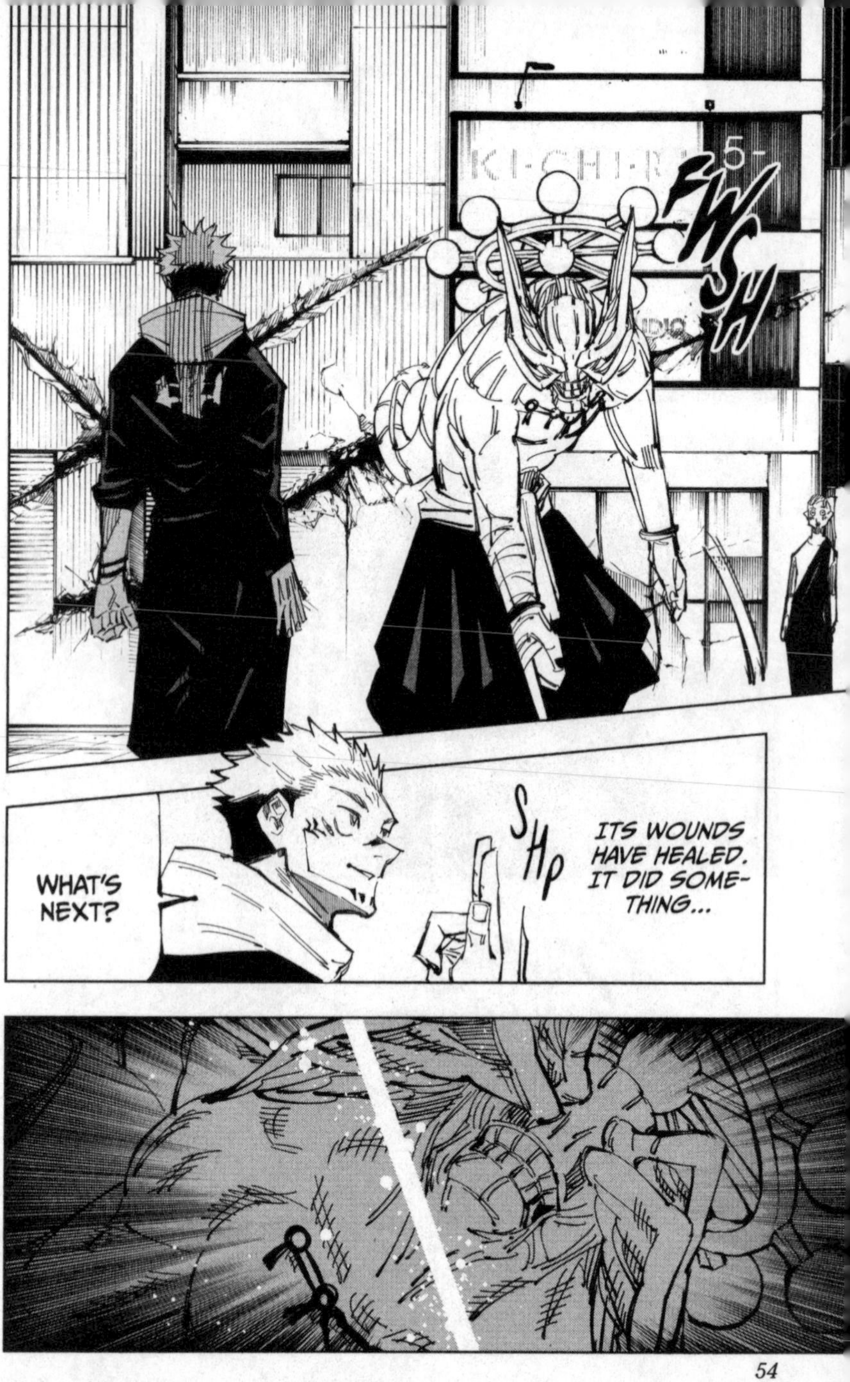
FWSH
ITS WOUNDS HAVE HEALED. IT DID SOME-THING...
SHP
WHAT'S NEXT?

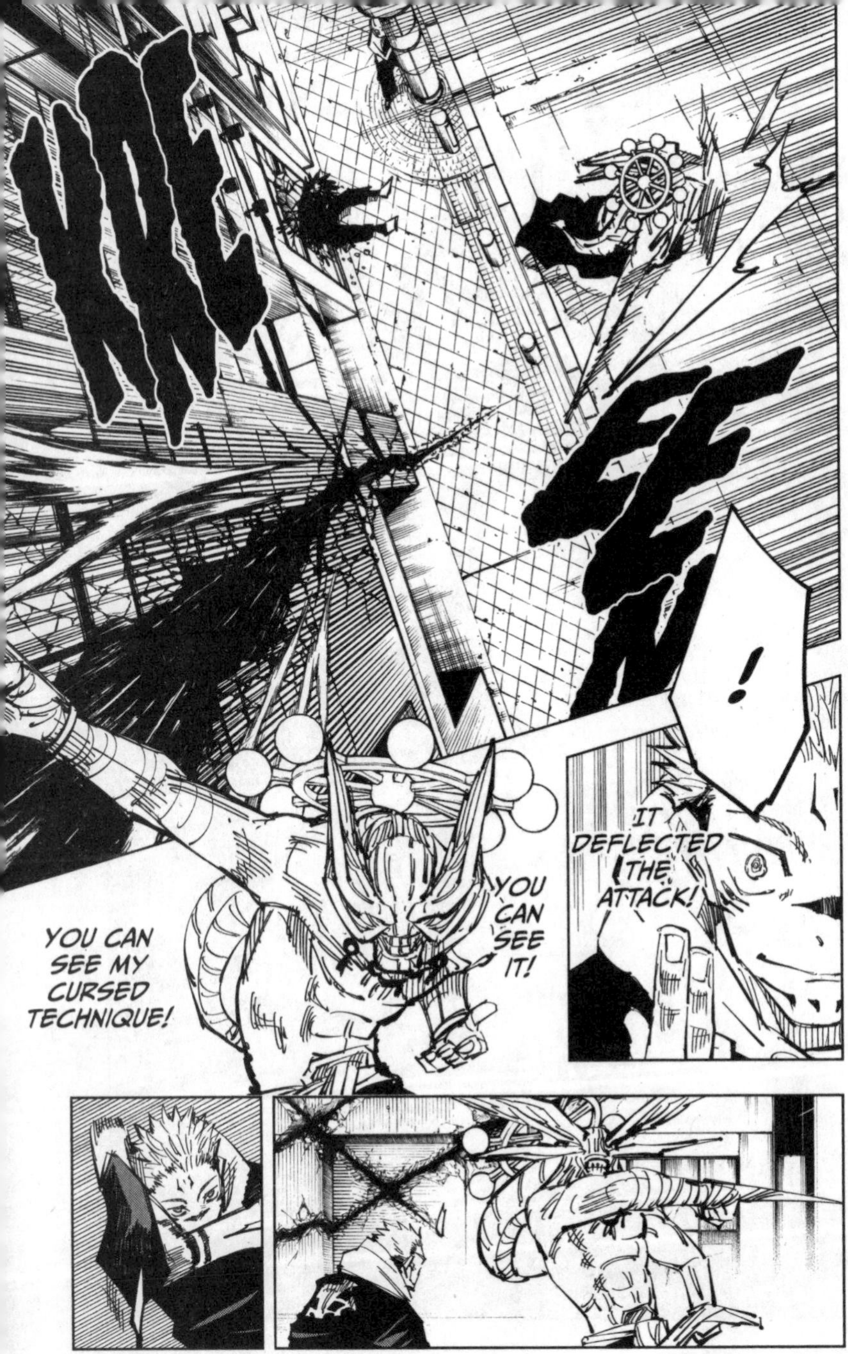
!
IT DEFLECTED THE ATTACK!
YOU CAN SEE IT!
YOU CAN SEE MY CURSED TECHNIQUE!

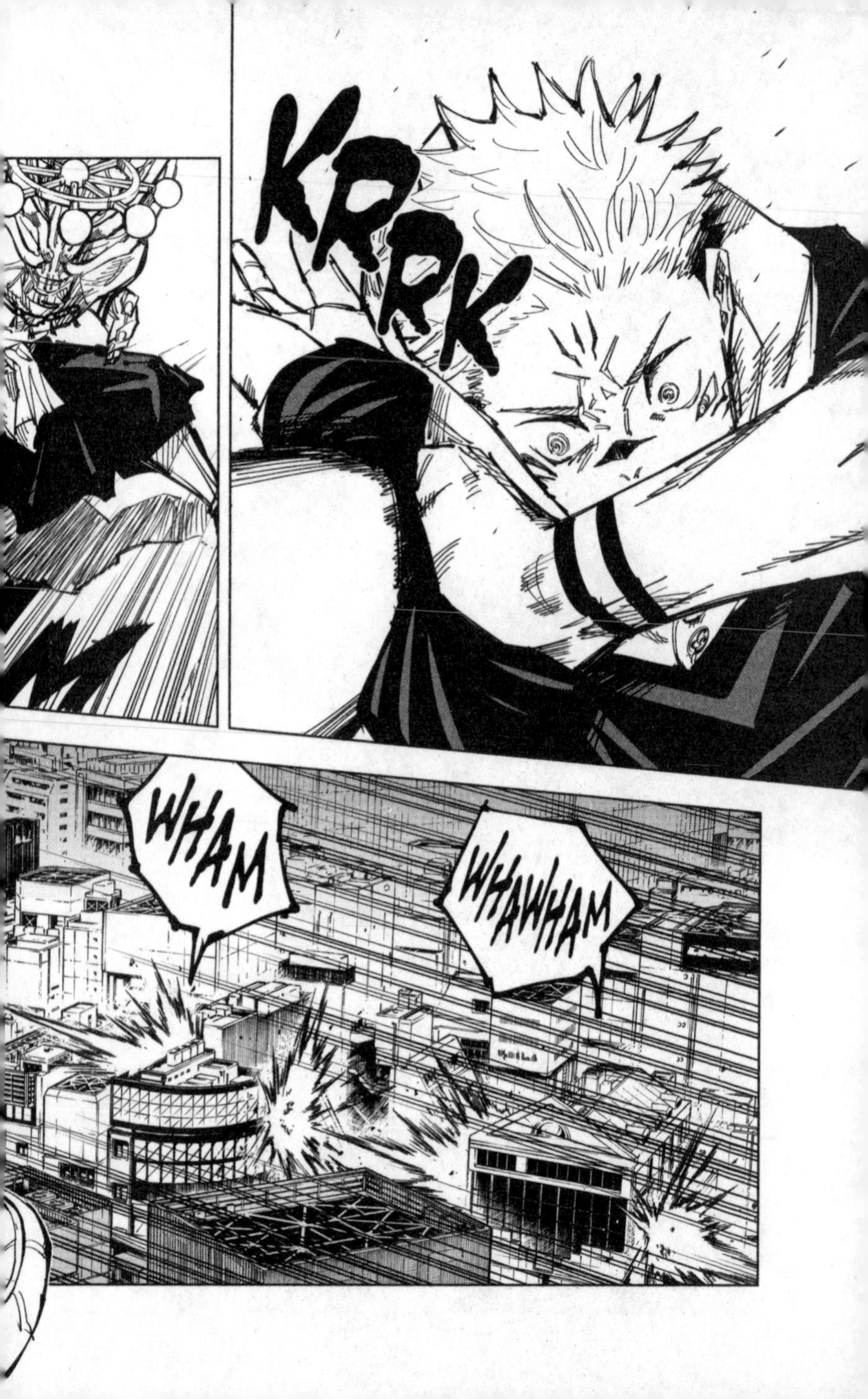
KRRK
WHAM
WHAWHAM

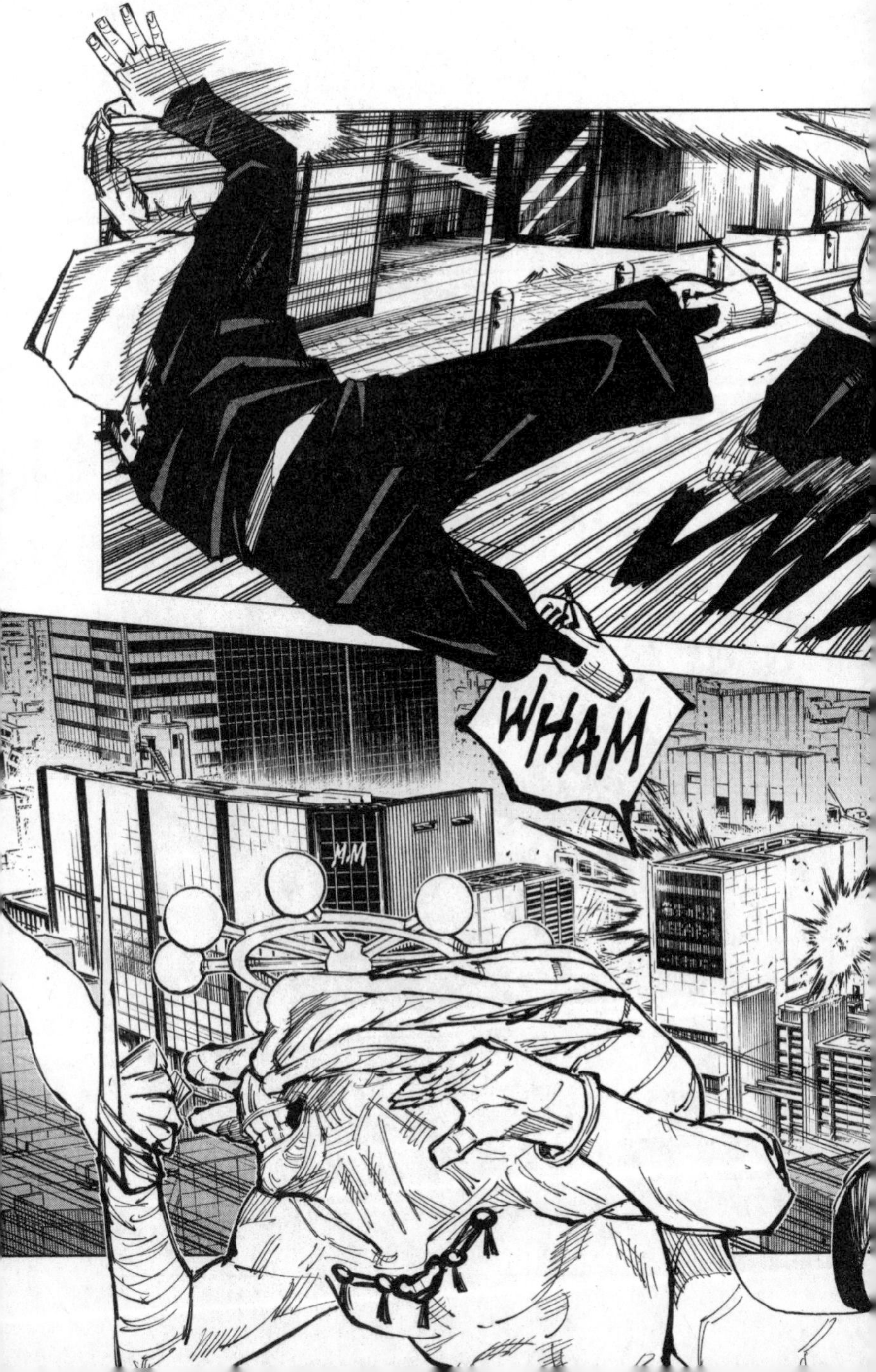
WHAM

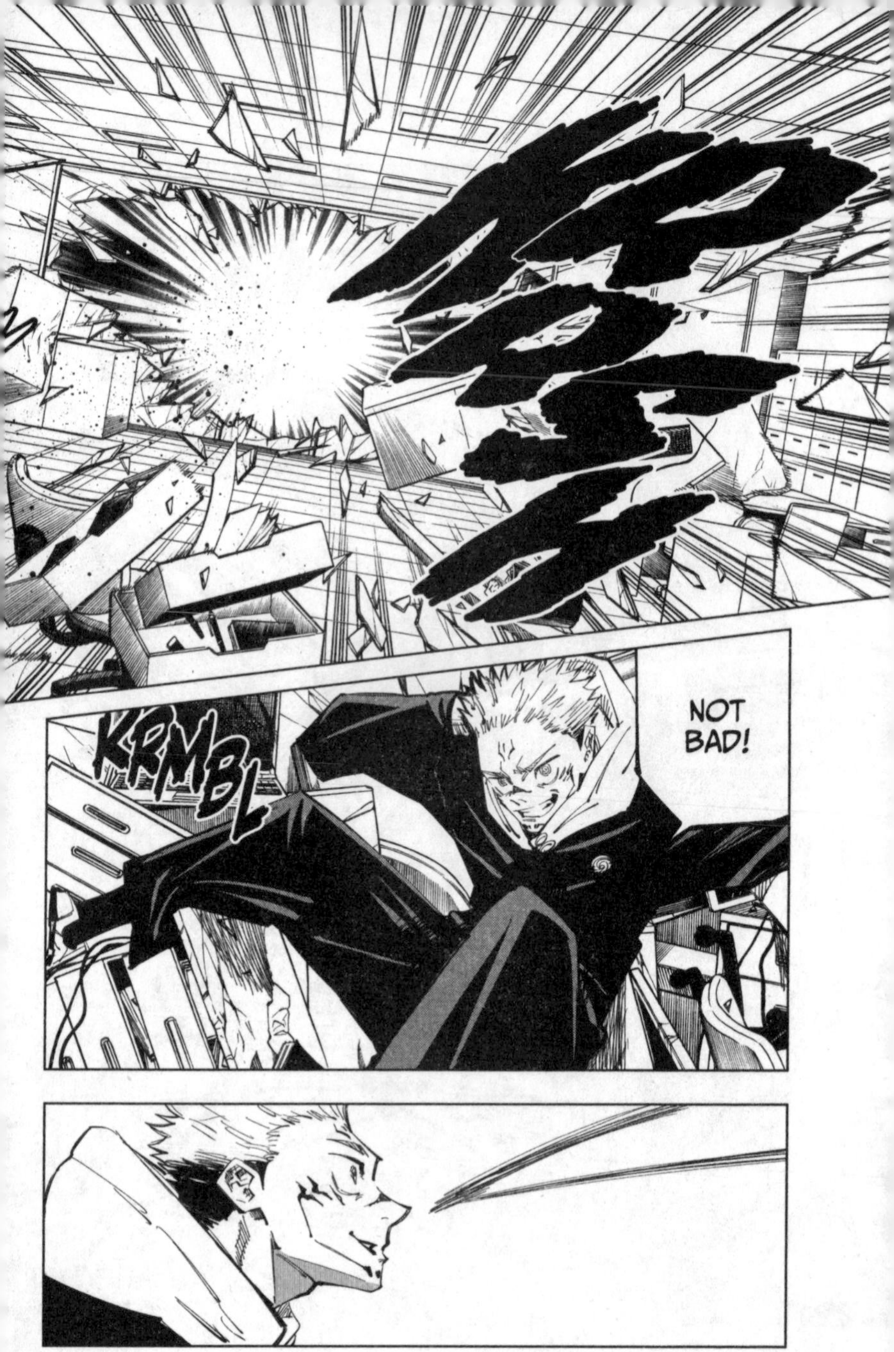
NOT BAD!
KRMBL

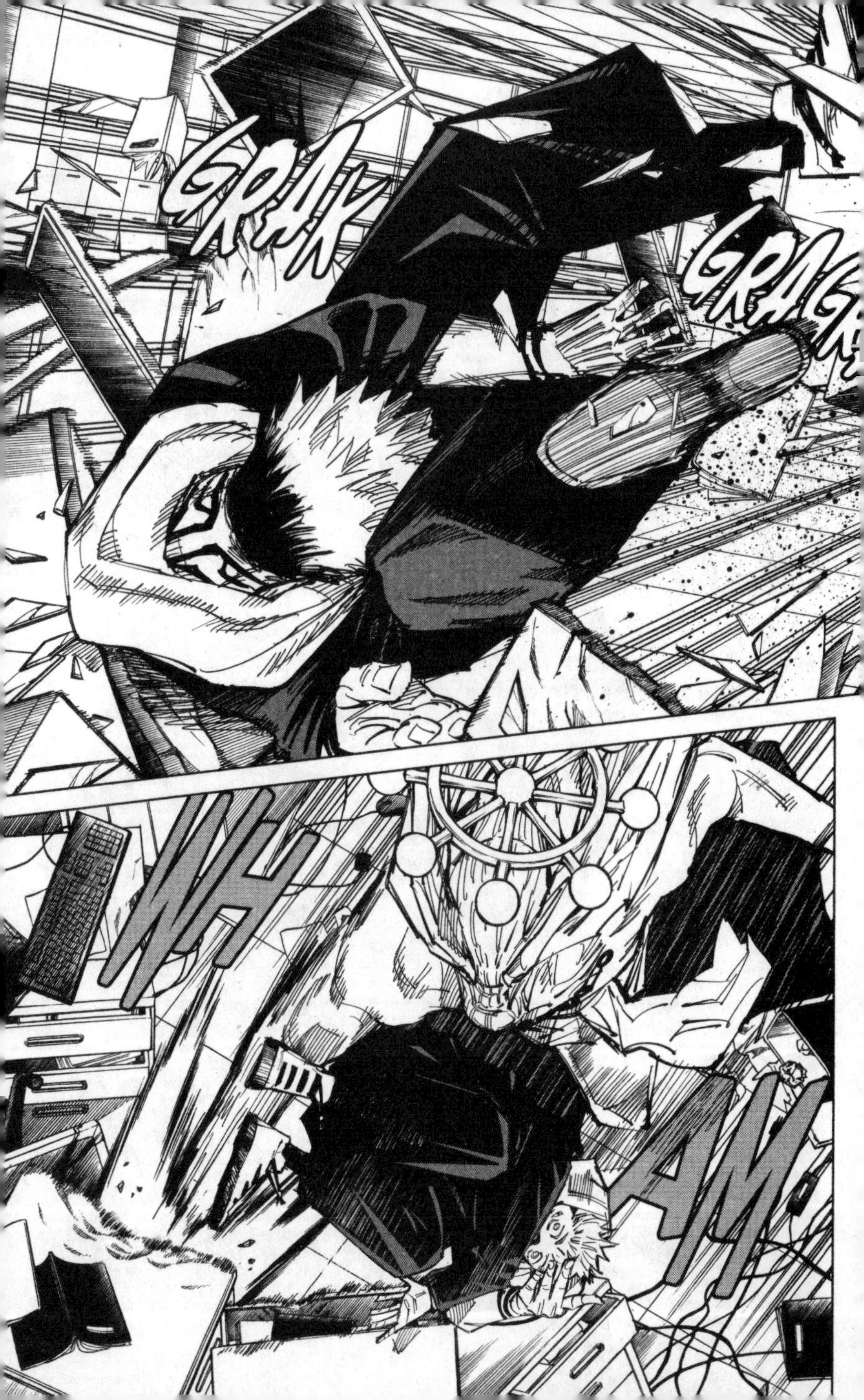
GRAK
GRAG
WH
AM

KRK

FWM

MY
TURN.

FZZT...

62

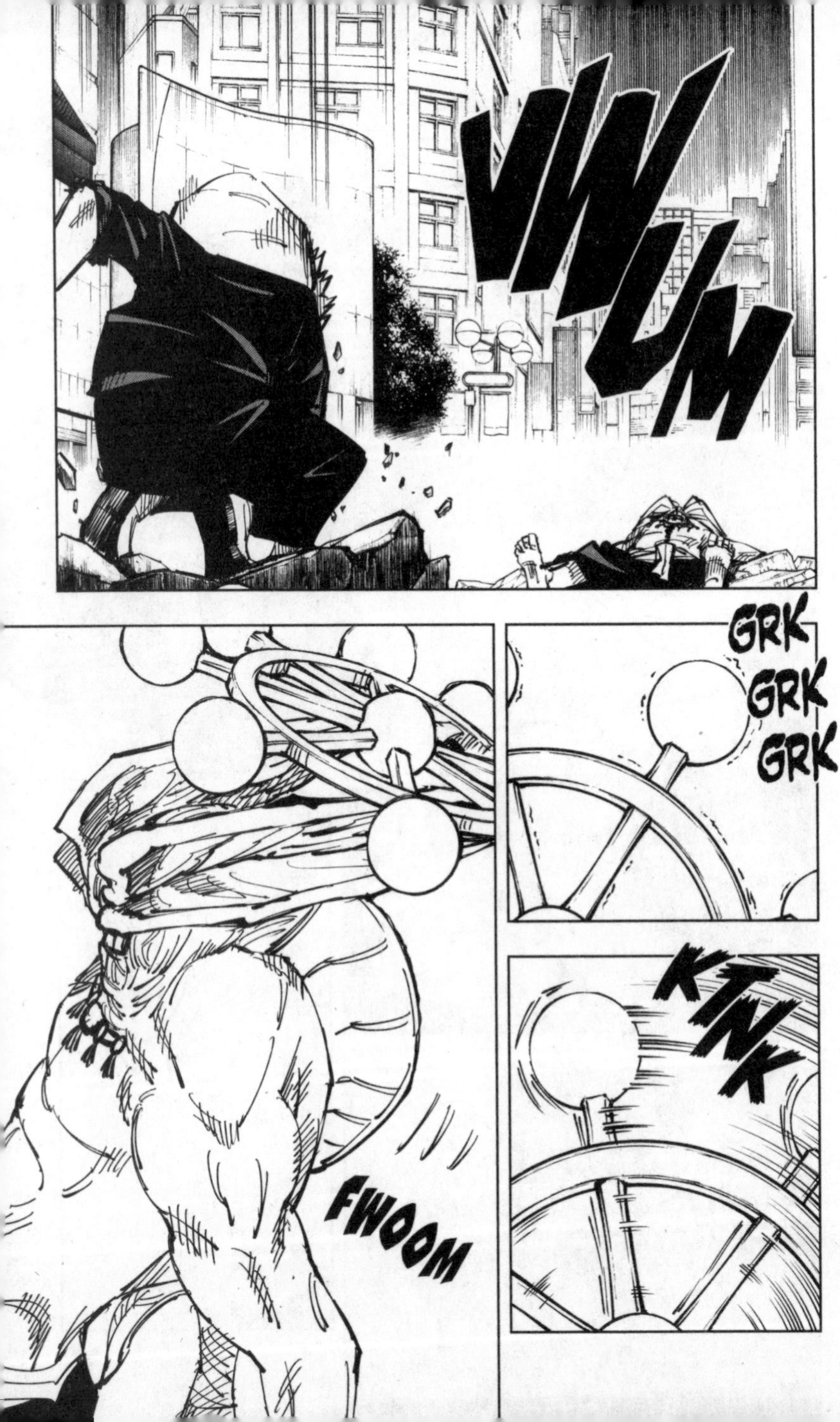
VWUM
GRK
GRK
GRK
KTNK
FWOOM

JUST AS I THOUGHT.

KRRK

...THE SECOND WAS IMBUED WITH CURSED ENERGY.

UNLIKE THE FIRST ATTACK, WHICH WAS IMBUED WITH POSITIVE ENERGY...

THAT SECOND ATTACK...

IT'S SIMILAR TO YAMATA NO OROCHI.

BOTH OCCURRED AFTER THAT WHEEL ON ITS BACK TURNED.

AS FOR MY ATTACK... IT WAS ABLE TO RECOGNIZE DISMANTLE.

64

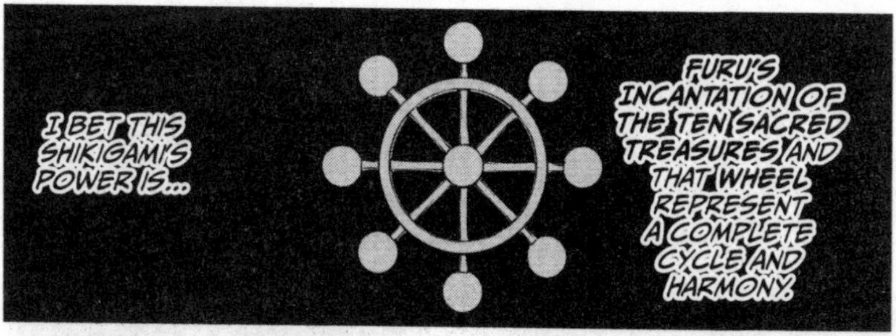
FURU'S INCANTATION OF THE TEN SACRED TREASURES AND THAT WHEEL REPRESENT A COMPLETE CYCLE AND HARMONY.
I BET THIS SHIKIGAMI'S POWER IS...

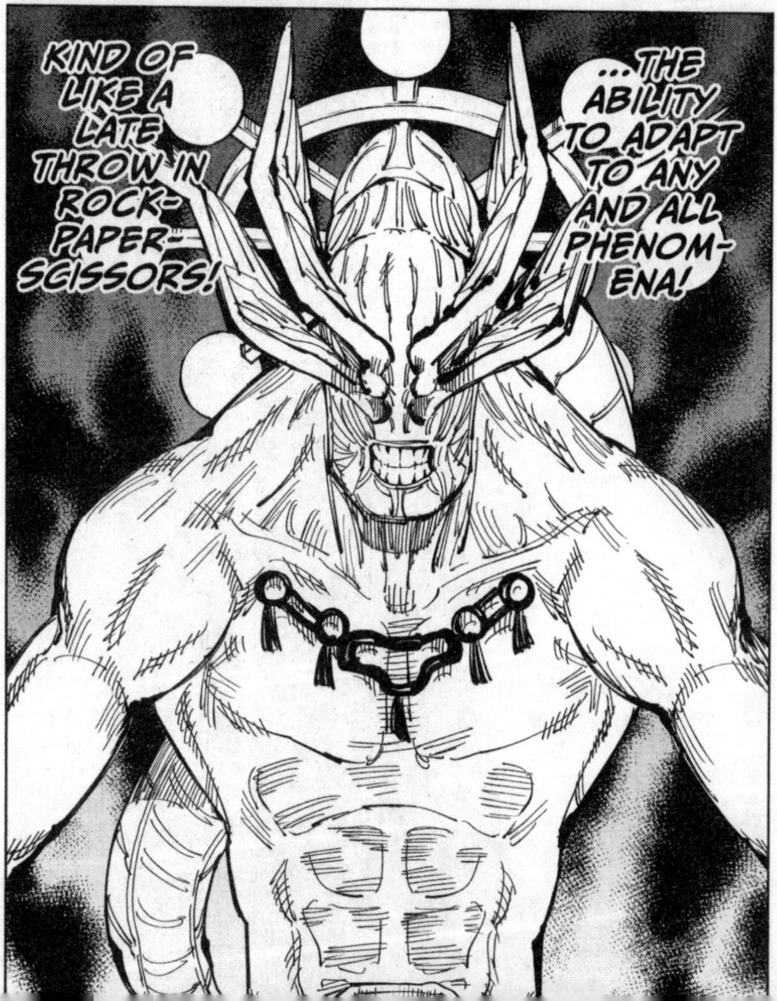
...THE ABILITY TO ADAPT TO ANY AND ALL PHENOM-ENA!
KIND OF LIKE A LATE THROW IN ROCK-PAPER-SCISSORS!

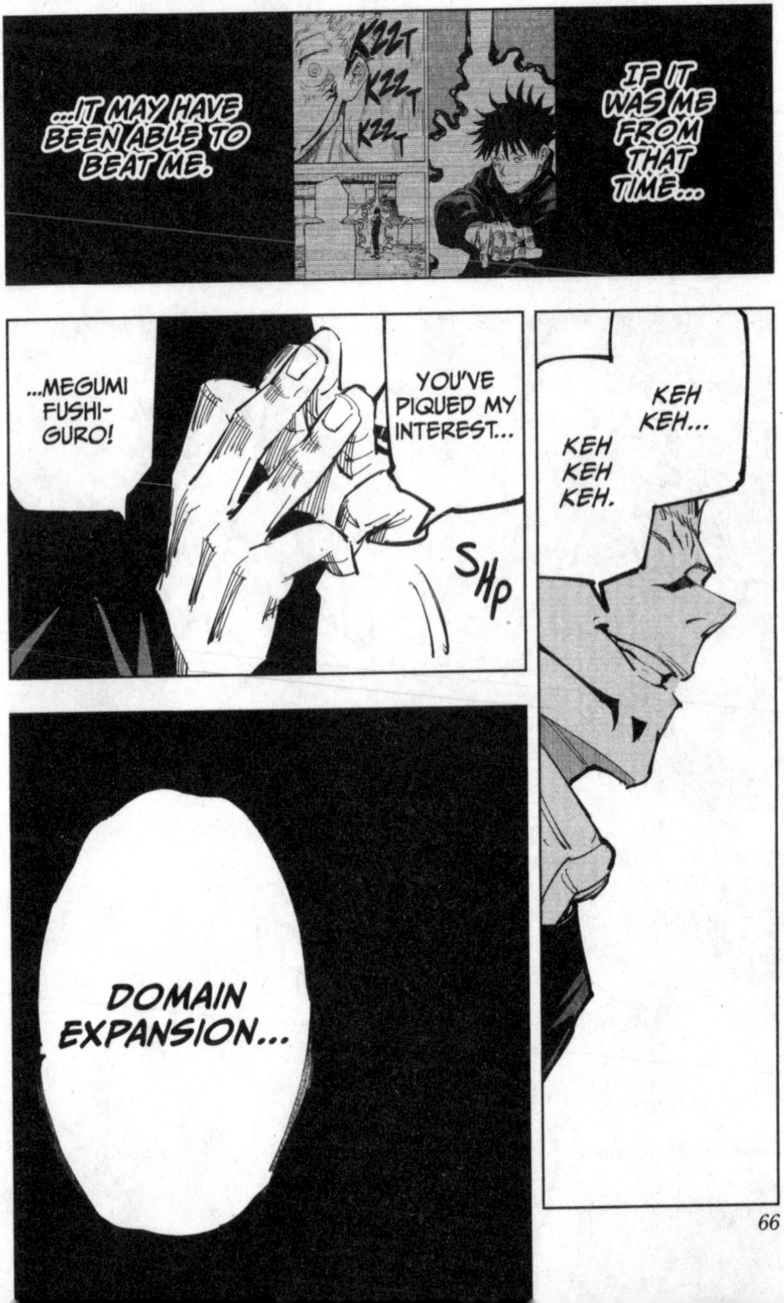

IF IT WAS ME FROM THAT TIME...
KZZT KZZT KZZT
...IT MAY HAVE BEEN ABLE TO BEAT ME.
KEH KEH...
KEH KEH KEH.
YOU'VE PIQUED MY INTEREST...
...MEGUMI FUSHI-GURO!
SHP
DOMAIN EXPANSION...

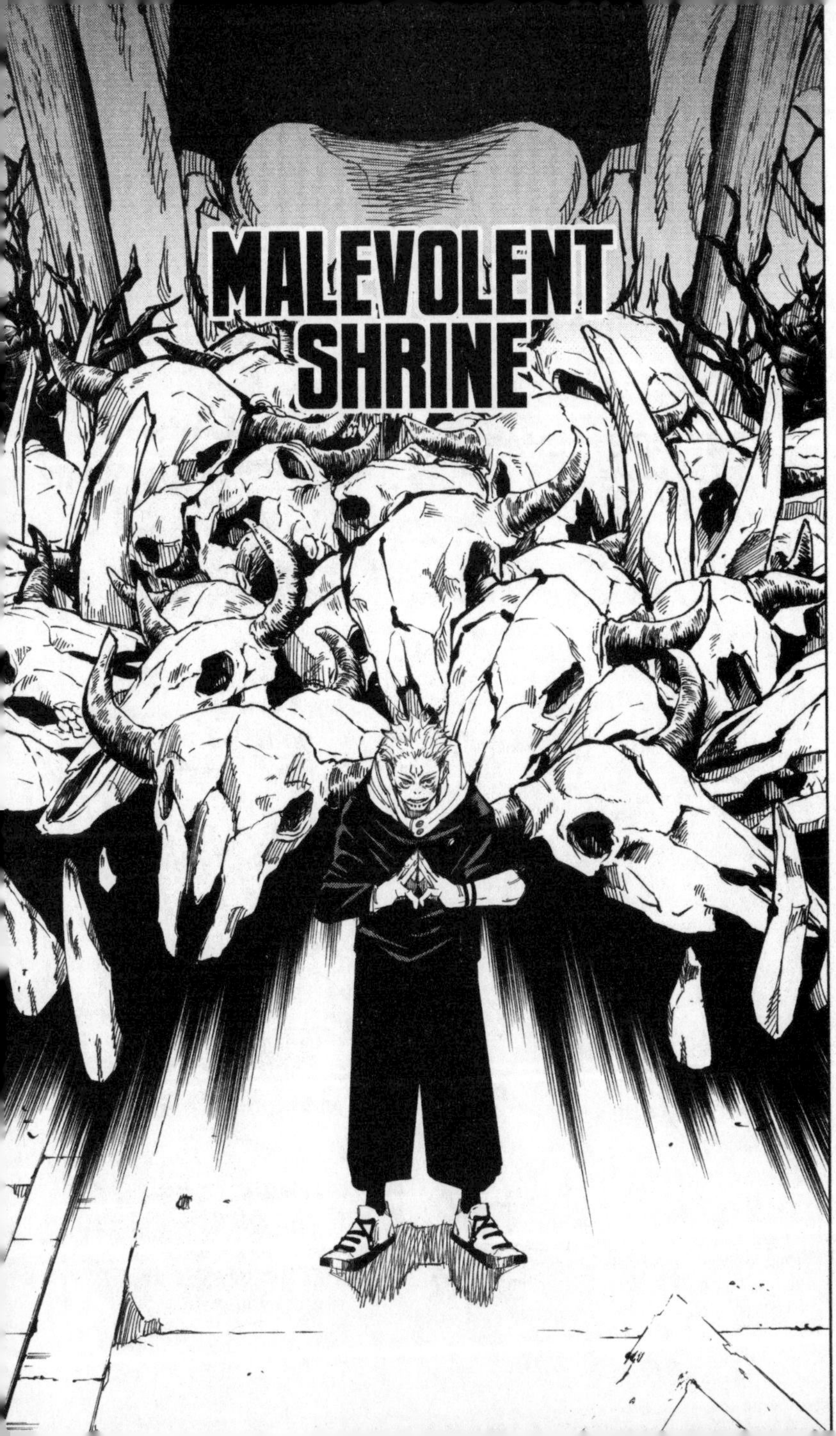
MALEVOLENT SHRINE

THE 2020 VALENTINES RANKINGS THAT I SERIOUSLY ALMOST FORGOT

RANKINGS (VALENTINES RECEIVED)	CHARACTER	AKUTAMI'S COMMENT
10 (4)	INO	MAYBE THE INCIDENT WAS STARTING ABOUT THAT TIME?
11 (3)	IEIRI	MACROSS F IN A SET WITH GOJO.
	IJICHI	COME ON, TETSUO!
	KAMO	HE LOST TO CHOSO... HA HA!
14 (2)	MEI MEI	AGE INDETERMINATE.
	MIWA	AFTER ALL, SHE'S CUTE!
	OZAWA	EVEN THOUGH SHE JUST BRIEFLY POPPED IN?

Chapter 119: The Shibuya Incident, Part 37

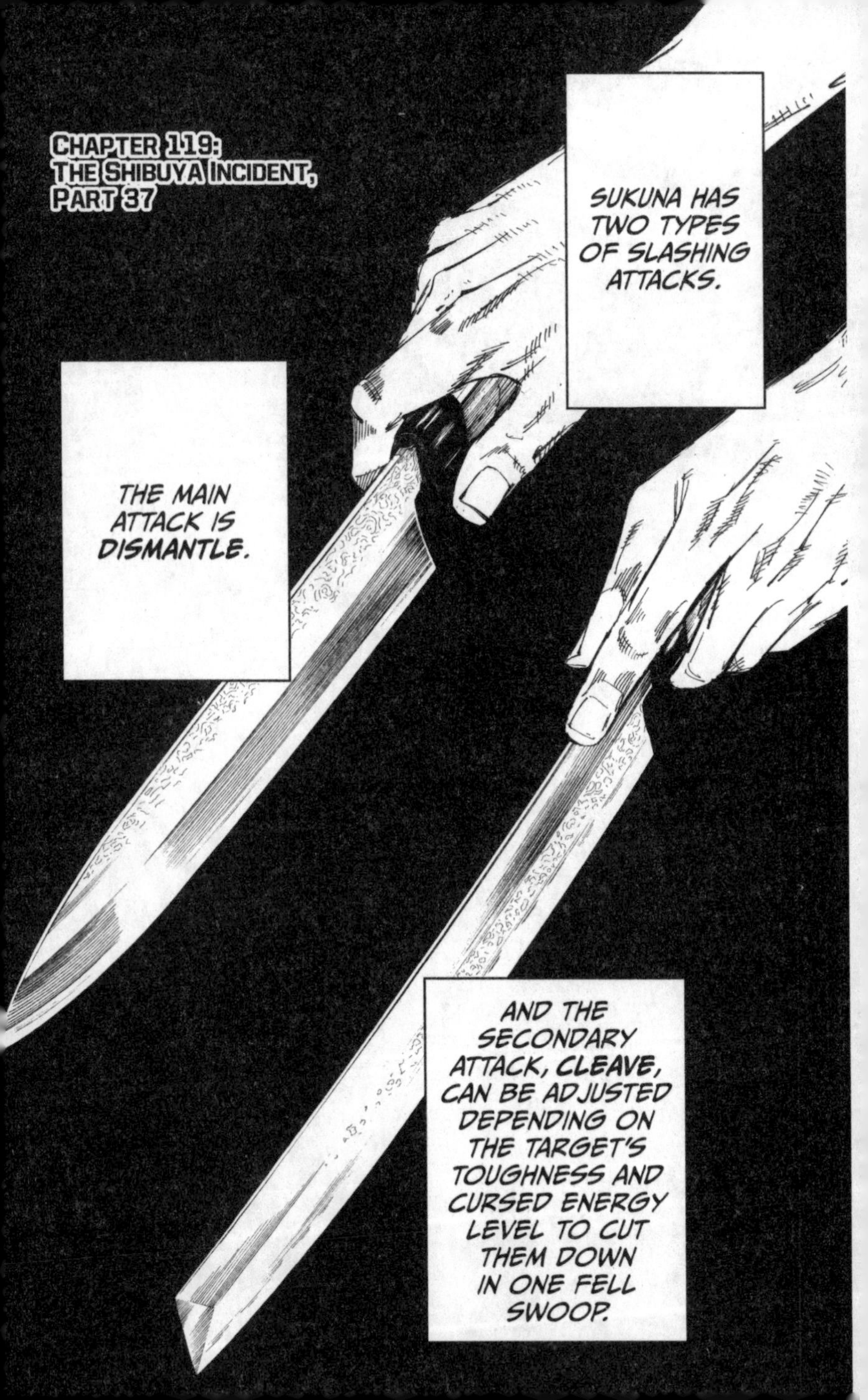
SUKUNA HAS TWO TYPES OF SLASHING ATTACKS.
THE MAIN ATTACK IS DISMANTLE.
AND THE SECONDARY ATTACK, CLEAVE, CAN BE ADJUSTED DEPENDING ON THE TARGET'S TOUGHNESS AND CURSED ENERGY LEVEL TO CUT THEM DOWN IN ONE FELL SWOOP.

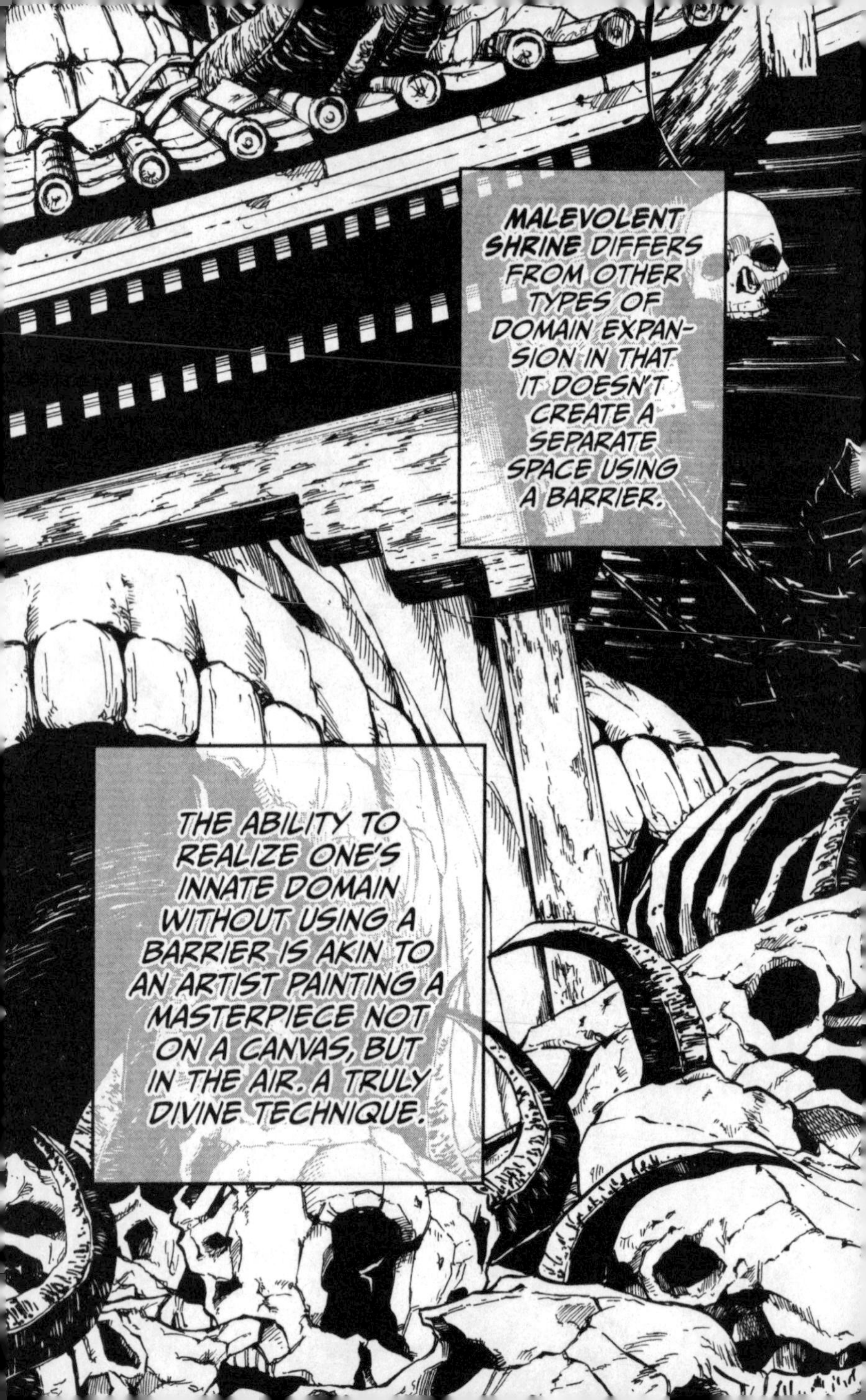
MALEVOLENT SHRINE DIFFERS FROM OTHER TYPES OF DOMAIN EXPANSION IN THAT IT DOESN'T CREATE A SEPARATE SPACE USING A BARRIER.
THE ABILITY TO REALIZE ONE'S INNATE DOMAIN WITHOUT USING A BARRIER IS AKIN TO AN ARTIST PAINTING A MASTERPIECE NOT ON A CANVAS, BUT IN THE AIR. A TRULY DIVINE TECHNIQUE.

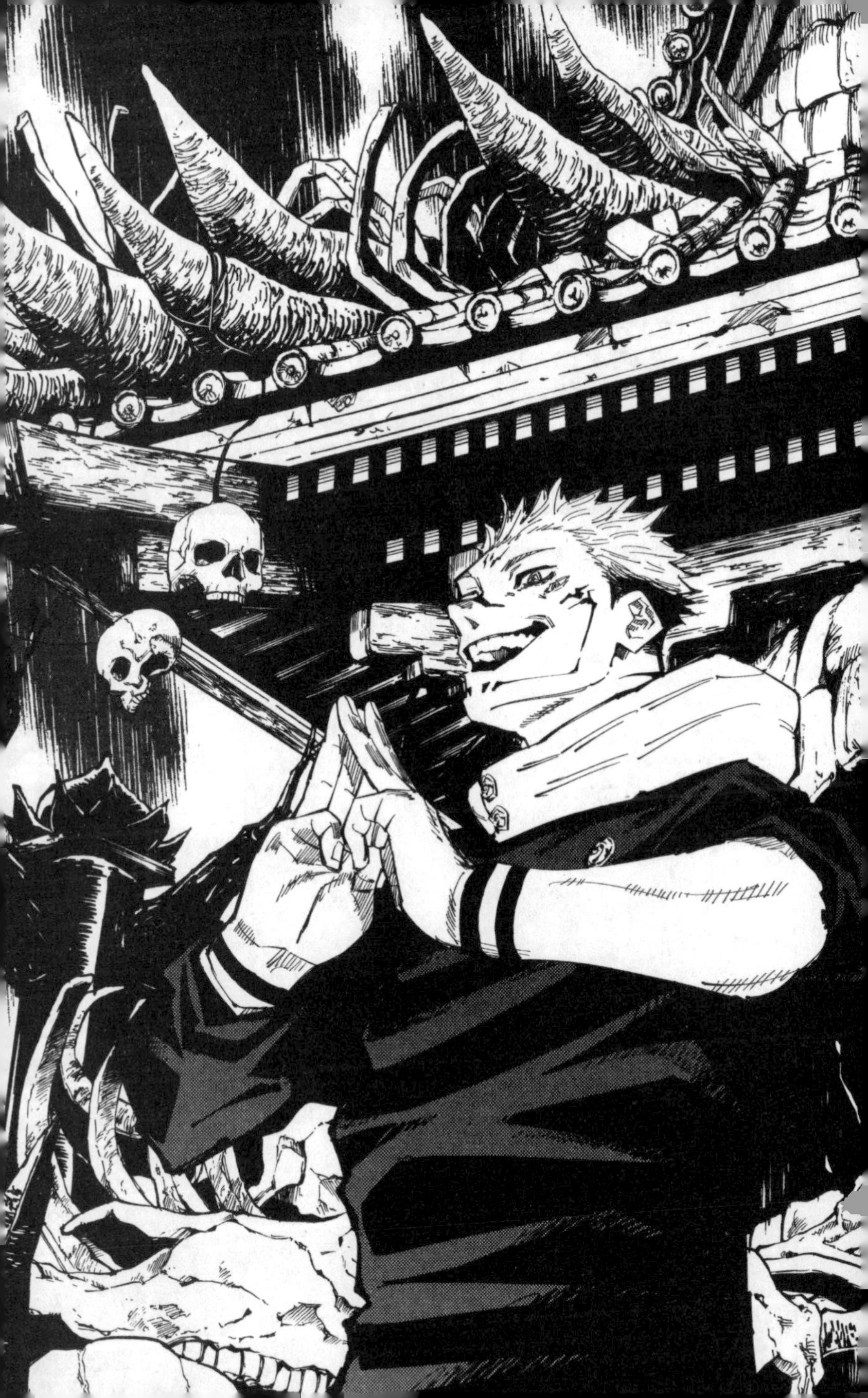

...TO A MAXIMUM RADIUS OF NEARLY 200 METERS.

FURTHERMORE, BY ALLOWING AN ESCAPE ROUTE, A *BINDING VOW* IS FORMED, WHICH VASTLY INCREASES THE GUARANTEED HIT'S EFFECTIVE AREA...

TAKING MEGUMI FUSHIGURO INTO ACCOUNT...

...SUKUNA NARROWED THE EFFECT'S RANGE TO A 140-METER RADIUS ABOVE THE SURFACE.

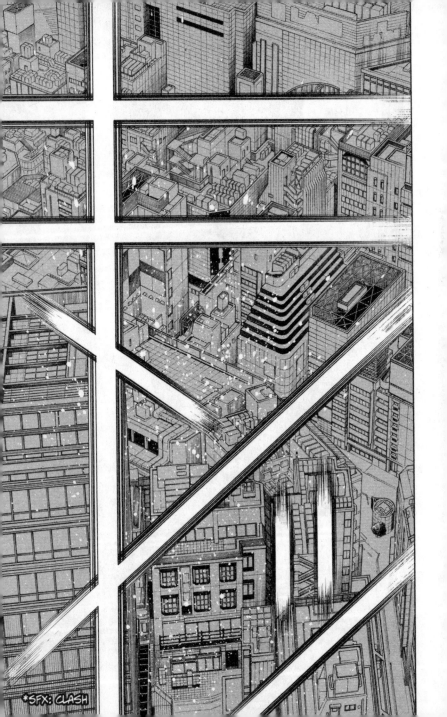

*SFX: CLASH

STILL NO RECEPTION.

HOW'S YOUR PHONE?

BUT...I DON'T THINK WE NEED TO WORRY ANYMORE.

HUH?

IT'D BE BAD IF BOTH OF OUR PHONES RAN OUT OF POWER.

DON'T USE YOURS TOO MUCH, KEIKO.

ME NEITHER...

TRUE...

THAT MEGA-PHONE GUY IS HERE.

74

OH RIGHT, THAT G—

FOR INANIMATE OBJECTS— DISMANTLE.

FOR ANYTHING WITH CURSED ENERGY WITHIN RANGE—CLEAVE.

UNTIL MALEVOLENT SHRINE IS GONE...

...IT WILL RELENTLESSLY ATTACK ALL TARGETS WITHIN THE EFFECTIVE RANGE OF ITS GUARANTEED HIT.

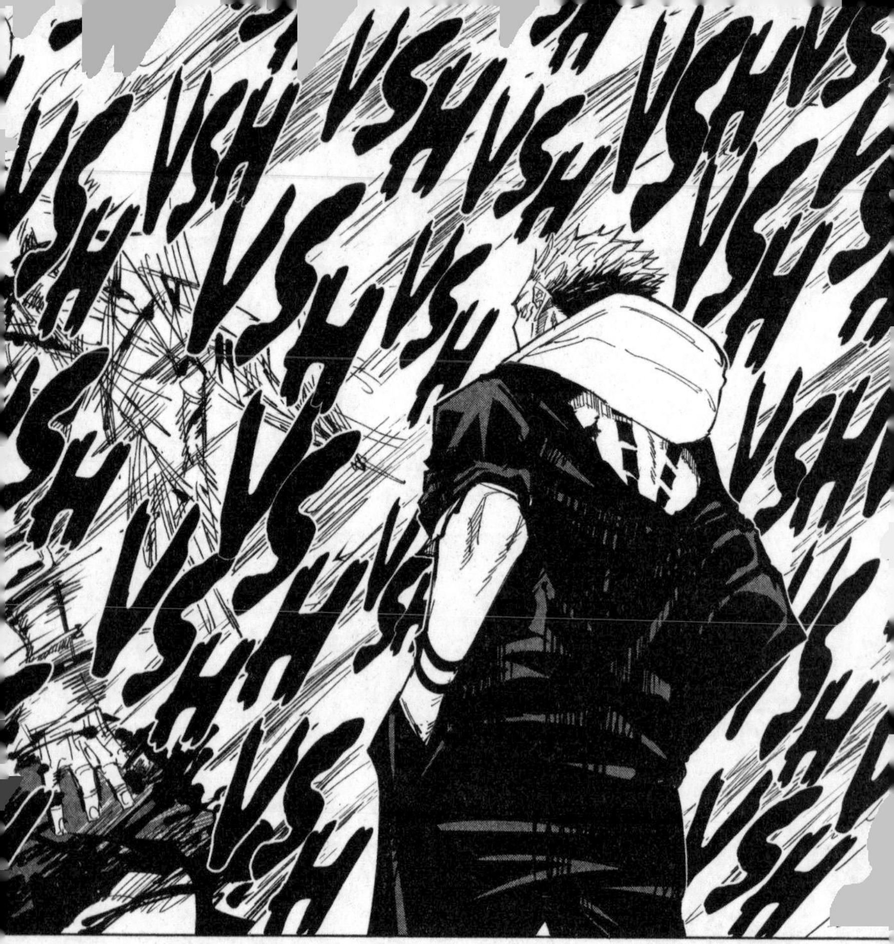
VSH VSH VSH VSH

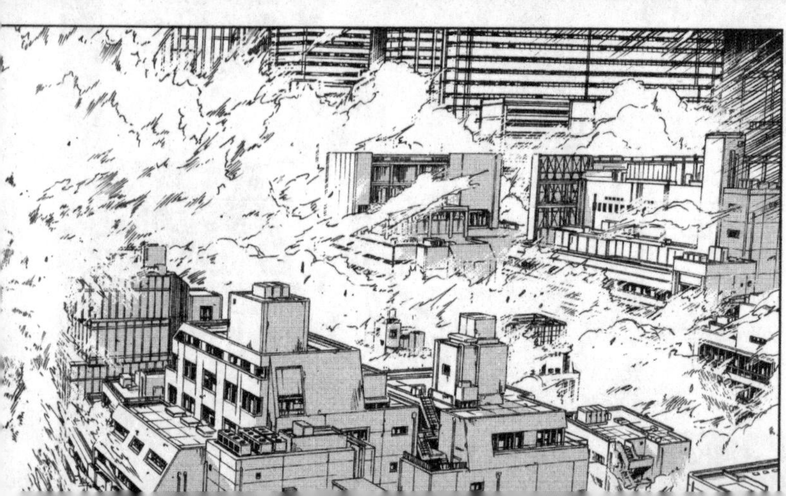

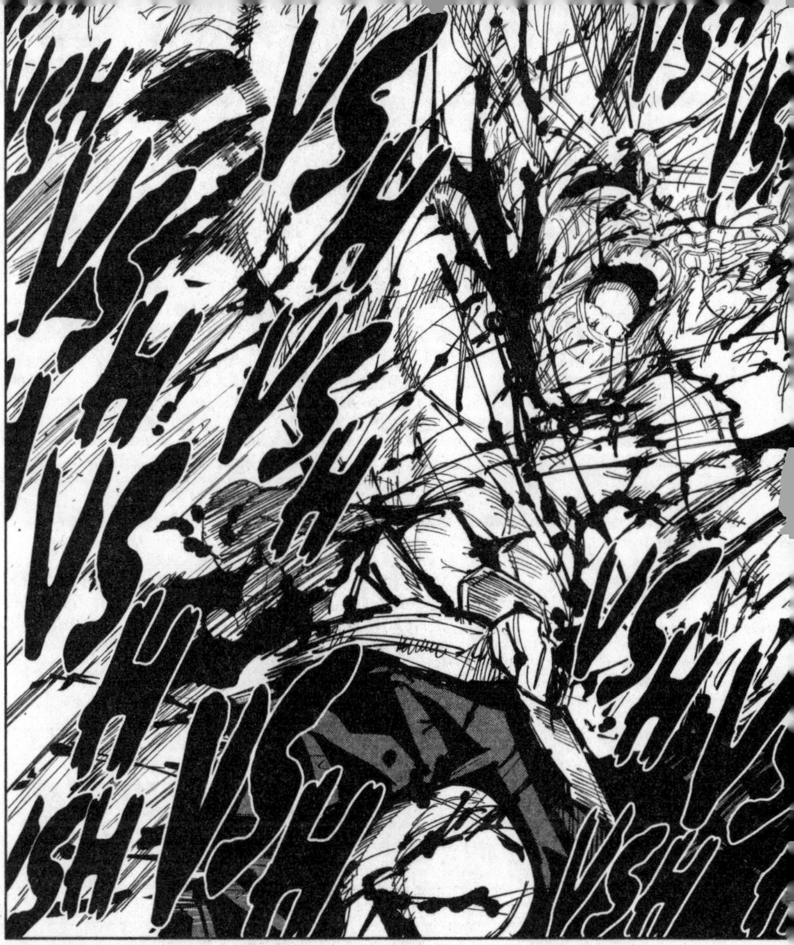
VSH VSH VSH VSH VSH
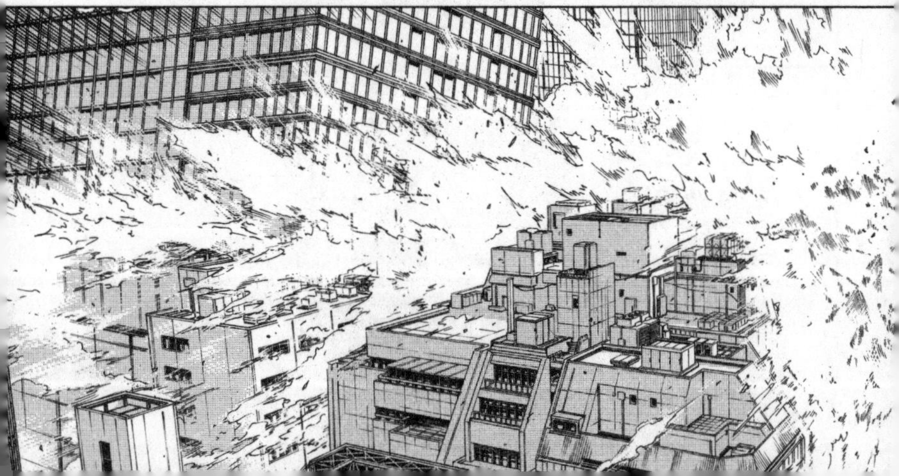

VWM

KRAK

THE ONLY WAY TO DEFEAT MAHORAGA...

...IS TO SLAUGHTER IT WITH A NEW ATTACK BEFORE IT CAN ADAPT.

CLEAVE FITS THE CRITERIA. HOWEVER...

KRAK

...IF IT HASN'T ADAPTED ONLY TO DISMANTLE...

...BUT TO SLASHING ATTACKS IN GENERAL, THEN...

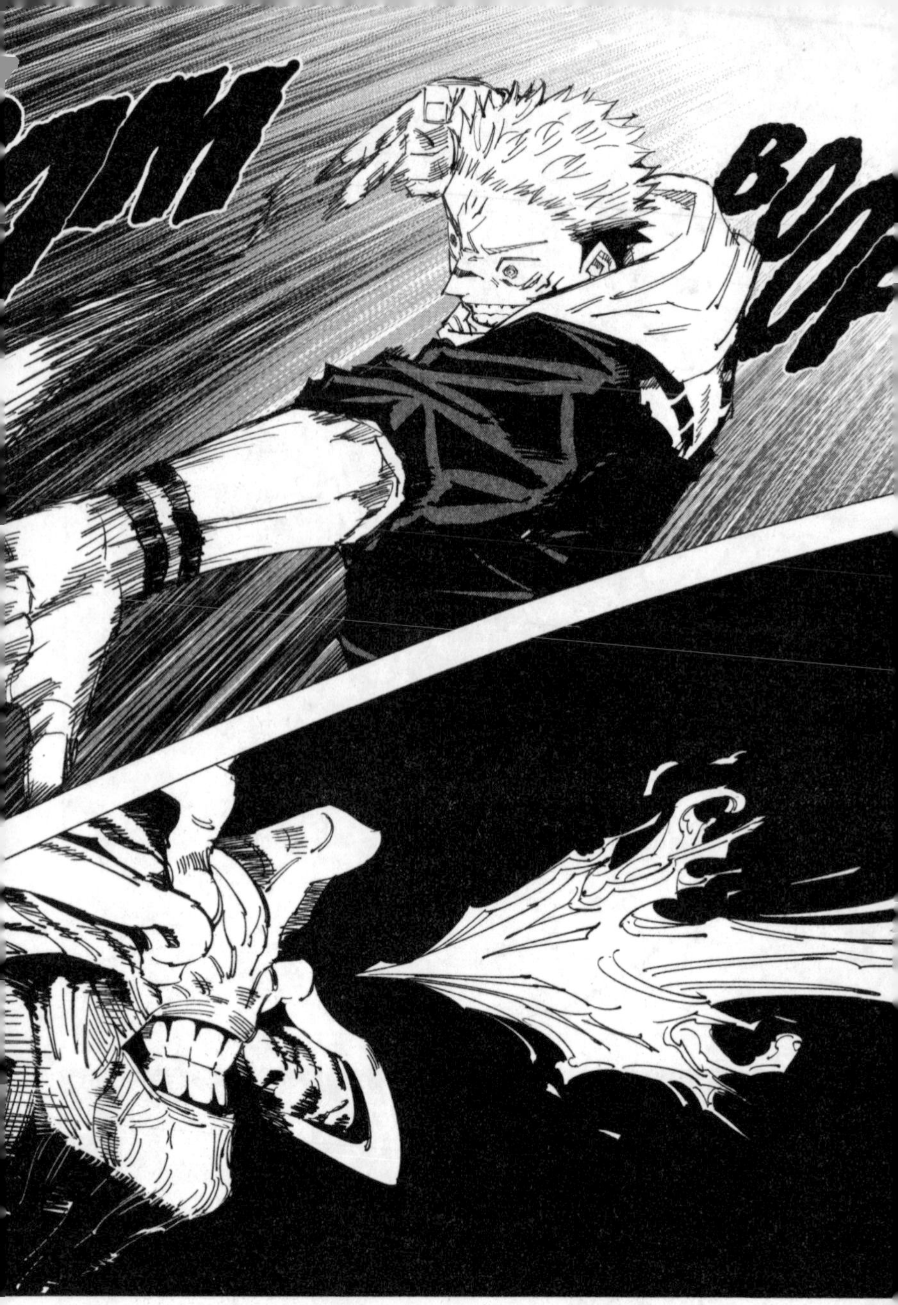

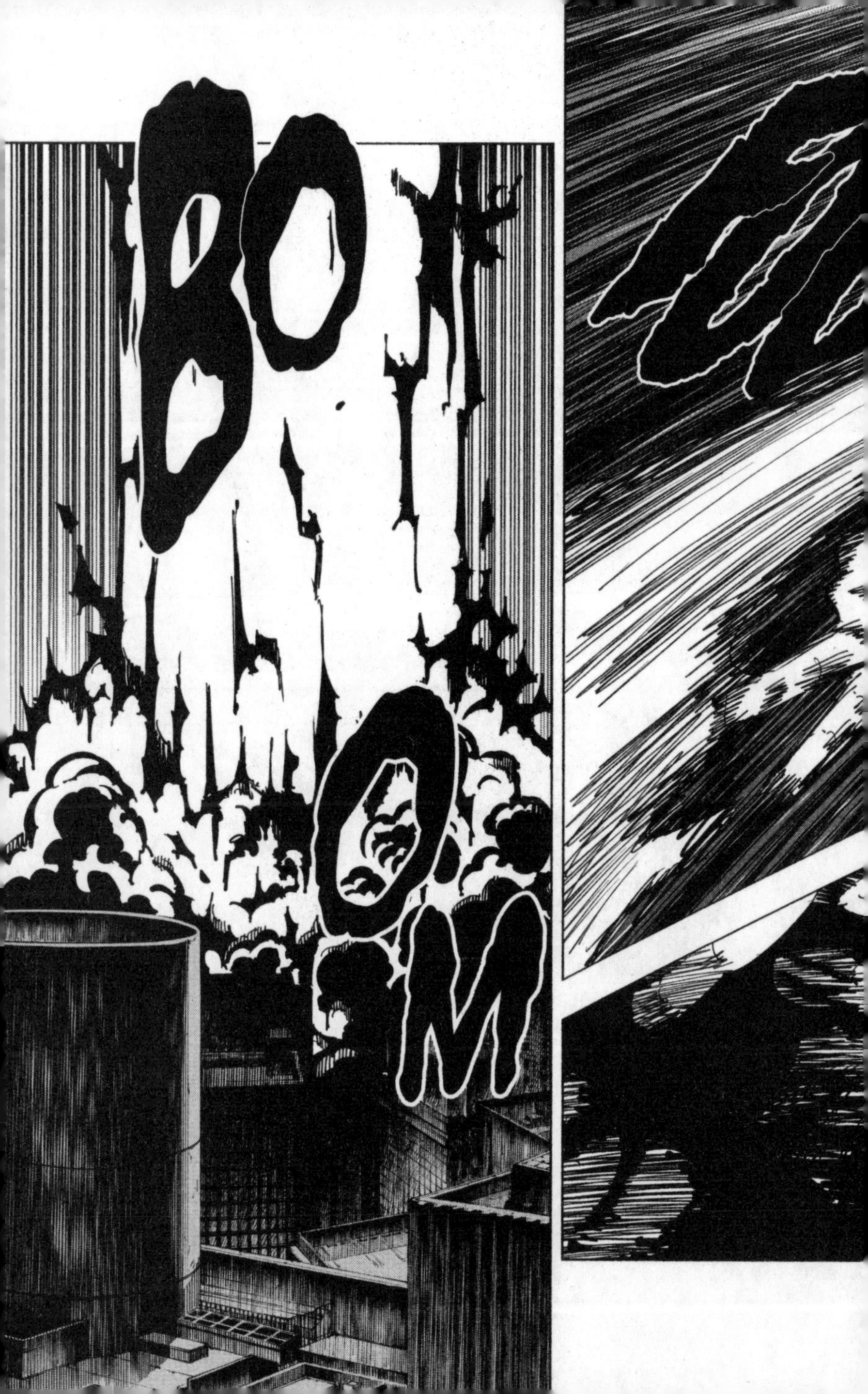
BOOM

FWIP

GLOOP

KLNK
KLNK

BEGONE.

WHAT'RE YOU LOOKING AT?

I'M OUTTA HERE!

I'LL BE ON MY WAY!

I...

MY LUCK NEVER RUNS OUT!

I SURVIVED AGAIN!

CURSE USER HARUTA SHIGEMO'S CURSED TECHNIQUE...

...STORES MIRACLES.

THE MARKINGS UNDER SHIGEMO'S EYES INDICATE HOW MANY MIRACLES HE HAS STORED, BUT EVEN HE IS NOT AWARE OF THIS FACT.

LITTLE EVERYDAY MIRACLES ARE ERASED FROM SHIGEMO'S MEMORY AND STORED.

FOR EXAMPLE...

4:44 44

HEY! ALL THE SAME NUMBER!

ONCE AGAIN, I LIVE...

THESE STORED MIRACLES ARE THEN RELEASED WHEN SHIGEMO'S LIFE IS IN DANGER.

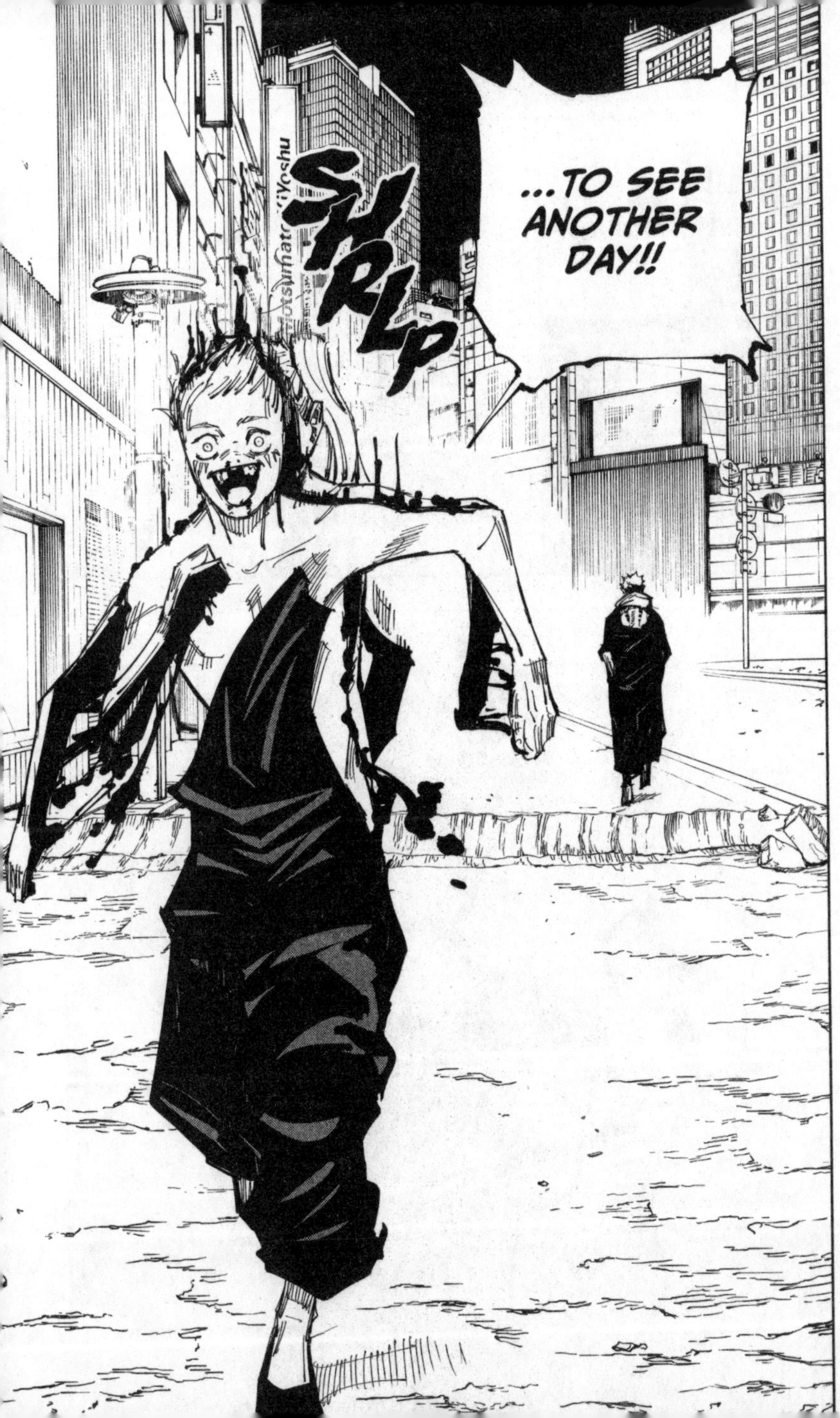
SHRLP
...TO SEE ANOTHER DAY!!

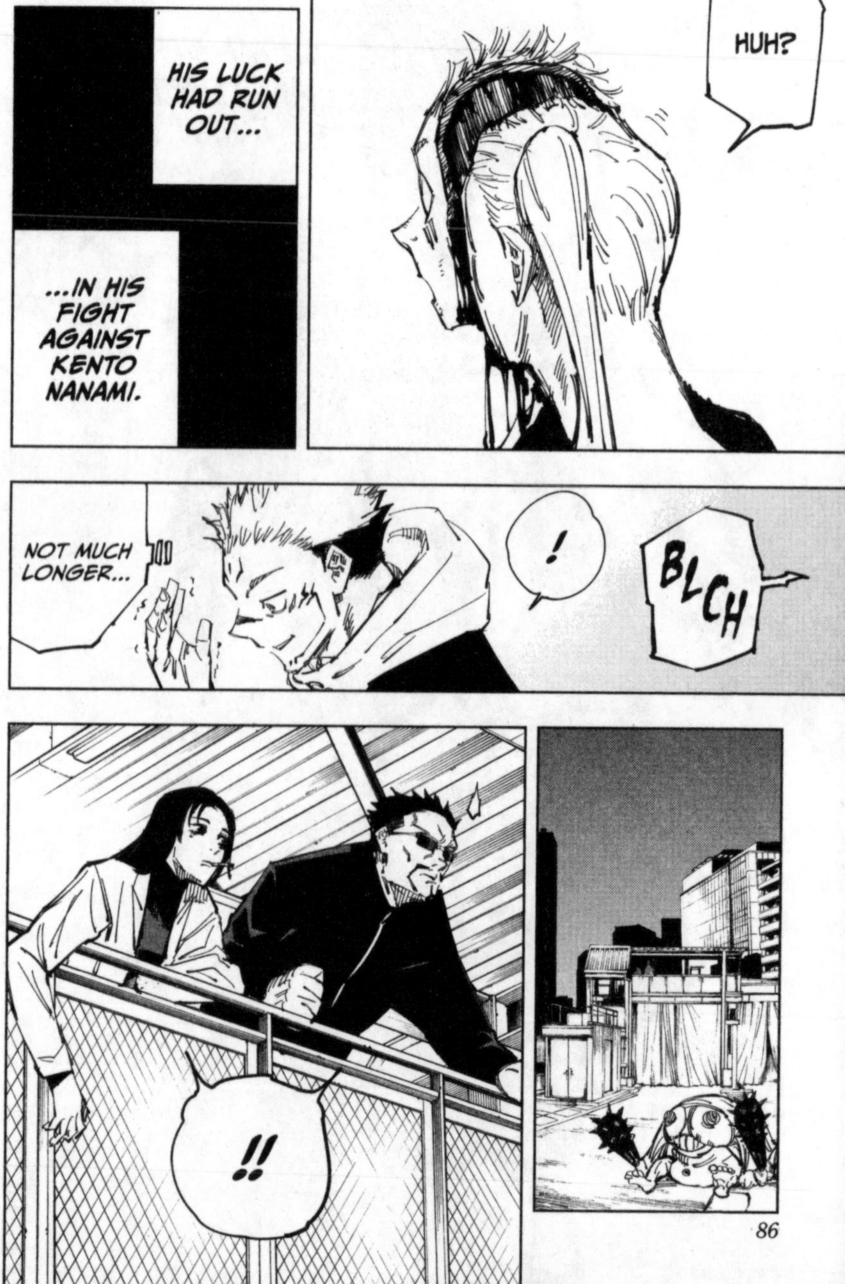
HUH?
HIS LUCK HAD RUN OUT...
...IN HIS FIGHT AGAINST KENTO NANAMI.
BLCH
!
NOT MUCH LONGER...
!!

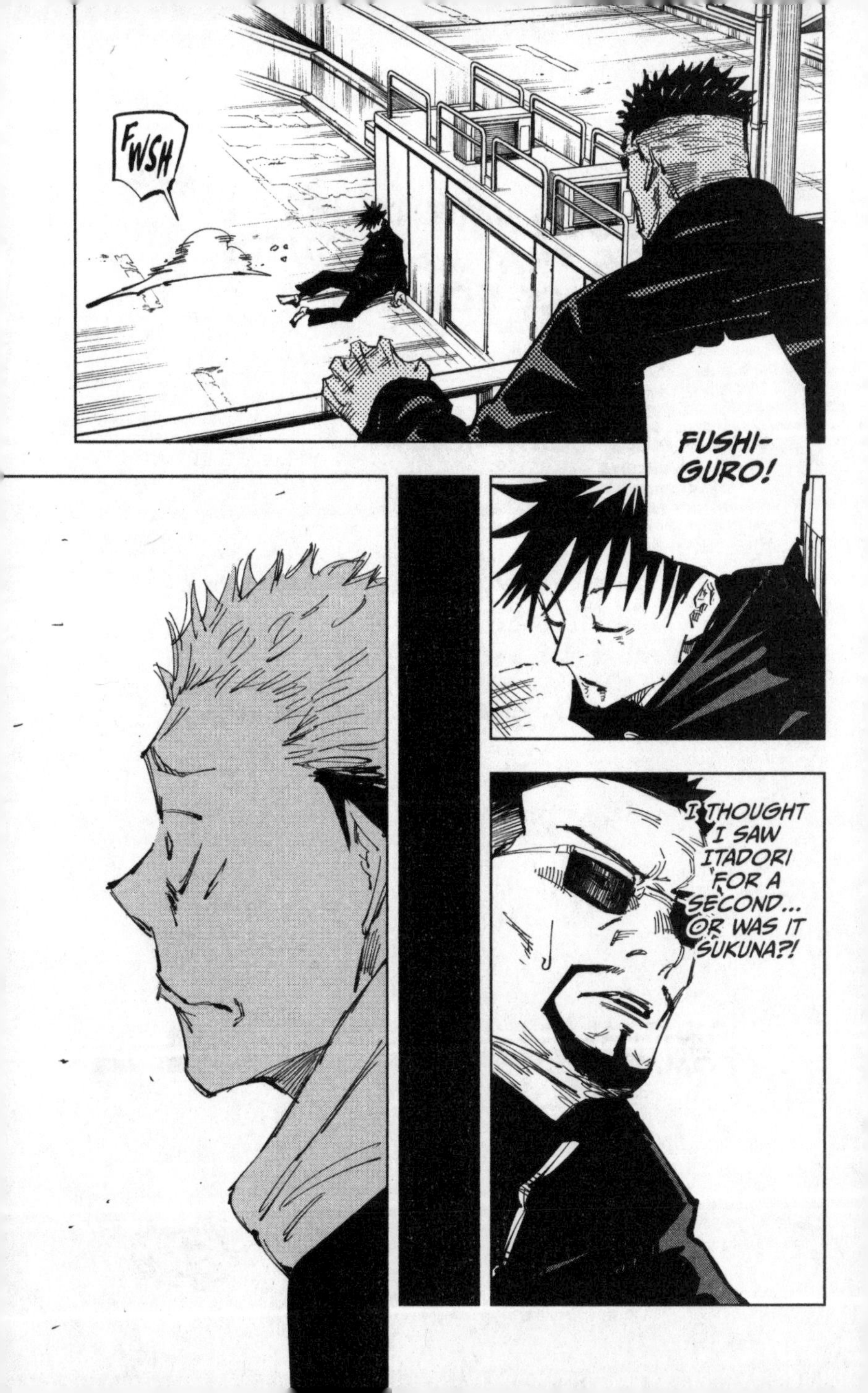
FWSH
FUSHI-GURO!
I THOUGHT I SAW ITADORI FOR A SECOND... OR WAS IT SUKUNA?!

THE 2020 VALENTINES RANKINGS THAT I SERIOUSLY ALMOST FORGOT

RANKINGS (VALENTINES RECEIVED)	CHARACTER	
17 (1)	OKKOTSU	SUKUNA
	PAPAGURO	HAIBARA
	PANDA	JUNPEI
	HANAMI	KAMO (NORITOSHI)

GENERAL COMMENT

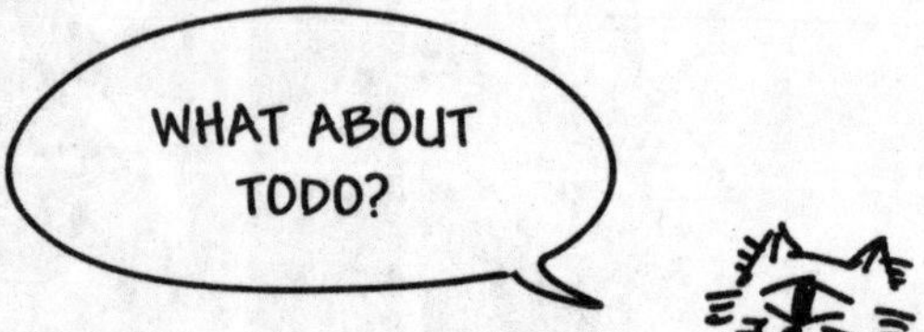
WHAT ABOUT TODO?

11:14 P.M.
DOGENZAKA,
IN FRONT OF SHIBUYA 109

TAKE A GOOD LOOK.

HEY, BRAT.

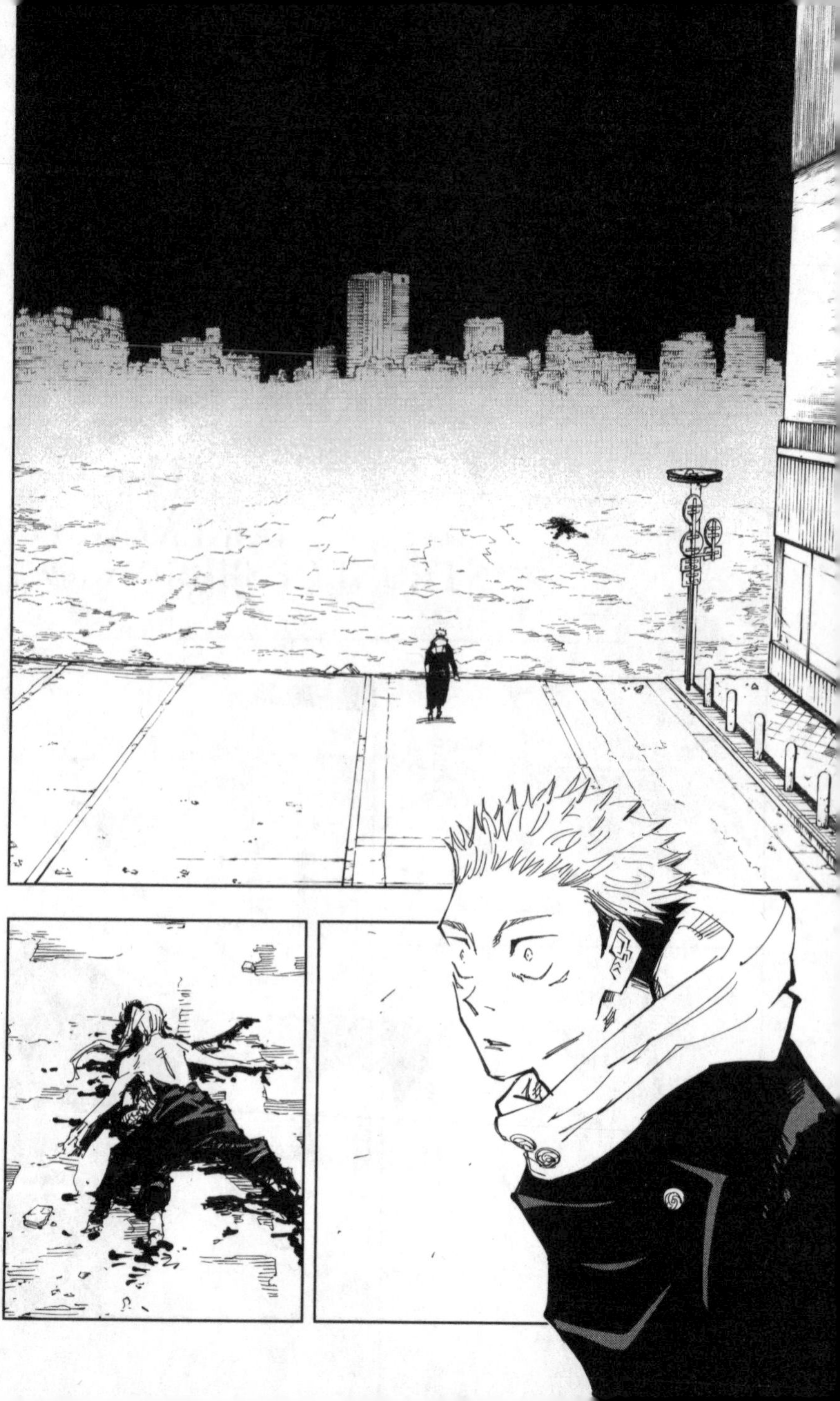

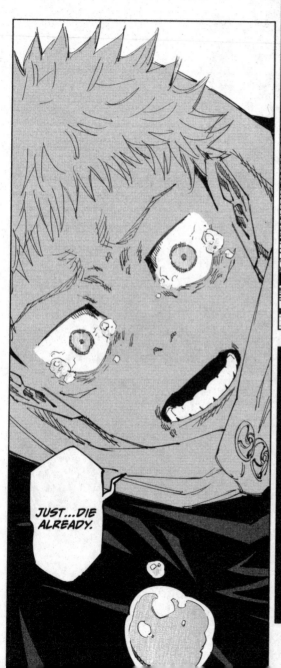

92

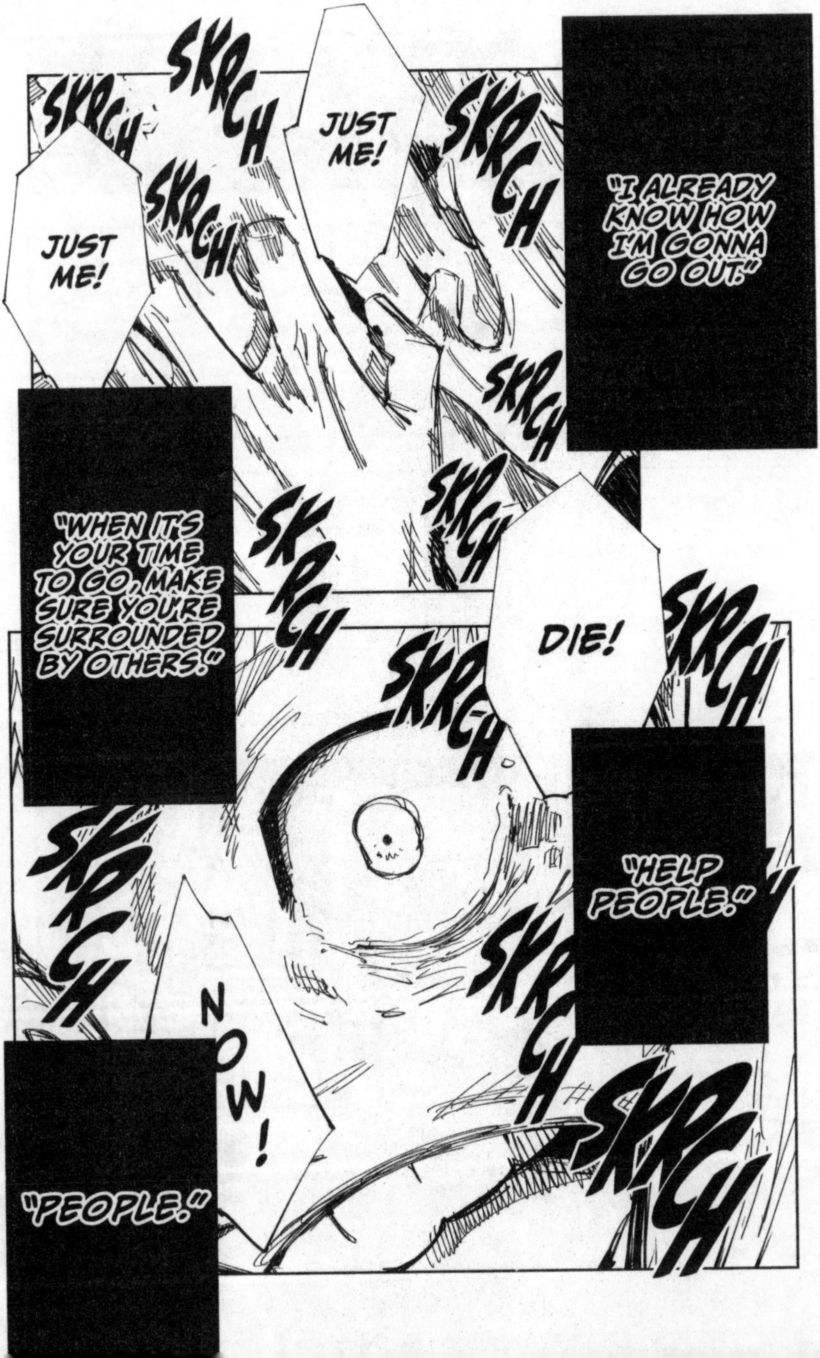
"I ALREADY KNOW HOW I'M GONNA GO OUT."
SKRCH
SKRCH
JUST ME!
SKRCH
SKRCH
SKRCH
JUST ME!
"WHEN IT'S YOUR TIME TO GO, MAKE SURE YOU'RE SURROUNDED BY OTHERS."
SKRCH
SKRCH
SKRCH
DIE!
SKRCH
SKRCH
"HELP PEOPLE."
SKRCH
SKRCH
SKRCH
NOW!
"PEOPLE."

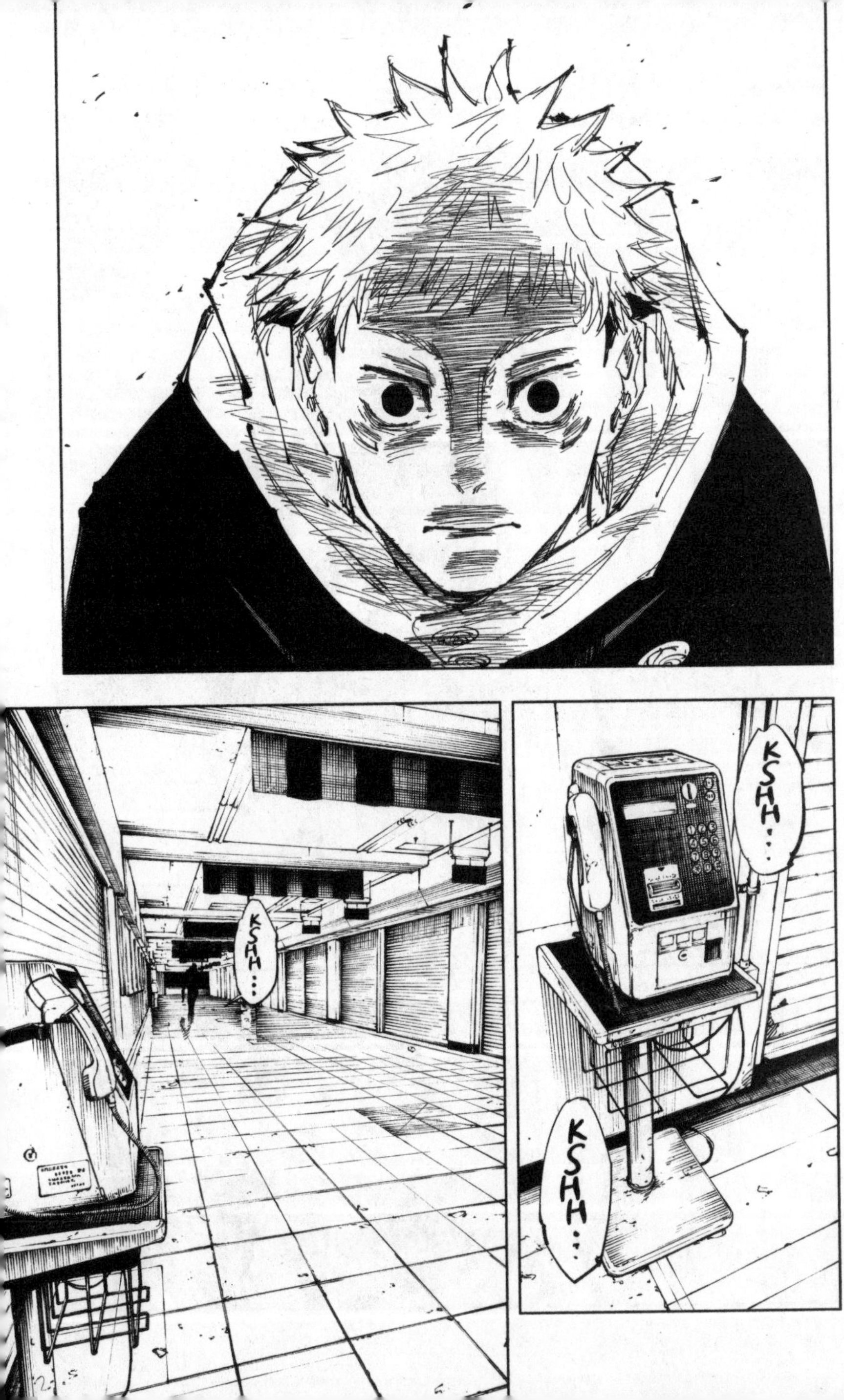
KSHH...
KSHH...
KSHH...

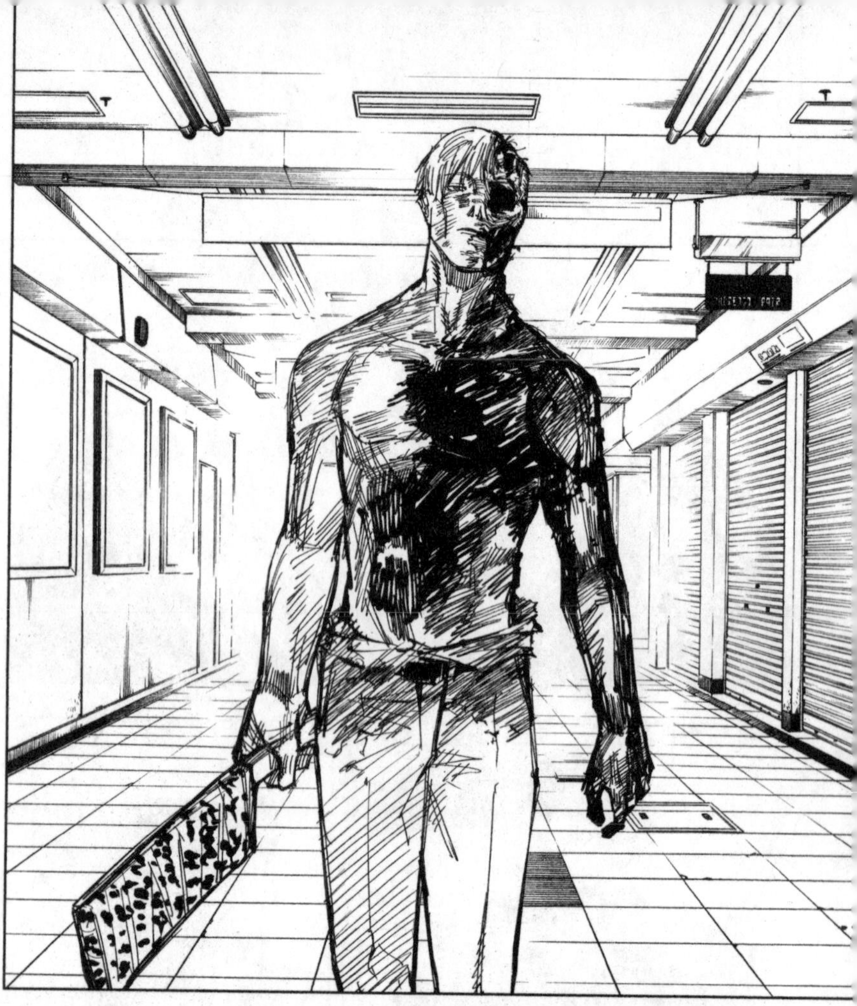
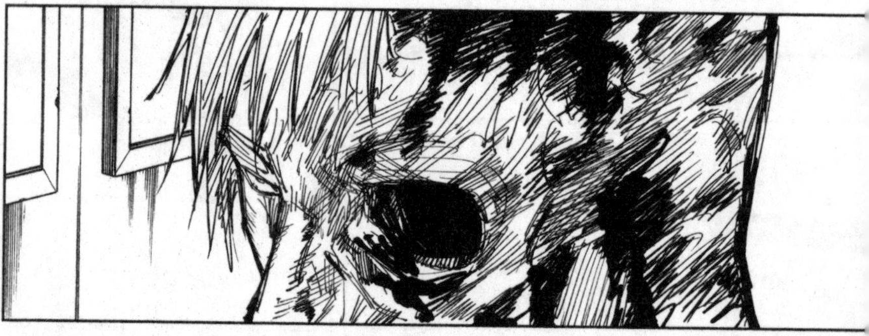

PHOTO ID

←出口 A₇

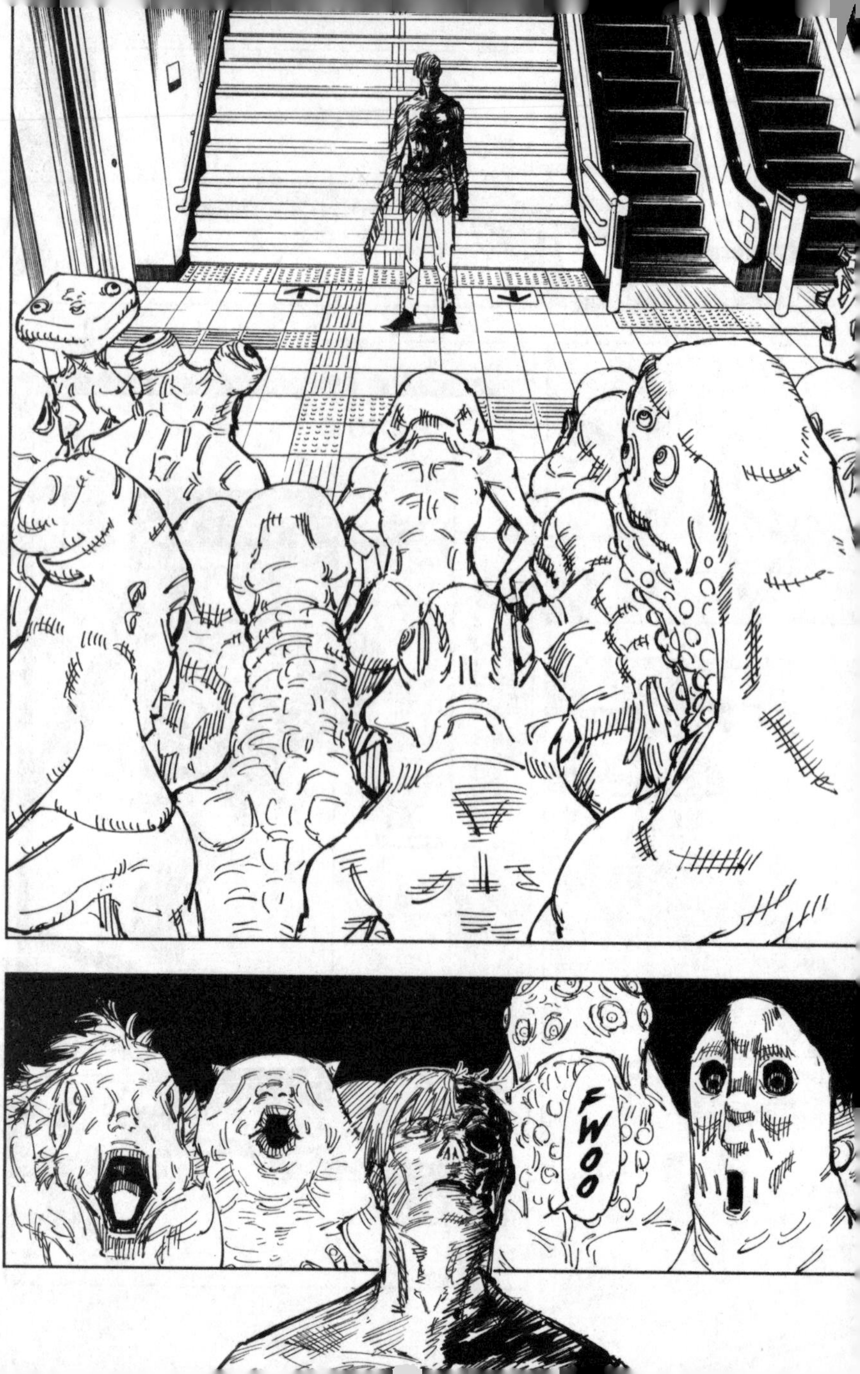
FWOO

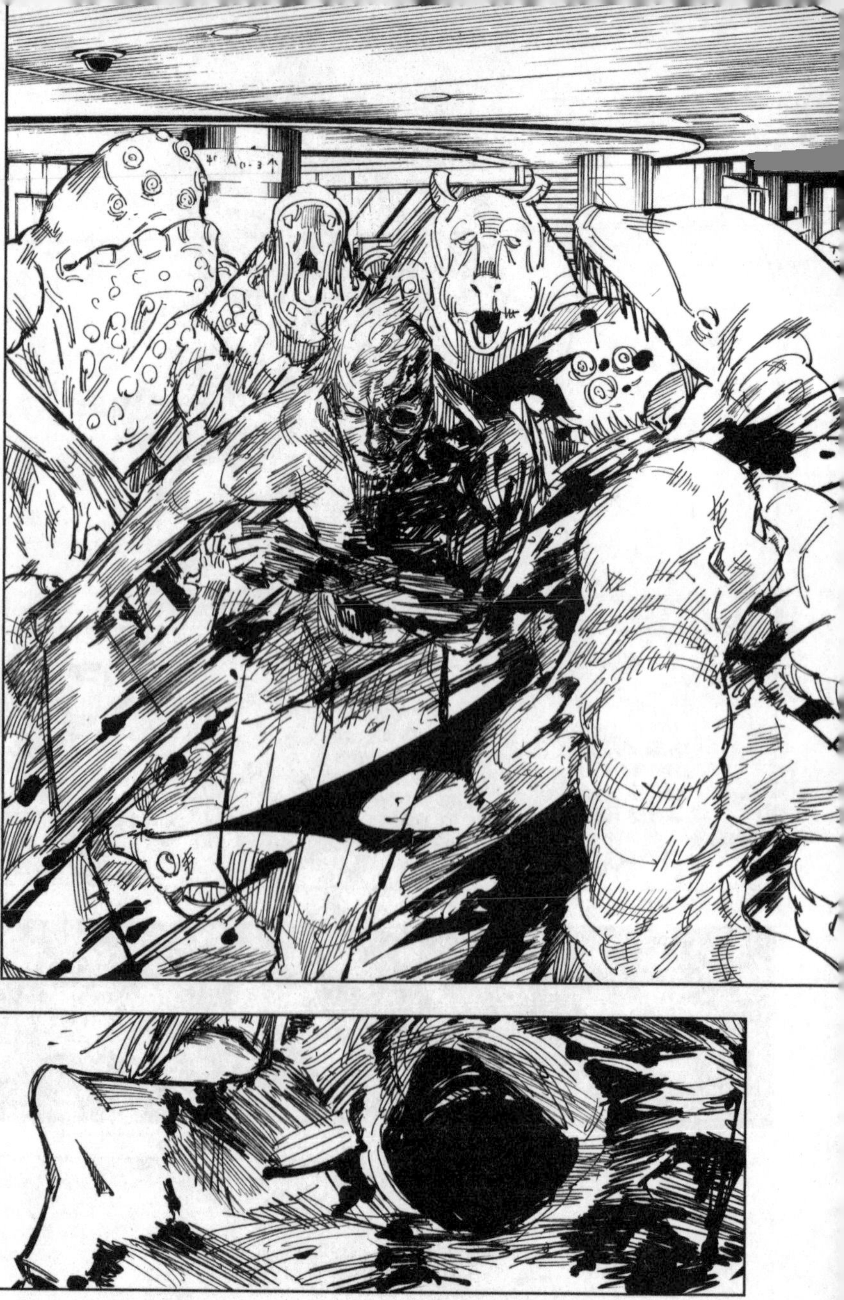

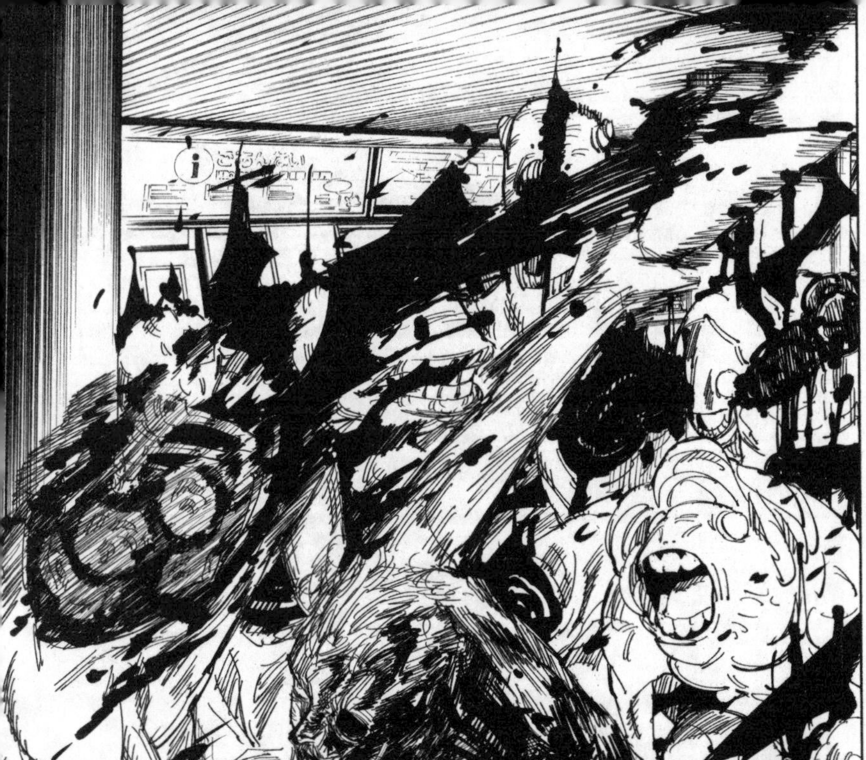
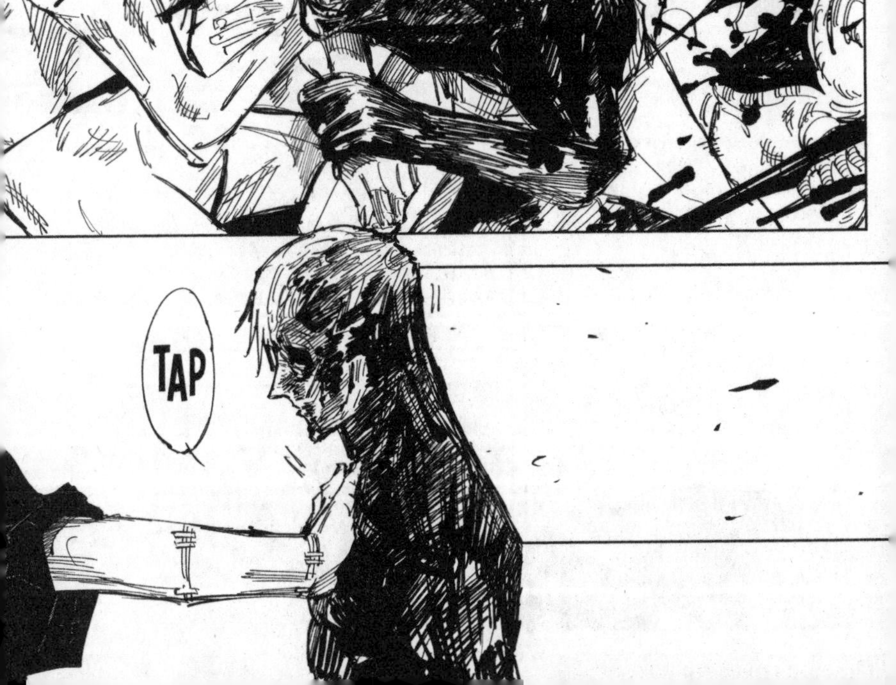
TAP

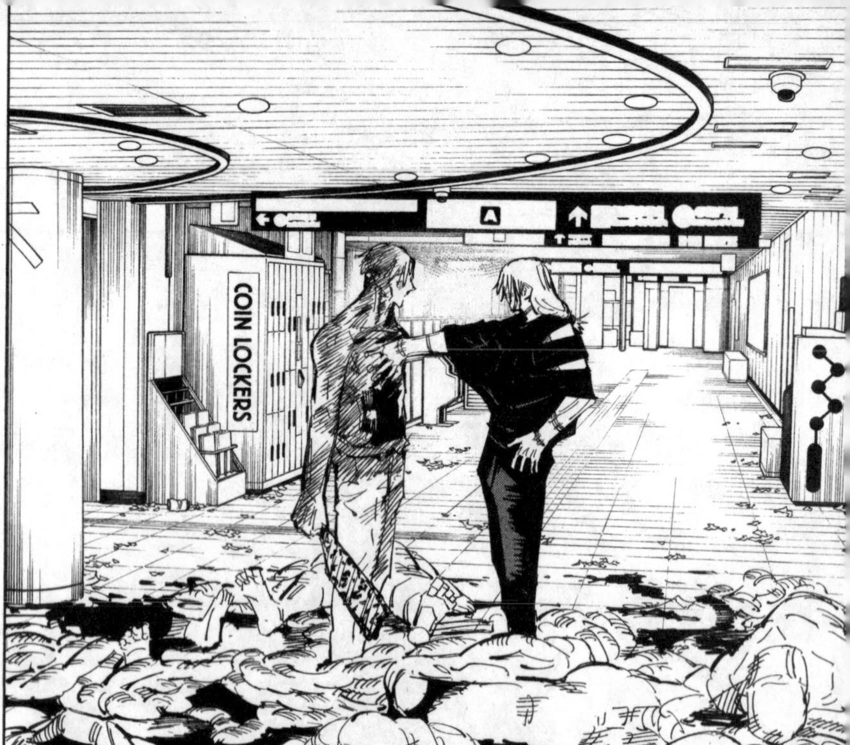
COIN LOCKERS

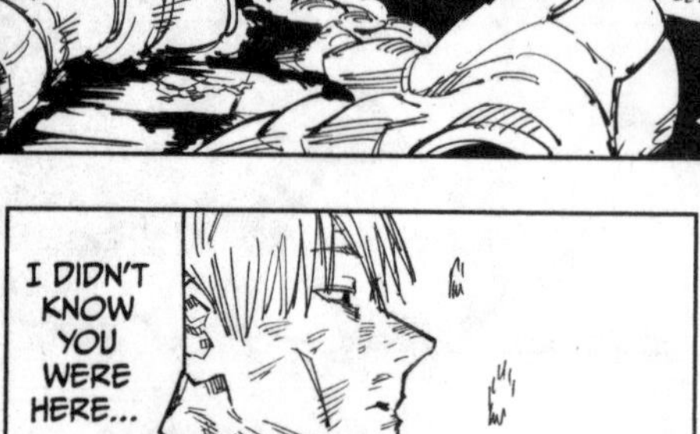
I DIDN'T KNOW YOU WERE HERE...

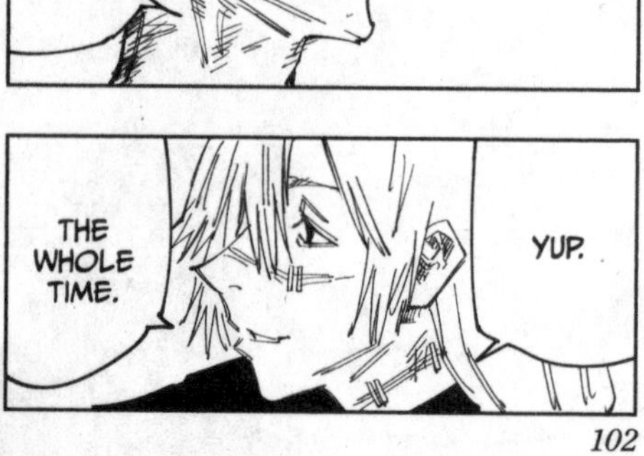
YUP.
THE WHOLE TIME.

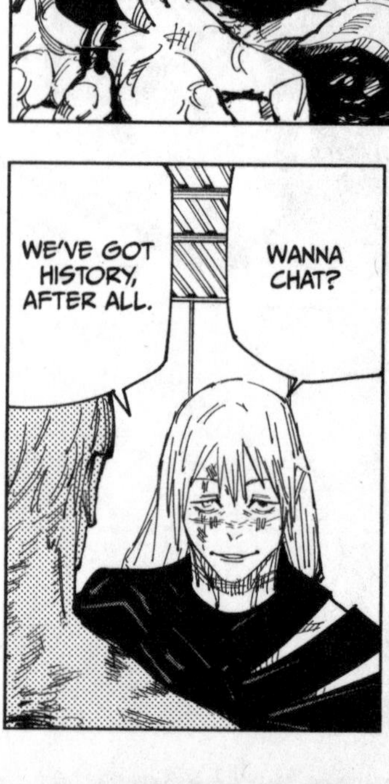
WANNA CHAT?
WE'VE GOT HISTORY, AFTER ALL.

I RAN. EVEN THOUGH I RAN AWAY, I CAME BACK WITH THE VAGUE REASON OF FINDING THE WORK WORTHWHILE.

WHAT WAS I TRYING TO DO ANYWAY?

HAIBARA...

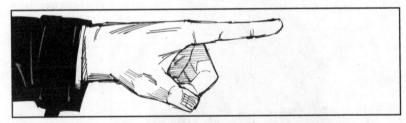

NANA-
MIN!

ITADORI.

IT'LL JUST
END UP
BECOMING
A CURSE
FOR HIM.

NO, HAIBARA.
THAT'S NOT
RIGHT. I CAN'T
SAY THAT
TO HIM.

ITADORI...

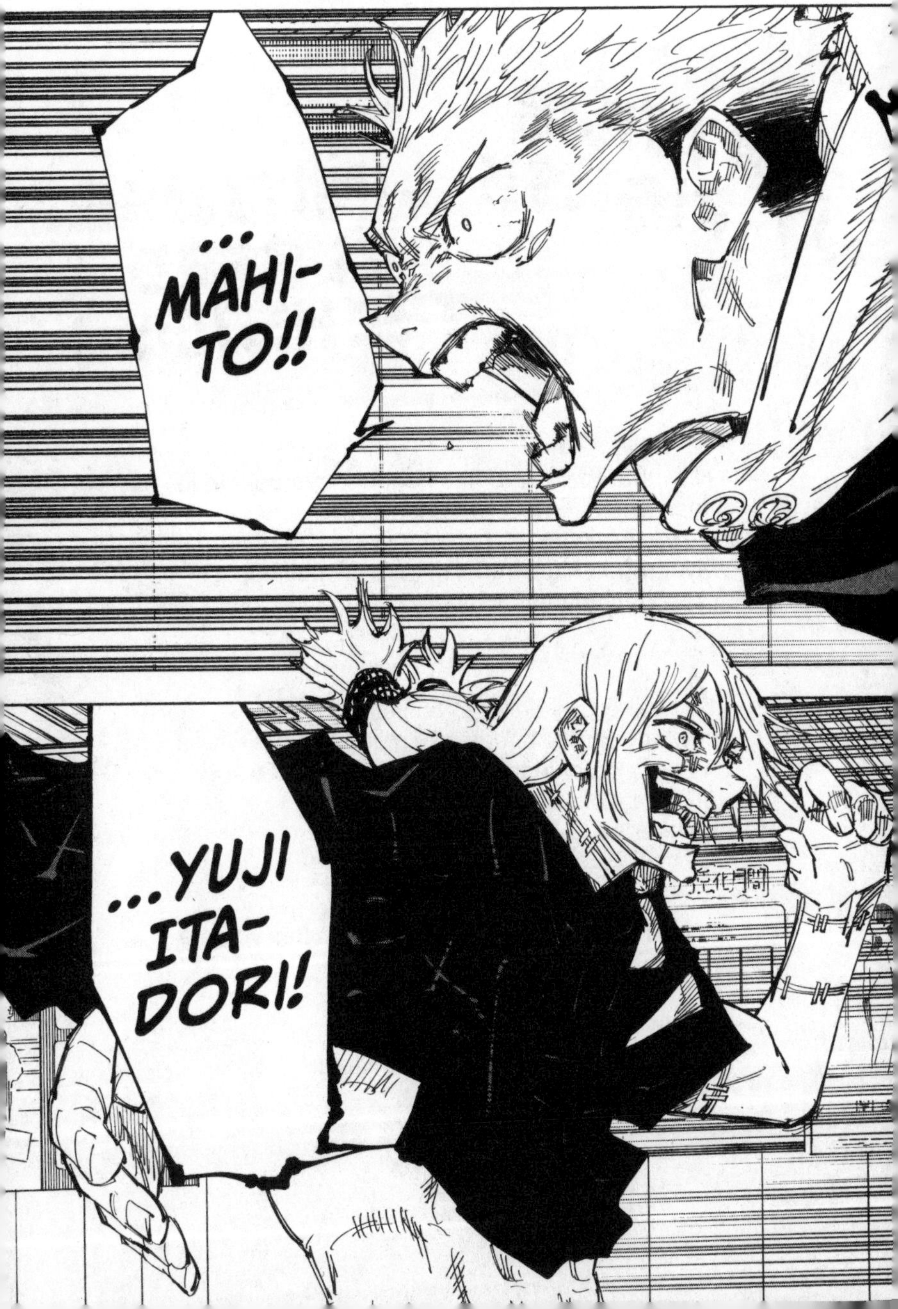
...MAHITO!!
...YUJI ITADORI!

GETTING IT RIGHT!! LIMITLESS CURSED TECHNIQUE

• Now that the anime has begun, more people in Japan and overseas will check out *Jujutsu Kaisen*. Because of that, I can't keep bluffing my way through stuff. Yes, I'm talking about Gojo's cursed technique.

• So I asked my editor to find someone knowledgeable about mathematics for their input, and the inquiry in the *Jump* editorial staff turned up T-san, who has a master's degree in engineering (information geometry)!!

• I hope to share what I've learned in this volume and the next.

• I should've done this from the start!!

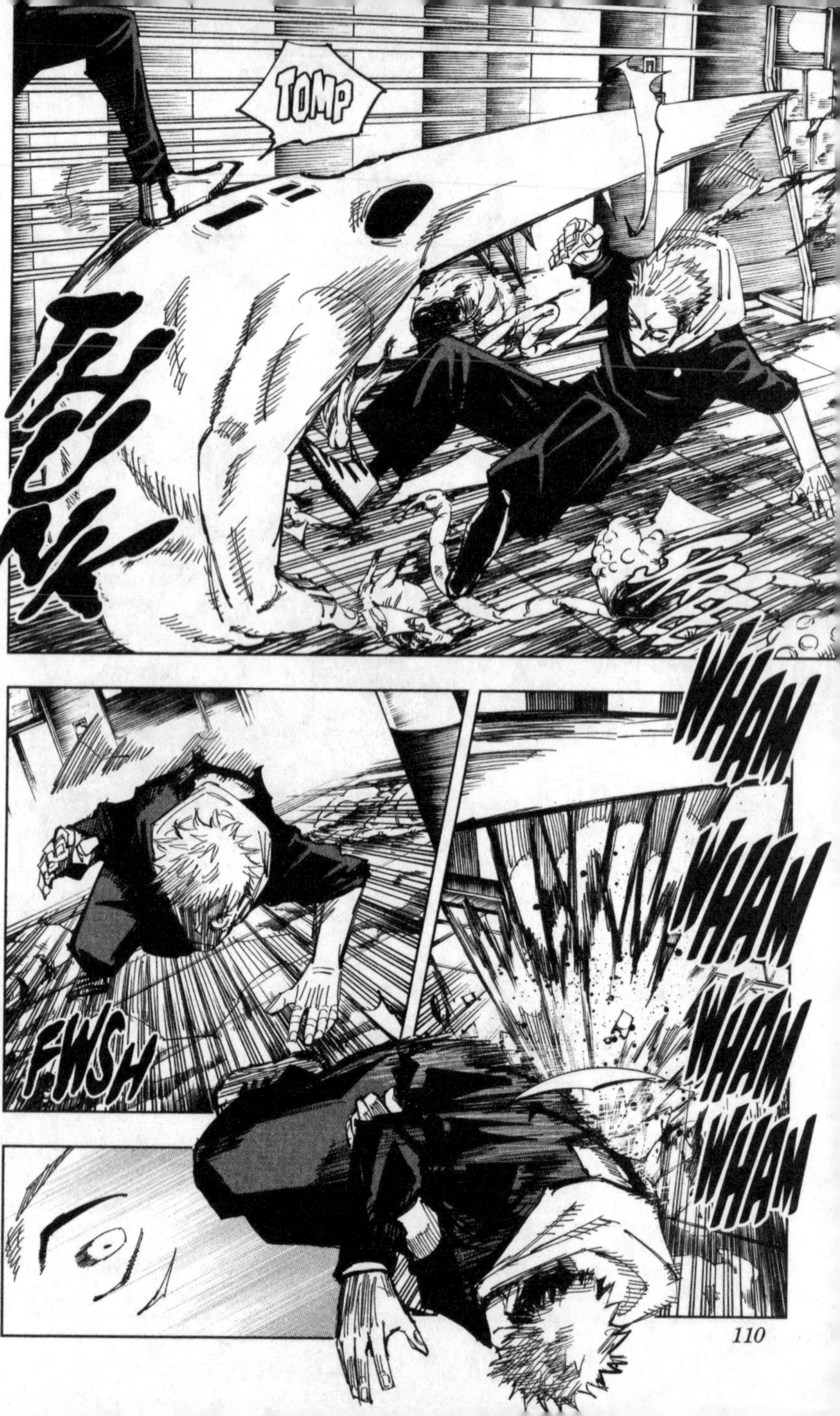
TOMP
THUNK
WHAM WHAM WHAM WHAM WHAM
FWSH

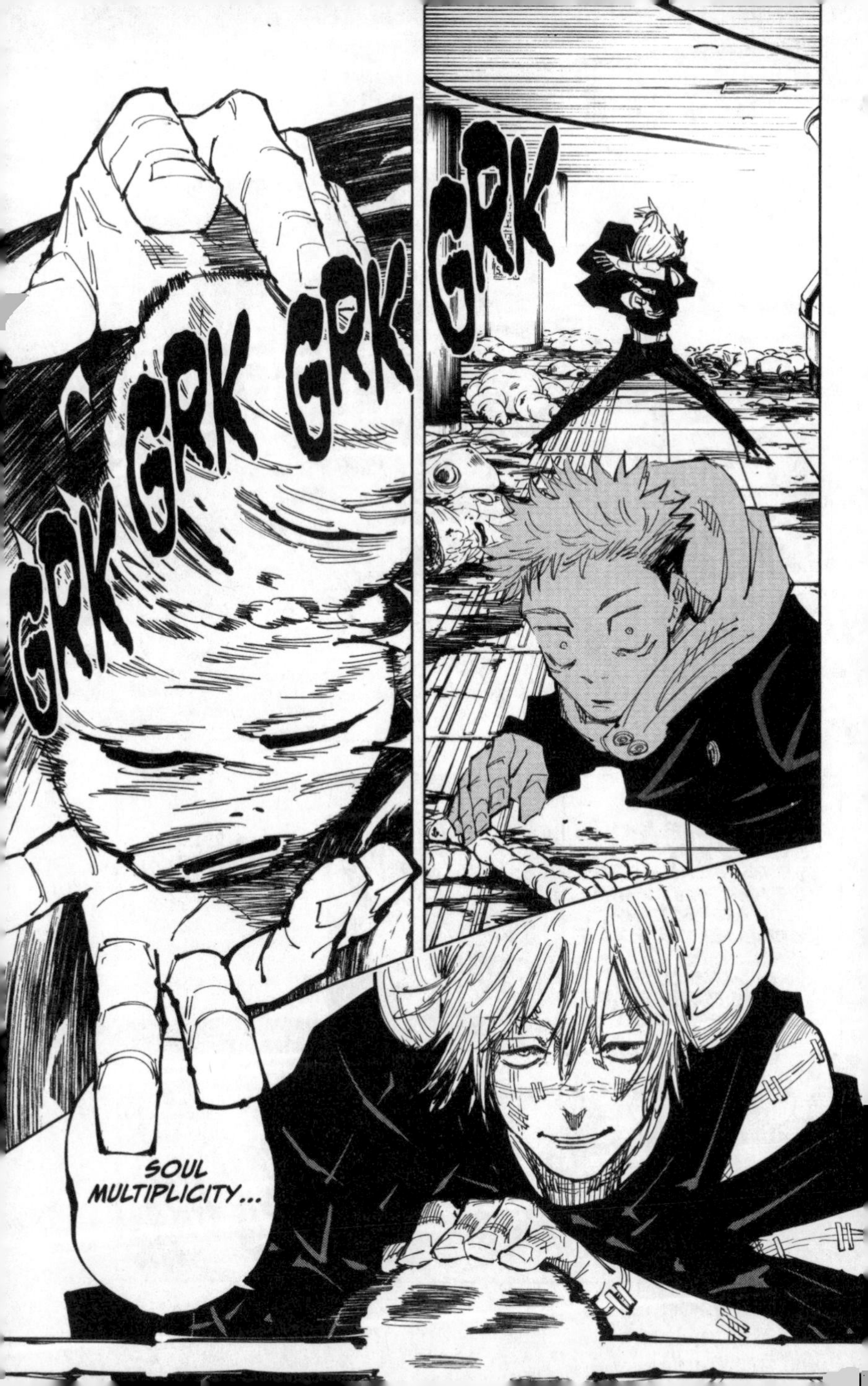
GRK GRK GRK GRK GRK
SOUL MULTIPLICITY...

BODY REPEL!!

GNK GNK GNK

BODY REPEL—
SOUL MULTIPLICITY CREATES A REACTION DUE TO THE REJECTION OF FUSION. BY USING THIS EFFECT AND INCREASING THE SOUL'S ENERGY, THE OVER-WHELMING OUTPUT CAN BE DIRECTED AT AN OPPONENT.

SOUL MULTIPLICITY—A TECHNIQUE THAT MERGES TWO OR MORE SOULS.

GRAK GRAK GRAK GRAK

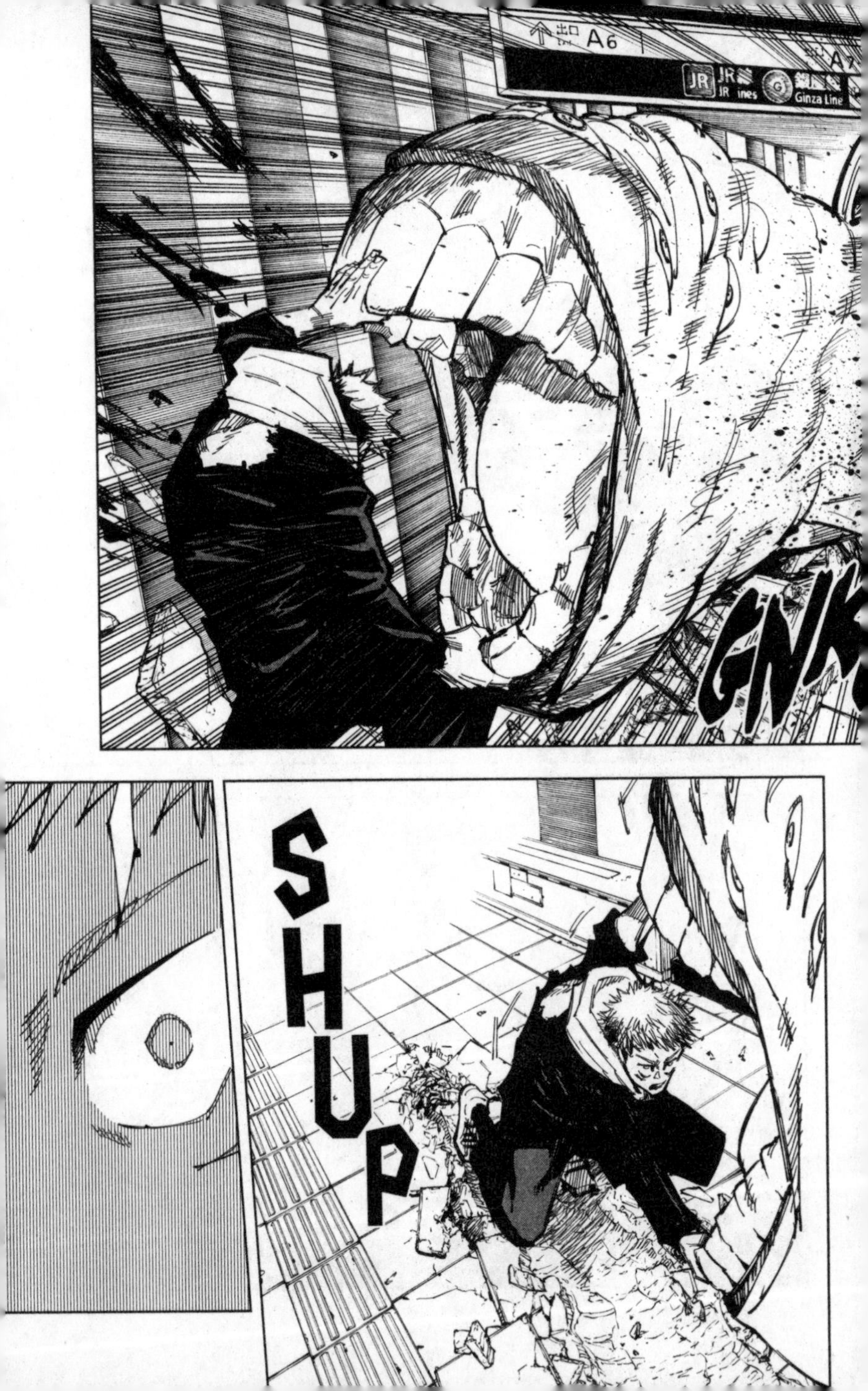
A6
JR
Ginza Line
GNK
SHUP

BOO!

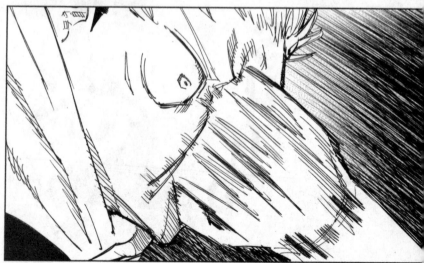

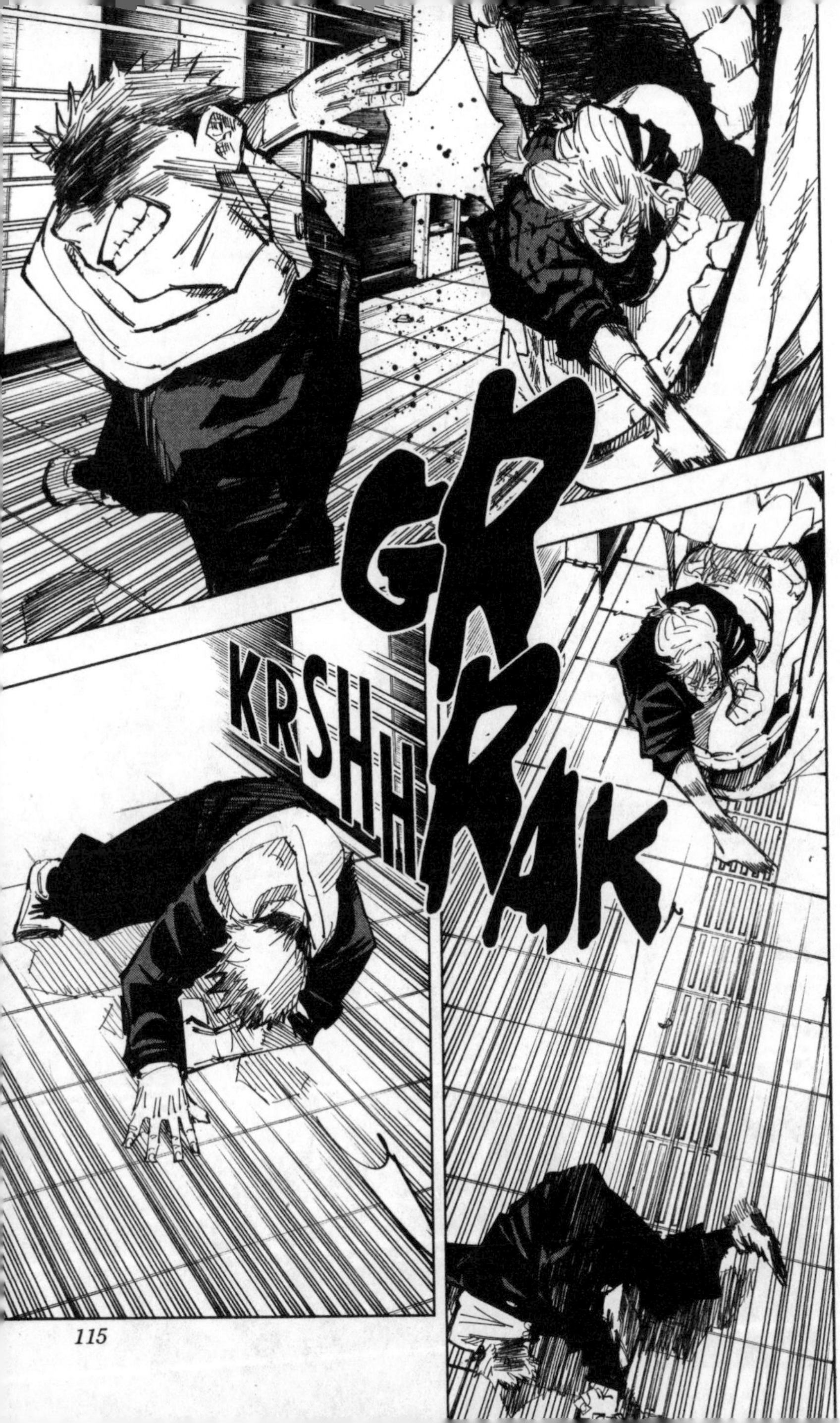
GRRAK
KRSHH

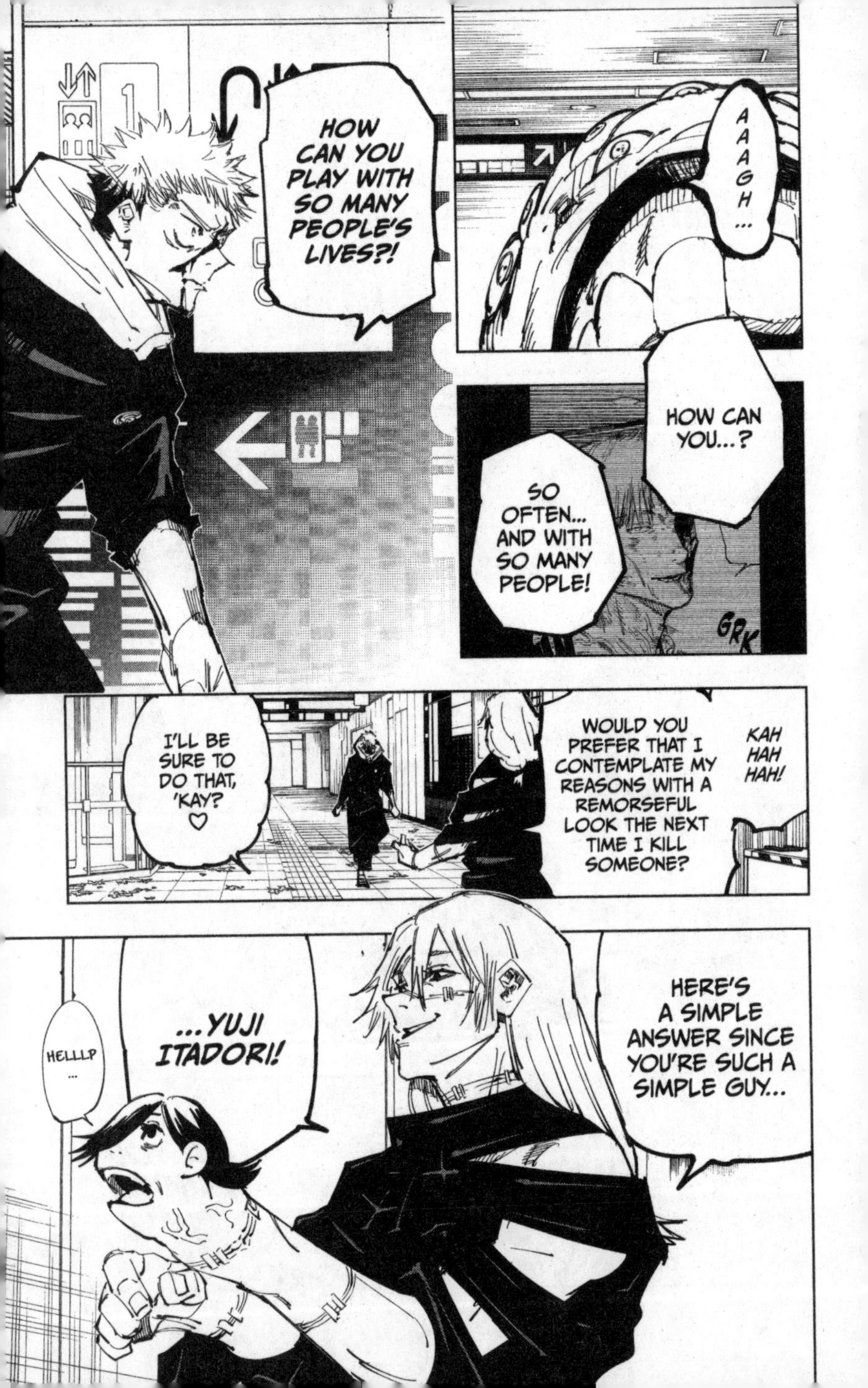
AAAGH...
HOW CAN YOU...?
SO OFTEN... AND WITH SO MANY PEOPLE!
GRK
HOW CAN YOU PLAY WITH SO MANY PEOPLE'S LIVES?!
WOULD YOU PREFER THAT I CONTEMPLATE MY REASONS WITH A REMORSEFUL LOOK THE NEXT TIME I KILL SOMEONE?
KAH HAH HAH!
I'LL BE SURE TO DO THAT, 'KAY? ♡
HERE'S A SIMPLE ANSWER SINCE YOU'RE SUCH A SIMPLE GUY...
...YUJI ITADORI!
HELLLP...

WHAT THE HELL?

YOU ARE ME.

SHNK

AAAGH!

'TIS JUST A CURSE SPOUTING NONSENSE.

GRK GRK

YEESH... NO NEED TO GET SO UPSET EVERY TIME.

BUT YOU KNOW WHAT?

FWOO ALL THAT BLAB-BERING...

YOU REALLY DON'T STOP TALKING.

UNTIL YOU ACCEPT THAT FACT...

I'LL MAKE SURE THOSE ARE YOUR DYING WORDS!

...THERE'S NO WAY YOU'LL EVER BEAT ME.

...A JUJUTSU SORCERER!

"YOU'VE GOT IT FROM HERE."

NANAMIN WOULDN'T LOSE HIS COOL.

NANA-MIN...

PROVE TO HIM THAT...

...I AM...

...YOU ARE...

I'LL STICK WITH MANIPULATING LIMBS, WHICH SHOULDN'T BE A PROBLEM TO SACRIFICE JUST LIKE A MOMENT AGO.

IDLE TRANSFIGURATION DOESN'T WORK ON ITADORI.

"I NEED TO FOCUS ON CONCENTRATING MY BODY'S FORM TO MAINTAIN TOUGHNESS"...

INCREASING MY SIZE BY MANIPULATING MY SOUL WOULD JUST MAKE ME A BIGGER TARGET. THAT MIGHT AS WELL BE SUICIDE.

MAINTAIN THIS FORM! AND WITH A PURE, RE-INFORCED HIT OF CURSED ENERGY...

MAXIMUM STRENGTH!

HE'S PLANNING TO PREDICT MY MOVEMENTS BY READING THE FLOW OF CURSED ENERGY.

...IS WHAT ITADORI MUST BE THINKING.

...CHANGE MY SOUL'S SHAPE.

I WON'T...

...ITADORI'S HEART!

...I'LL STAB...

消火栓

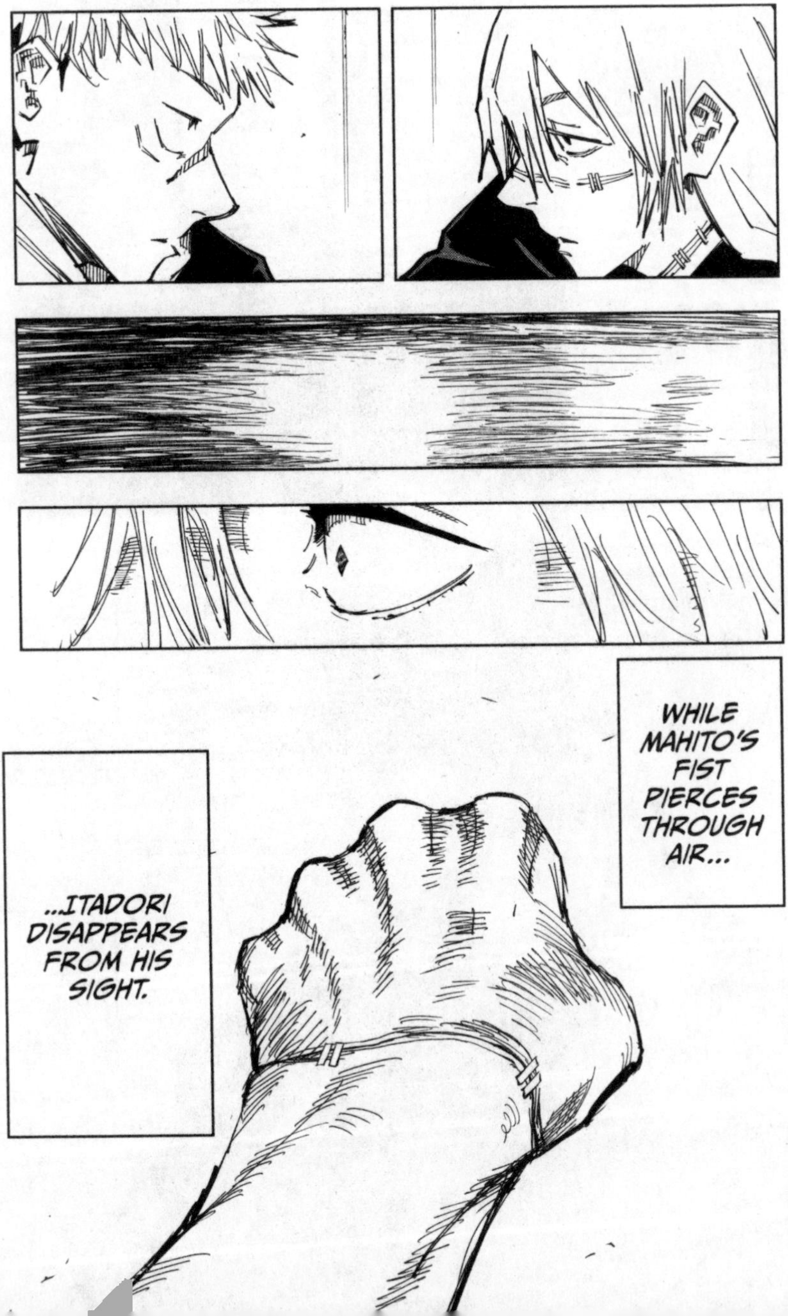
WHILE MAHITO'S FIST PIERCES THROUGH AIR...
...ITADORI DISAPPEARS FROM HIS SIGHT.

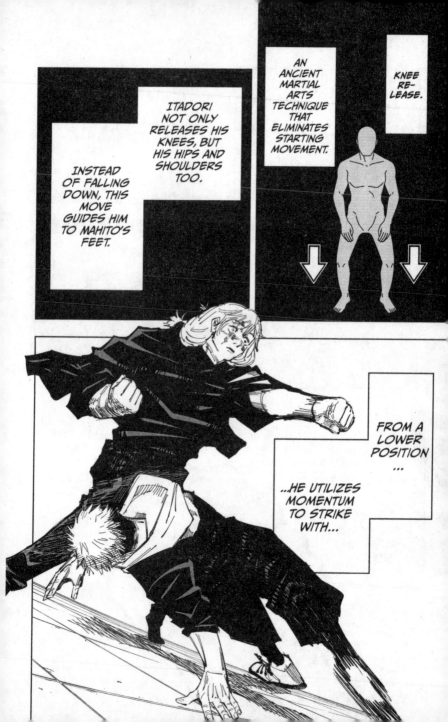

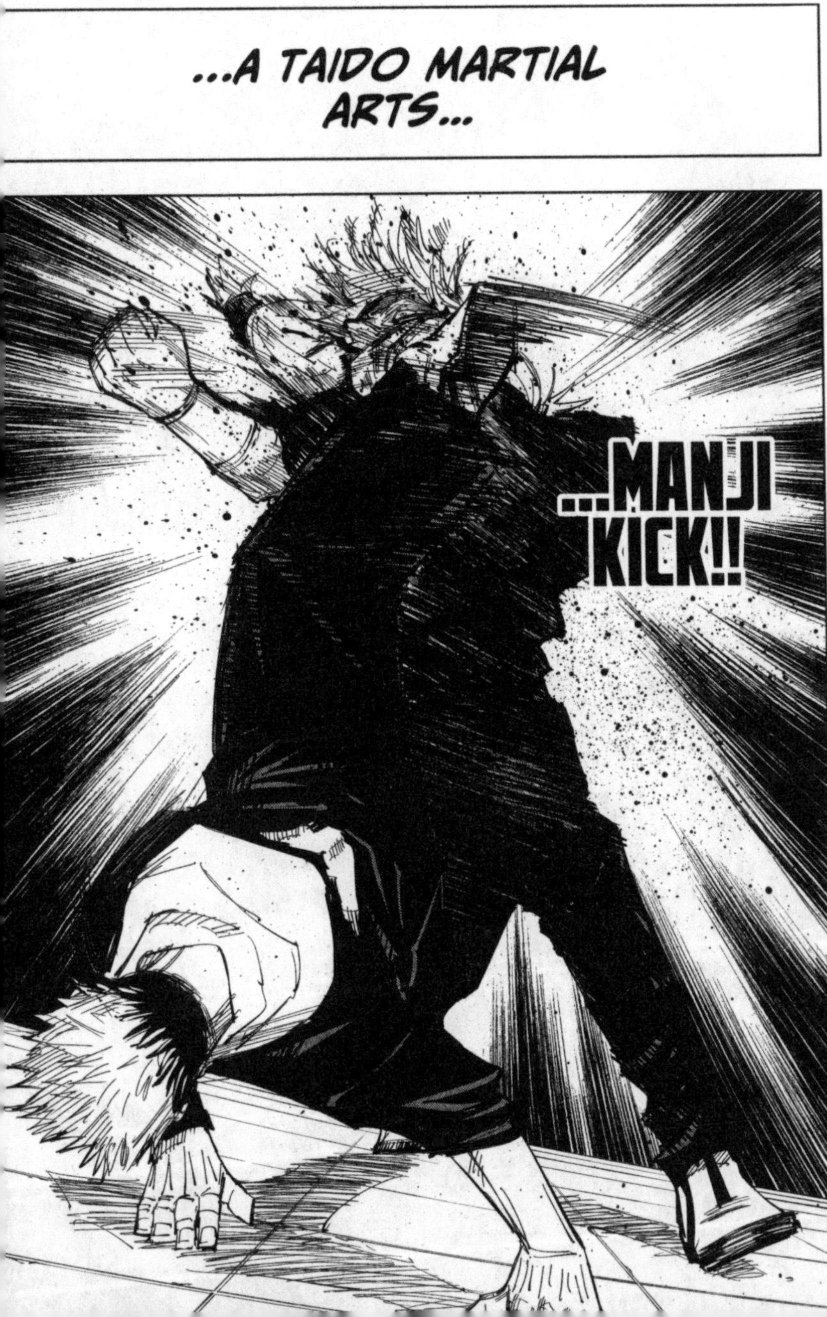
...A TAIDO MARTIAL ARTS...
...MANJI KICK!!

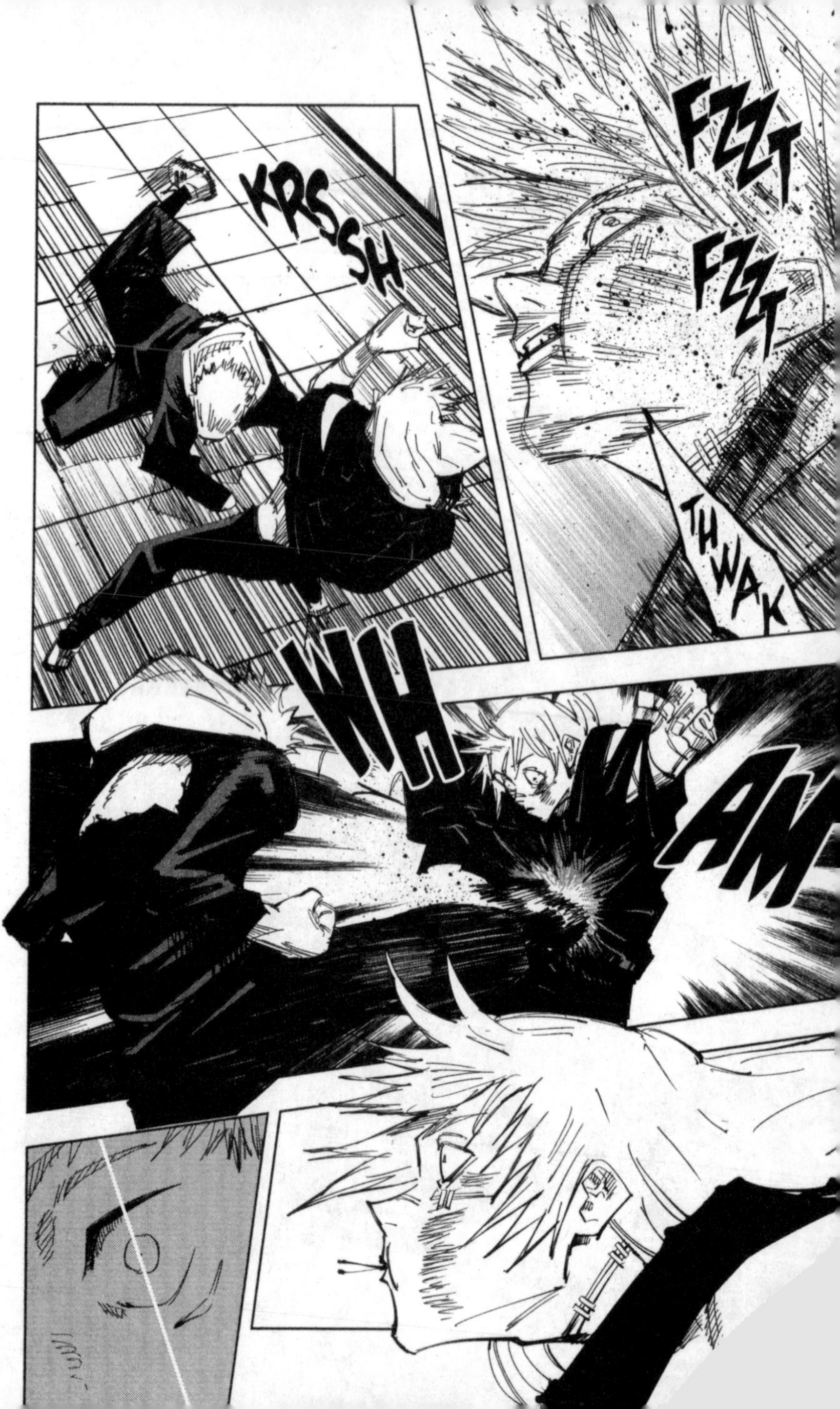
FZZT
FZZT
THWAK
KRSSH
WH
AM

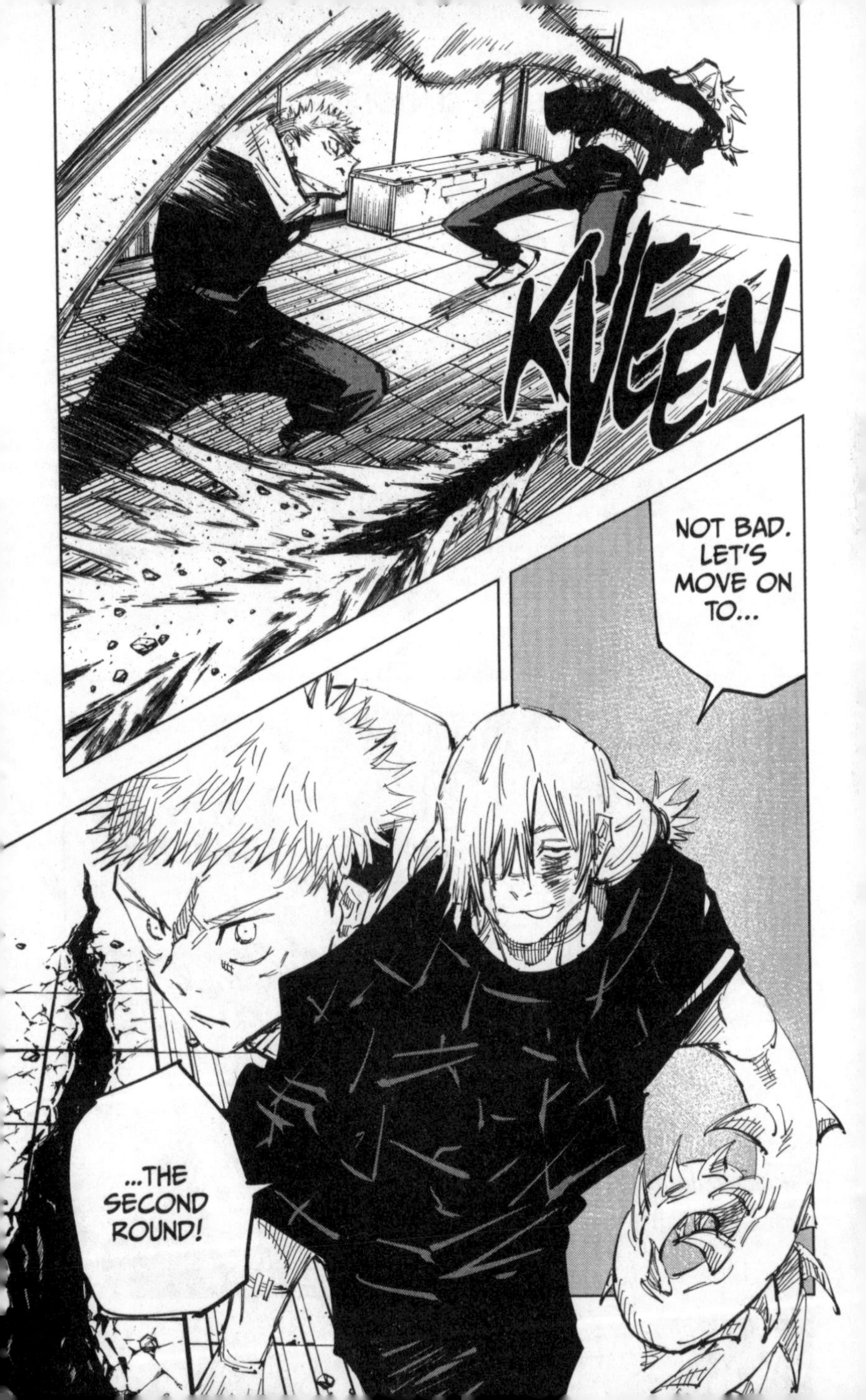
KVEEN
NOT BAD. LET'S MOVE ON TO...
...THE SECOND ROUND!

GETTING IT RIGHT!!
LIMITLESS CURSED TECHNIQUE ~INTRODUCTION~

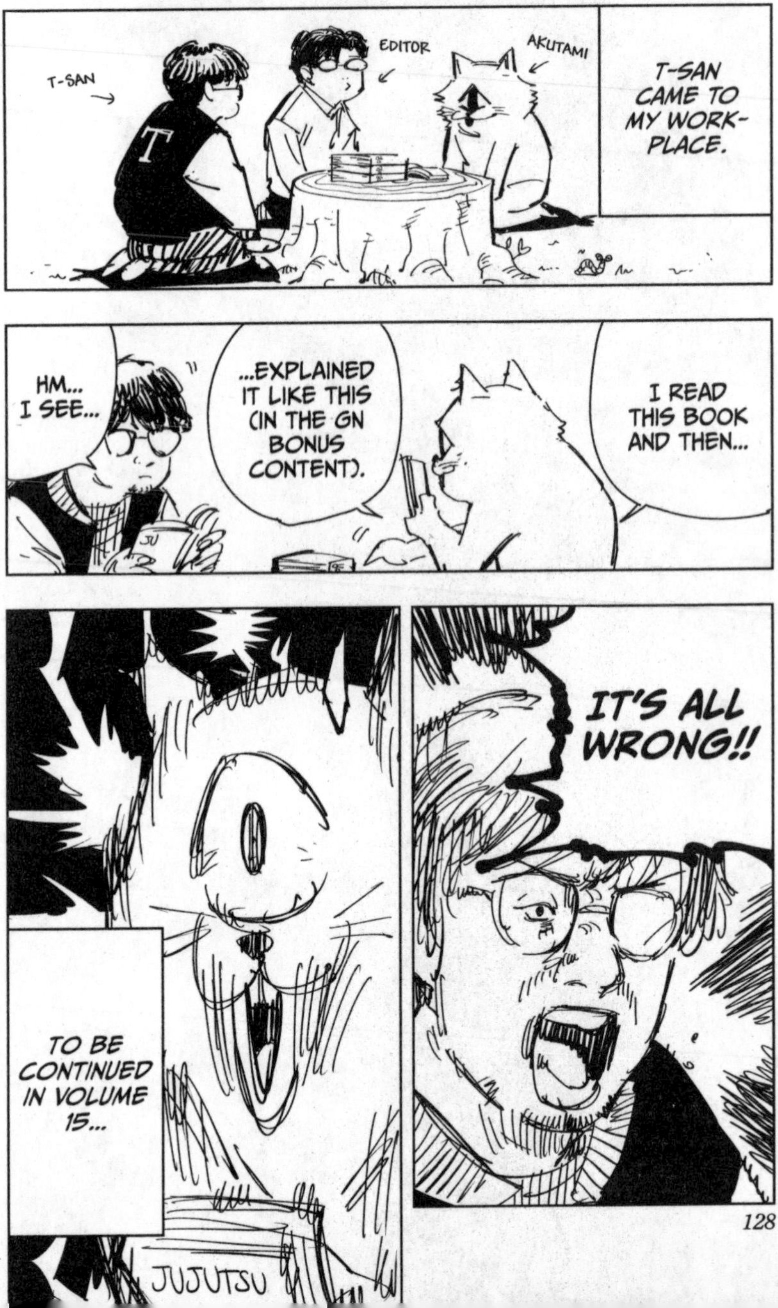

T-SAN CAME TO MY WORK-PLACE.
AKUTAMI
EDITOR
T-SAN
I READ THIS BOOK AND THEN...
...EXPLAINED IT LIKE THIS (IN THE GN BONUS CONTENT).
HM... I SEE...
IT'S ALL WRONG!!
TO BE CONTINUED IN VOLUME 15...
JUJUTSU

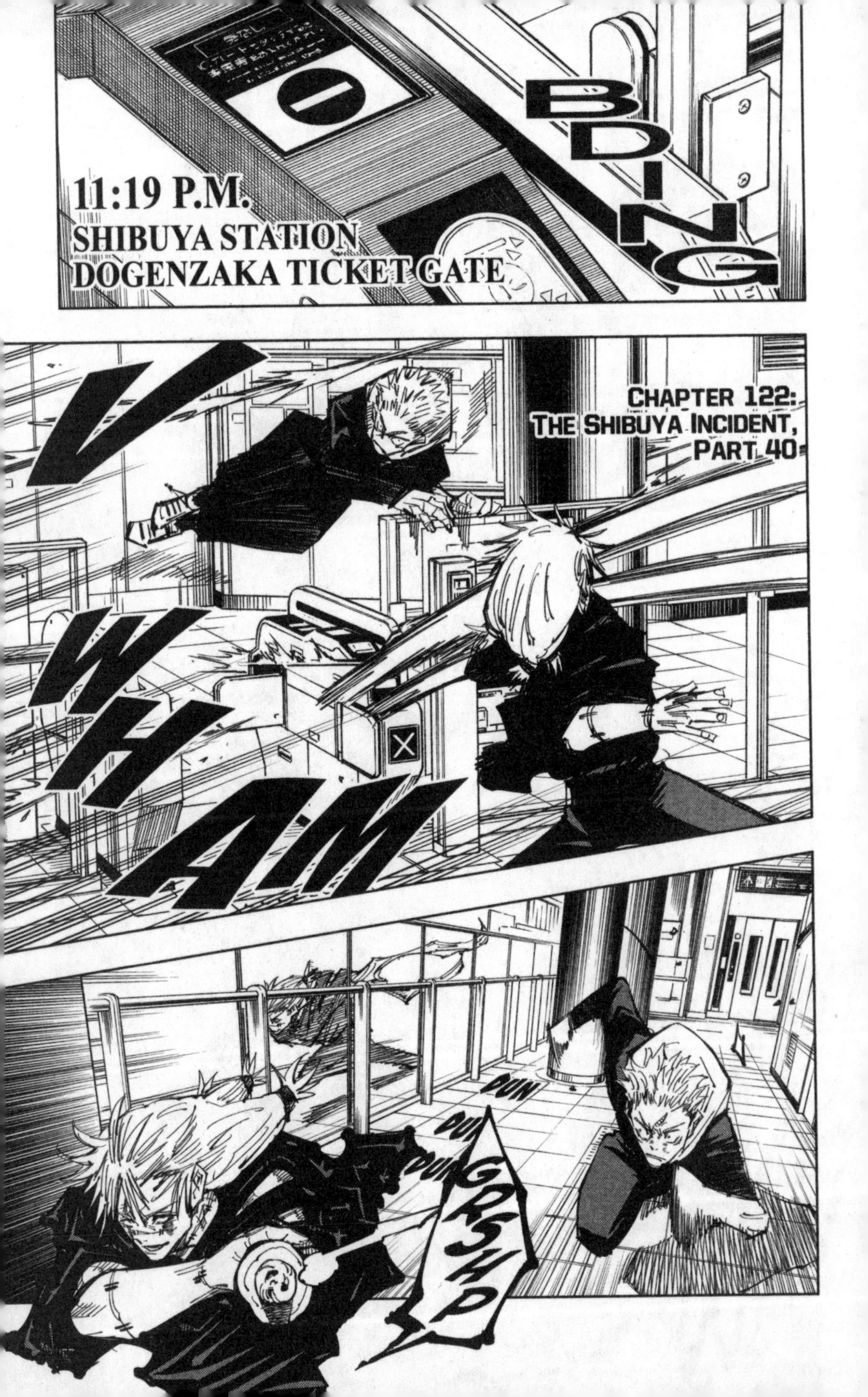
11:19 P.M.
SHIBUYA STATION
DOGENZAKA TICKET GATE
BDING
CHAPTER 122:
THE SHIBUYA INCIDENT,
PART 40
WHAM
DUN
DUN
DUN
GRSHP

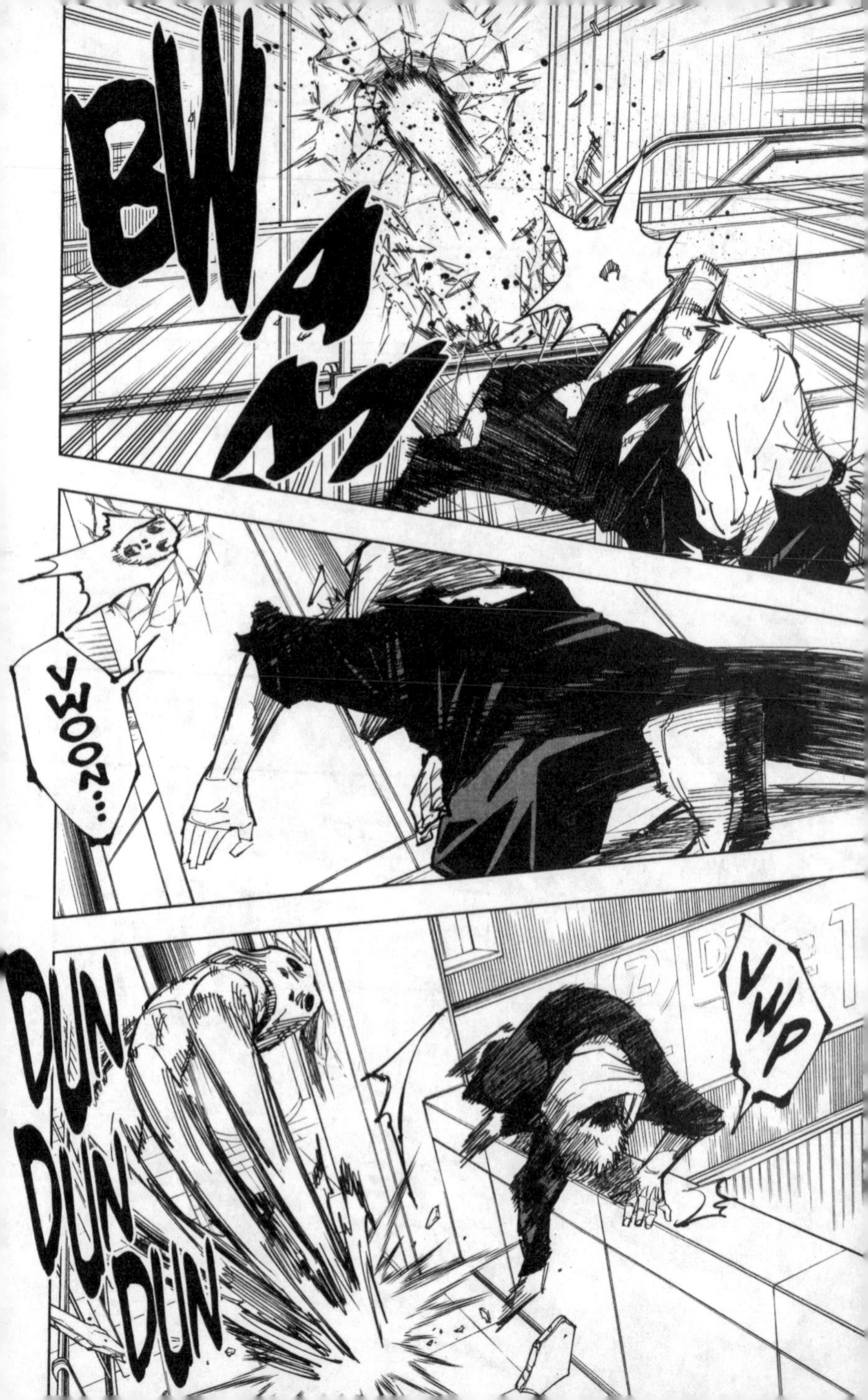
BWAM
VWOON...
VWP
DUN DUN DUN.

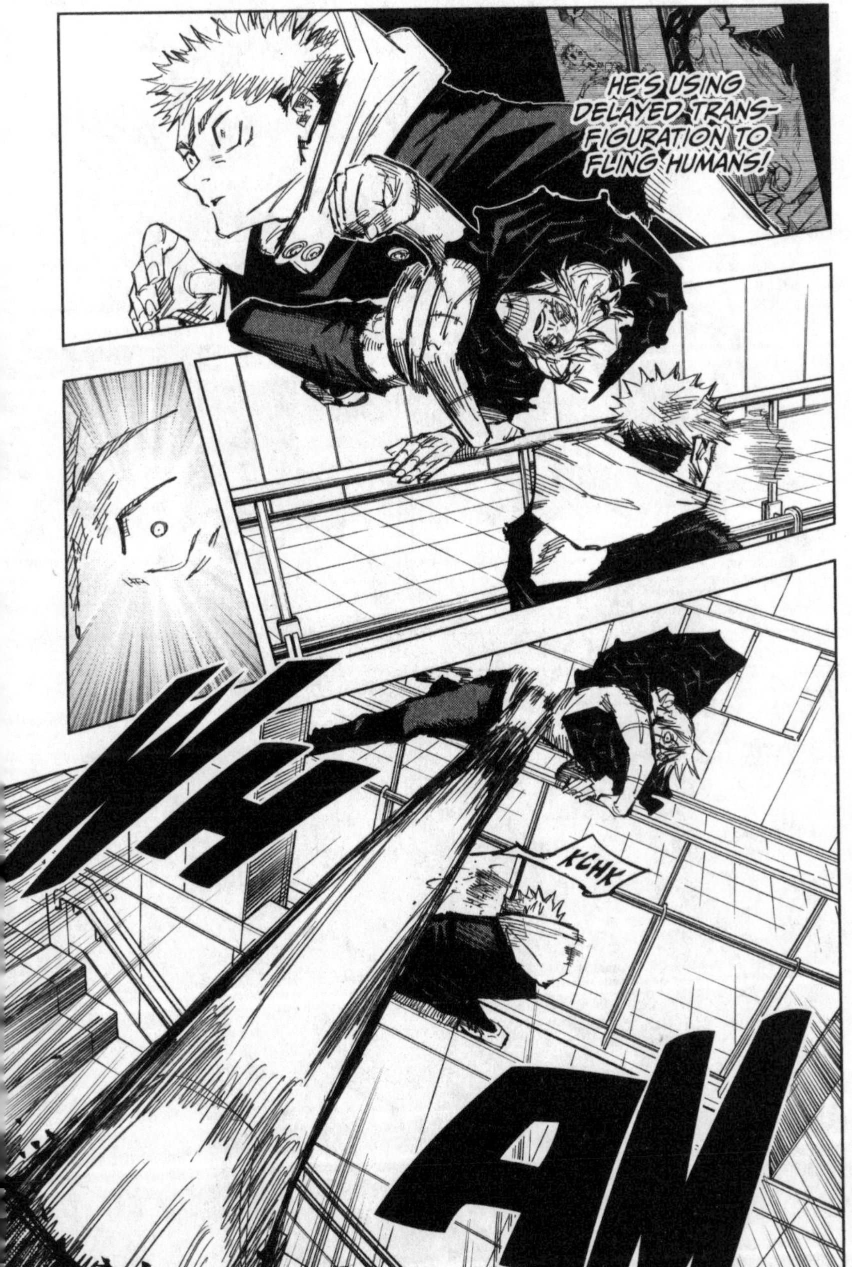
HE'S USING DELAYED TRANS-FIGURATION TO FLING HUMANS!
KCHK
WHAM

OHH... THAT WAS SCARY!

IF I TAKE A RISK AND MESS UP THE TIMING, I COULD END UP DEAD. I'LL STICK TO USING TRANSFIGURED HUMANS FOR NOW.

MWP MWP MWP

REDUCING RISK ISN'T THE ONLY REASON I'M USING TRANSFIGURED HUMANS.

HE HAS MORE MOVES NOW.

DELAYED TRANSFIGURATION, BODY DISMEMBERMENT, AND MERGING...

!

DUN

IT'S DANGEROUS OVER THERE WITH ALL THOSE MONSTERS!

HEY, COME THIS WAY!

A STUDENT?!

TRY TO STAY SOMEW—

SORRY, BUT NOWHERE'S SAFE IN SHIBUYA.

WHERE'S MAHITO...?

UPSTAIRS!

134

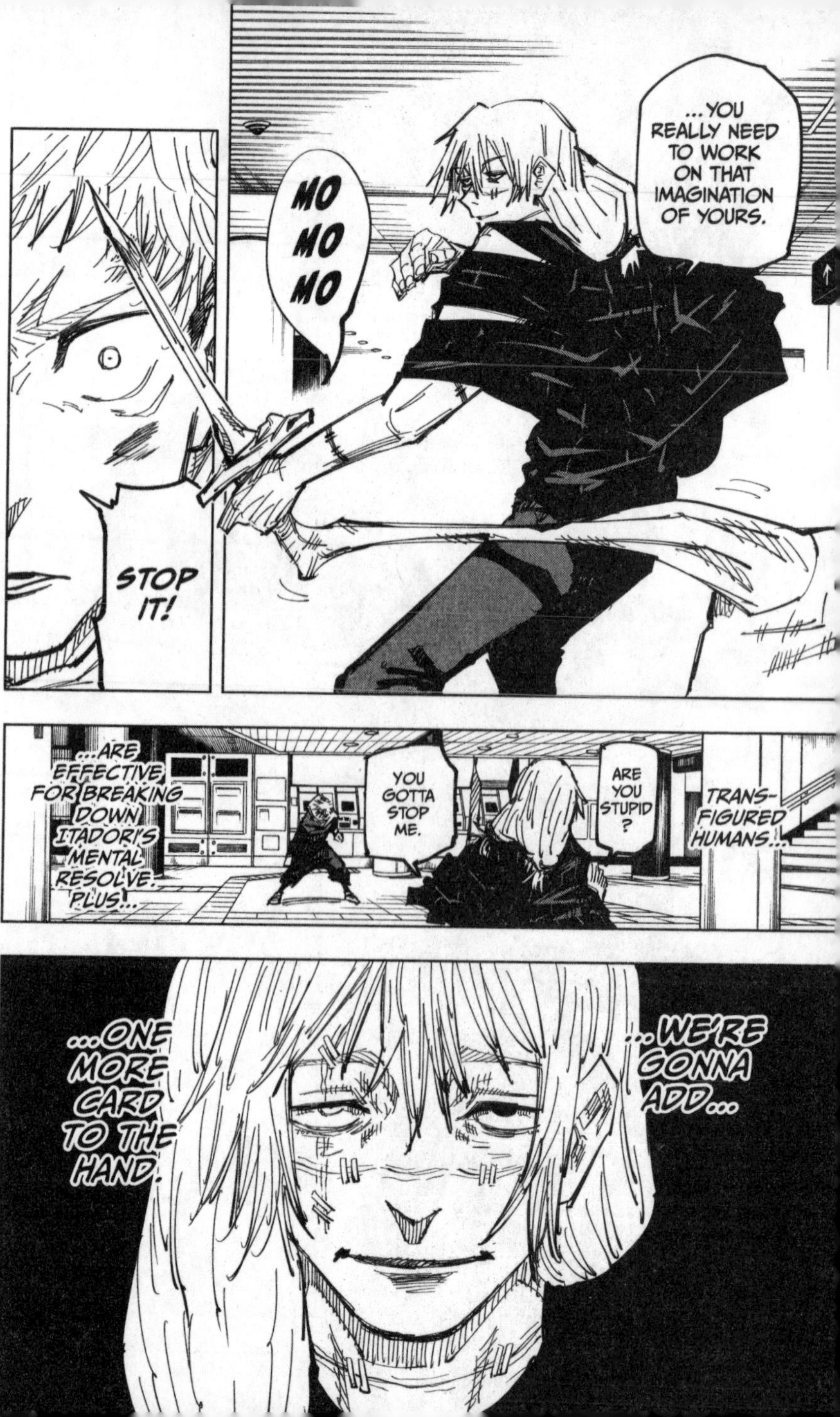
...YOU REALLY NEED TO WORK ON THAT IMAGINATION OF YOURS.
MO MO MO
STOP IT!
TRANS-FIGURED HUMANS...
ARE YOU STUPID?
YOU GOTTA STOP ME.
...ARE EFFECTIVE FOR BREAKING DOWN ITADORI'S MENTAL RESOLVE. PLUS...
...WE'RE GONNA ADD...
...ONE MORE CARD TO THE HAND.

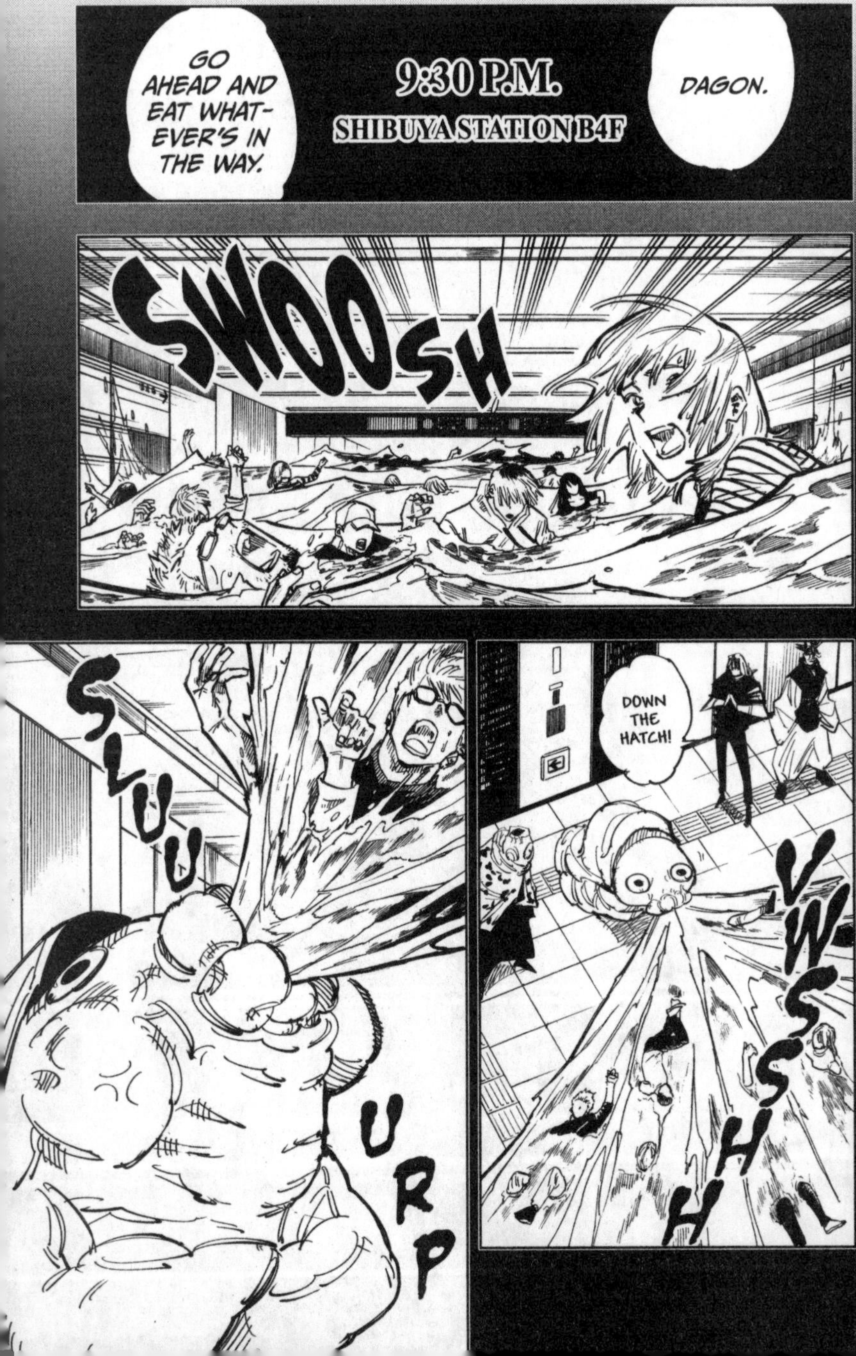
DAGON.
9:30 P.M.
SHIBUYA STATION B4F
GO AHEAD AND EAT WHAT-EVER'S IN THE WAY.
SWOOSH
DOWN THE HATCH!
VWSSHHH
SLUUU
URP

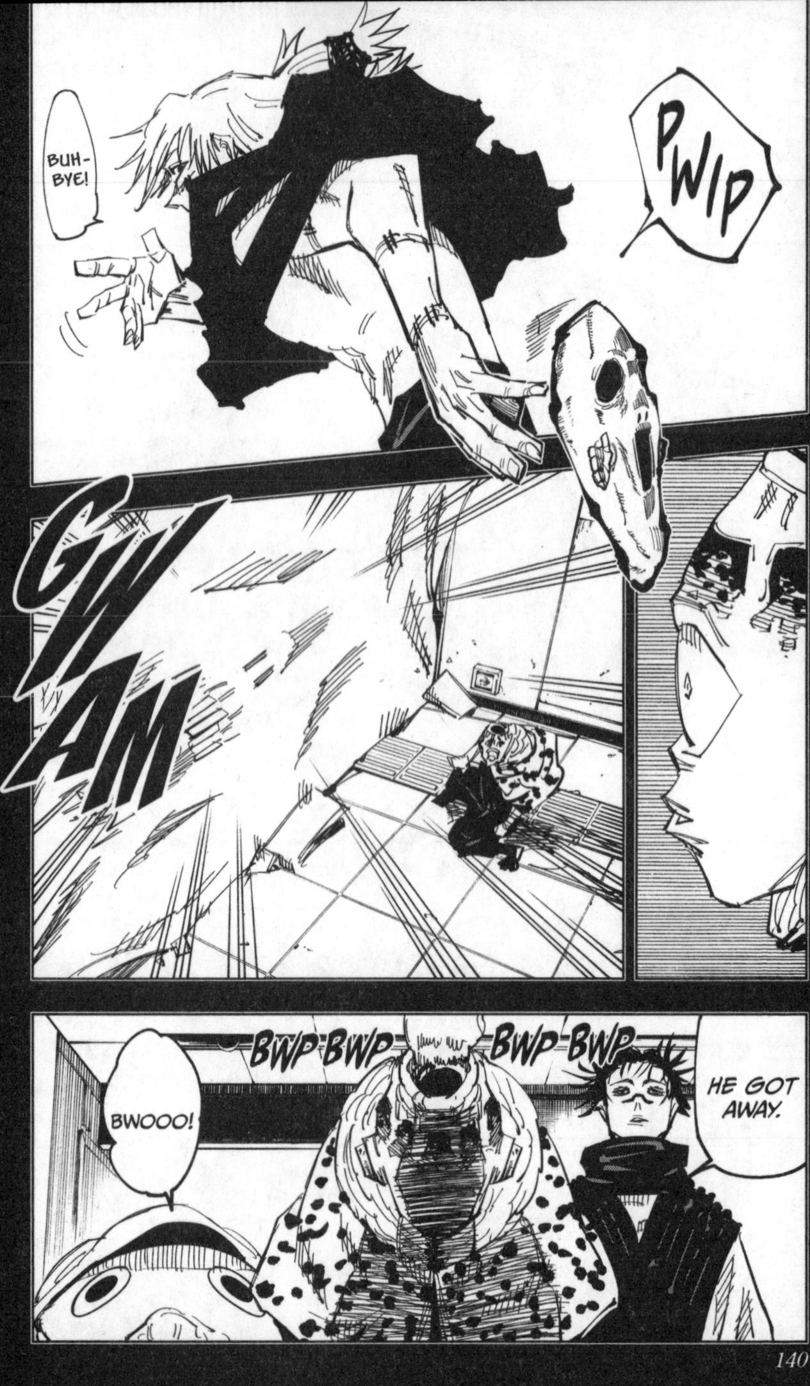
PWIP
BUH-BYE!
GWAM
HE GOT AWAY.
BWP BWP BWP BWP
BWOOO!

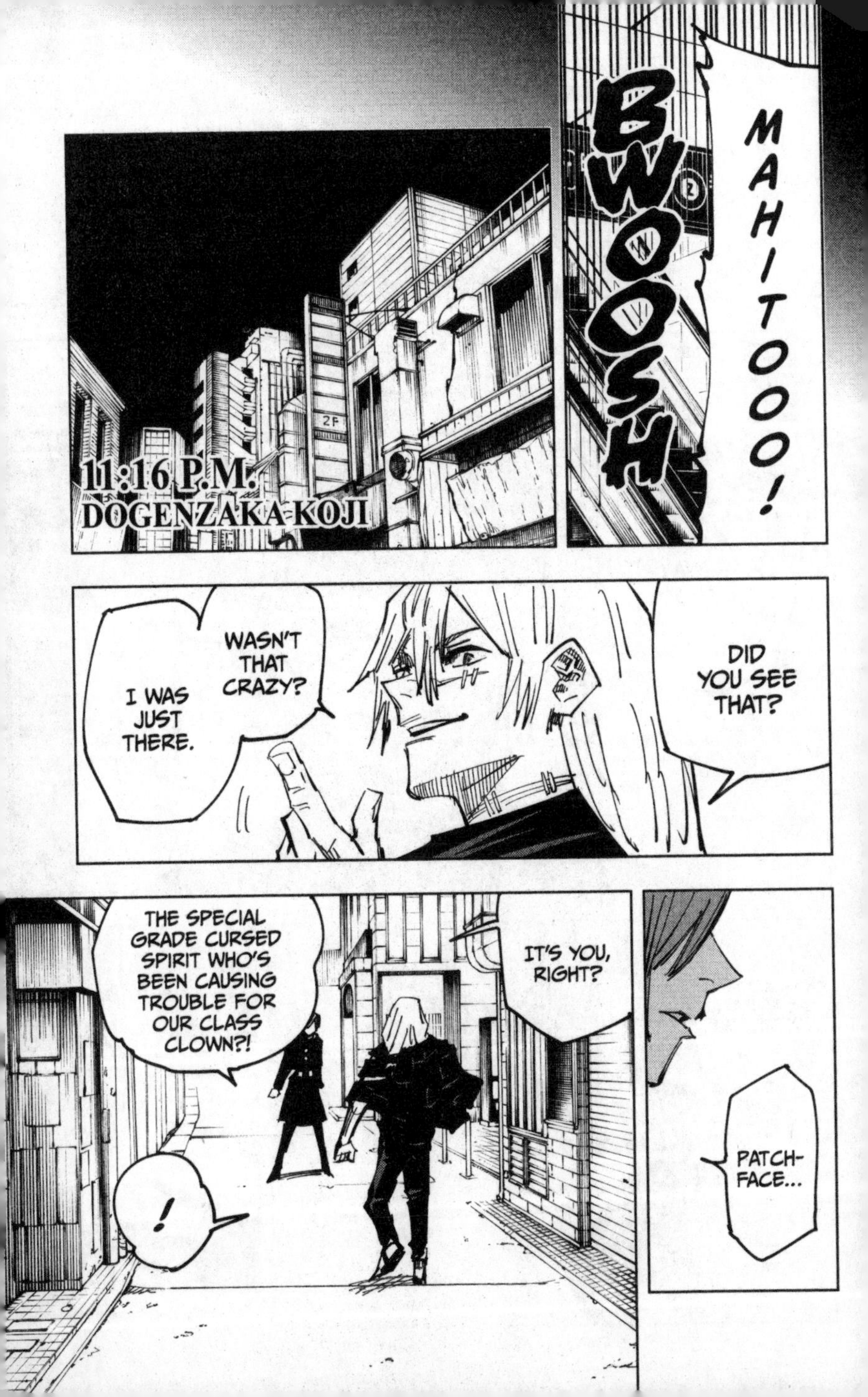
MAHITOOO!
BWOOSH
11:16 P.M.
DOGENZAKA KOJI
DID YOU SEE THAT?
WASN'T THAT CRAZY?
I WAS JUST THERE.
PATCH-FACE...
IT'S YOU, RIGHT?
THE SPECIAL GRADE CURSED SPIRIT WHO'S BEEN CAUSING TROUBLE FOR OUR CLASS CLOWN?!
!

AM I FAMOUS NOW?

AW, SHUCKS.

FAMOUS FOR BEING A COWARD AND RUNNING AWAY.

YEAH.

KEH KEH KEH

KILLING YOU SHOULD BE WORTHWHILE.

I LIKE YA ALREADY.

142

...NOT TO LET HIM TOUCH ME... THEY TOLD ME...

...SO YOU'LL HAVE TO AT LEAST LET ME SQUASH A FLEEING BUG LIKE YOU.

I THINK HIS CURSED TECHNIQUE HAS SOMETHING TO DO WITH THE SOUL...

I DON'T HAVE MUCH TO SHOW FOR TODAY...

SHK

...FROM BACK THEN.

REMEMBER THE FEELING...

...CURSED ENERGY!

FEEL THE CORE OF...

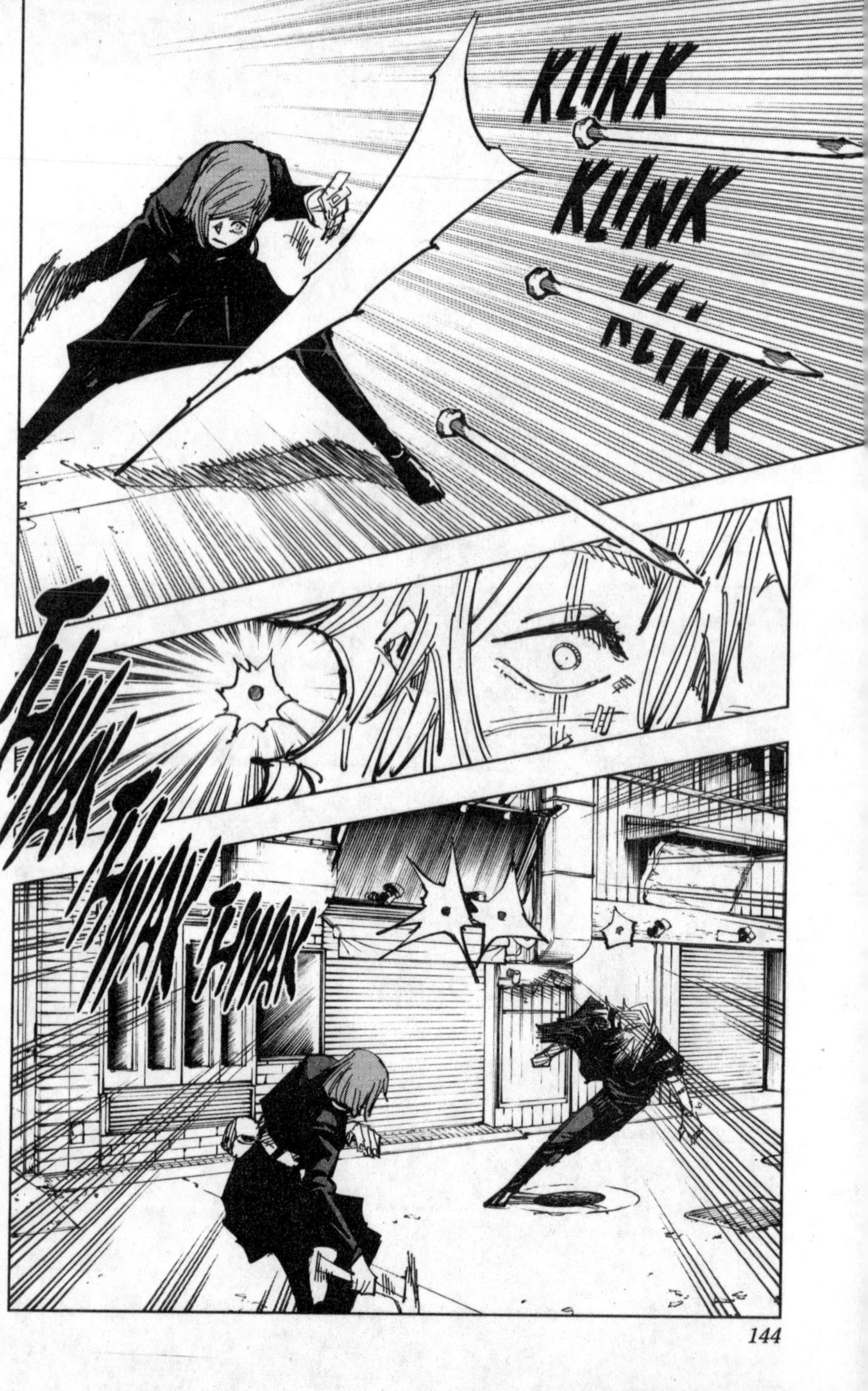
KLINK
KLINK
KLINK
KLINK
THWAK
THWAK
THWAK
THWAK

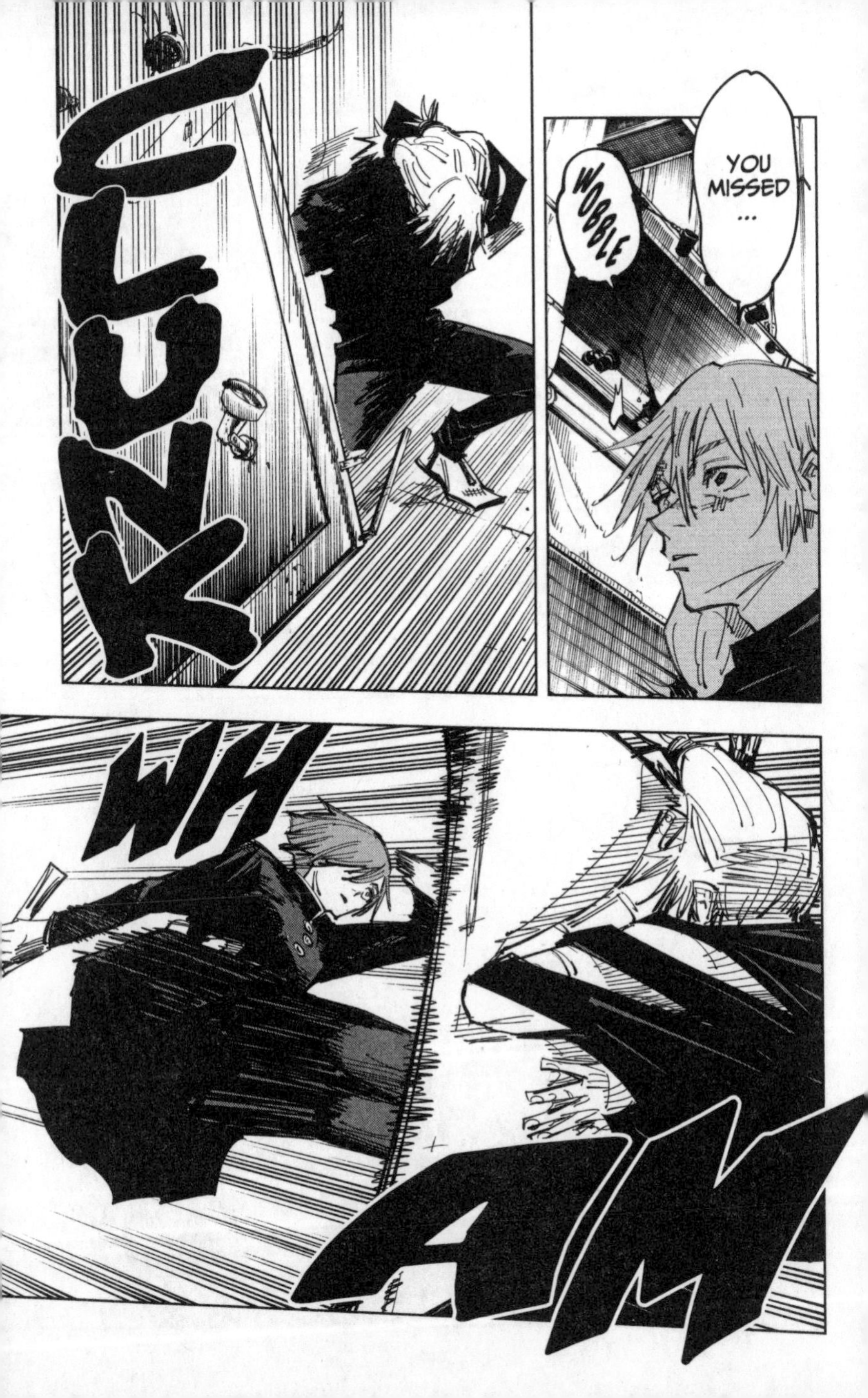
YOU MISSED ...
WOBBLE
WHAM

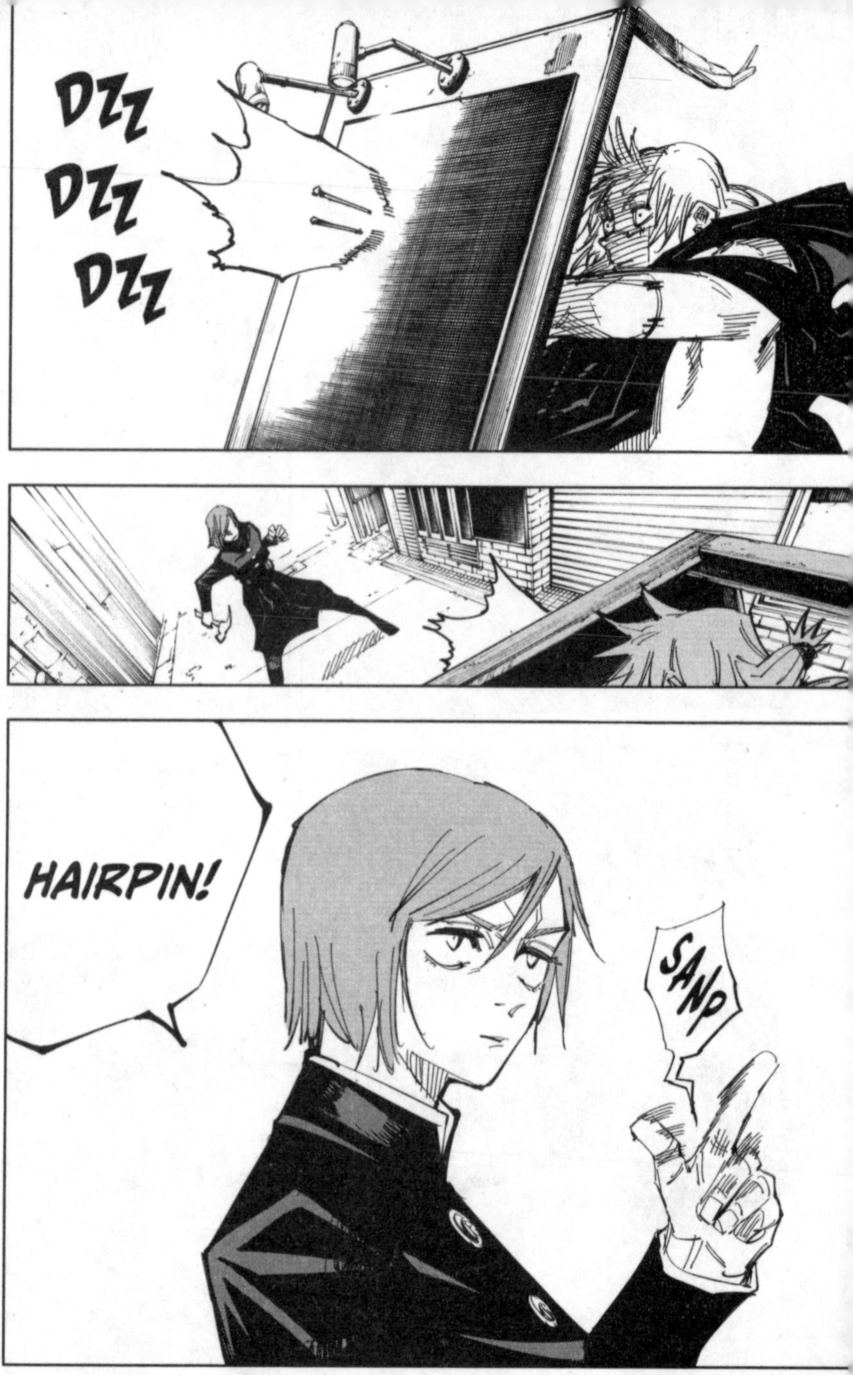
DZZ
DZZ
DZZ
HAIRPIN!
SNAP

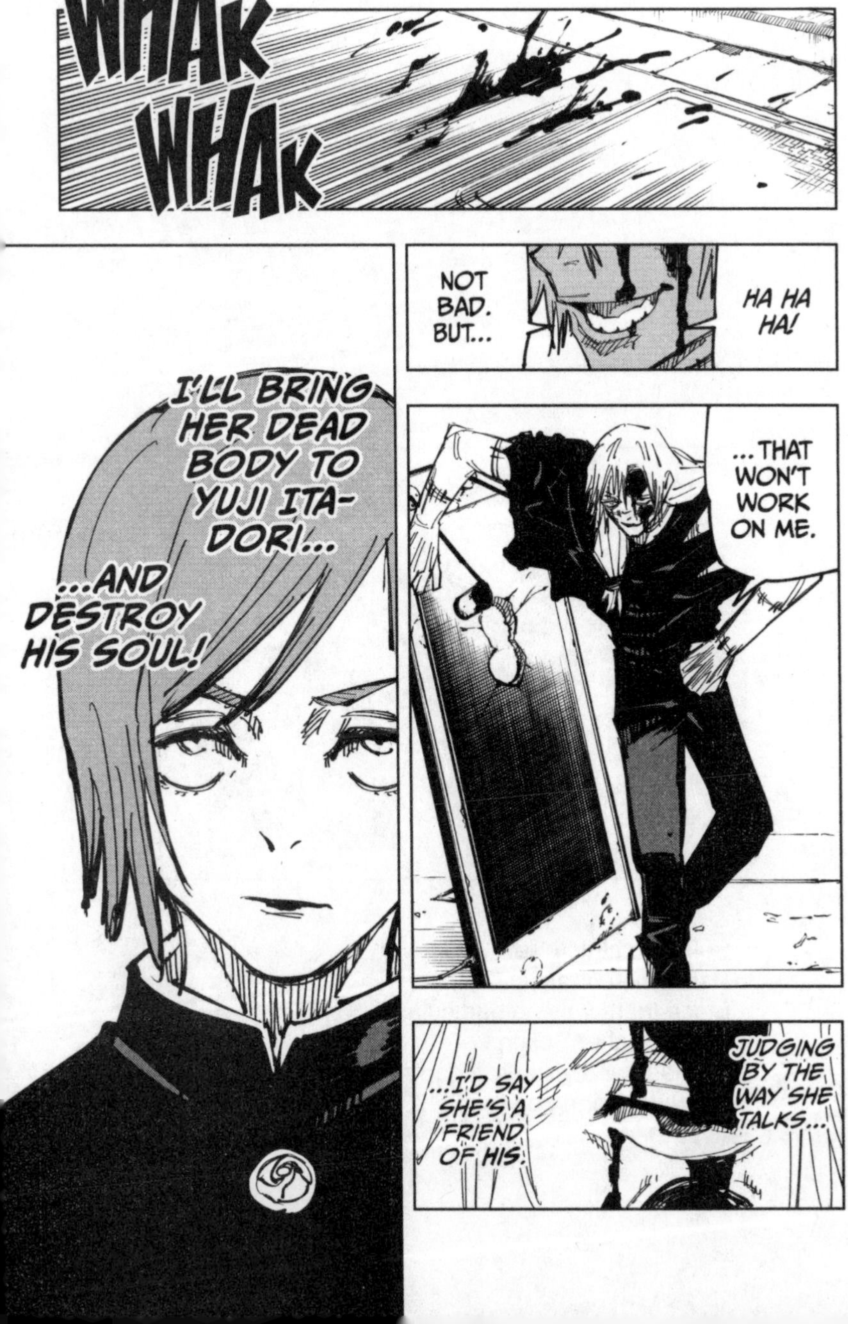
WHAK WHAK
HA HA HA!
NOT BAD. BUT...
...THAT WON'T WORK ON ME.
JUDGING BY THE WAY SHE TALKS...
...I'D SAY SHE'S A FRIEND OF HIS.
I'LL BRING HER DEAD BODY TO YUJI ITA-DORI...
...AND DESTROY HIS SOUL!

Extra Info

• Sukuna actually flew all the way
outside the curtain in this scene.
• Since there was no particular
effect on either Sukuna or
Mahoraga and visually it had no
particular bearing on the fight, I
left it out.

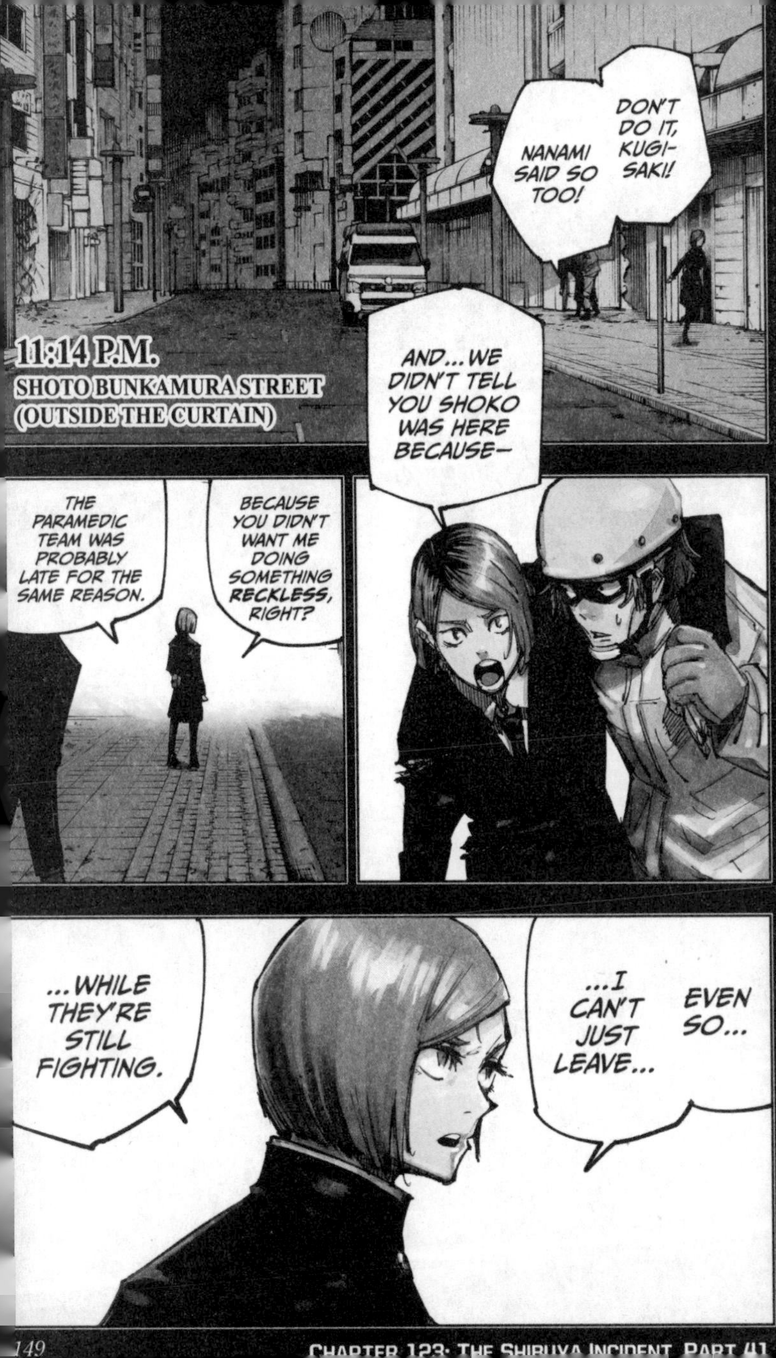
11:14 P.M.
SHOTO BUNKAMURA STREET (OUTSIDE THE CURTAIN)
DON'T DO IT, KUGI-SAKI!
NANAMI SAID SO TOO!
AND...WE DIDN'T TELL YOU SHOKO WAS HERE BECAUSE—
BECAUSE YOU DIDN'T WANT ME DOING SOMETHING RECKLESS, RIGHT?
THE PARAMEDIC TEAM WAS PROBABLY LATE FOR THE SAME REASON.
EVEN SO...
...I CAN'T JUST LEAVE...
...WHILE THEY'RE STILL FIGHTING.

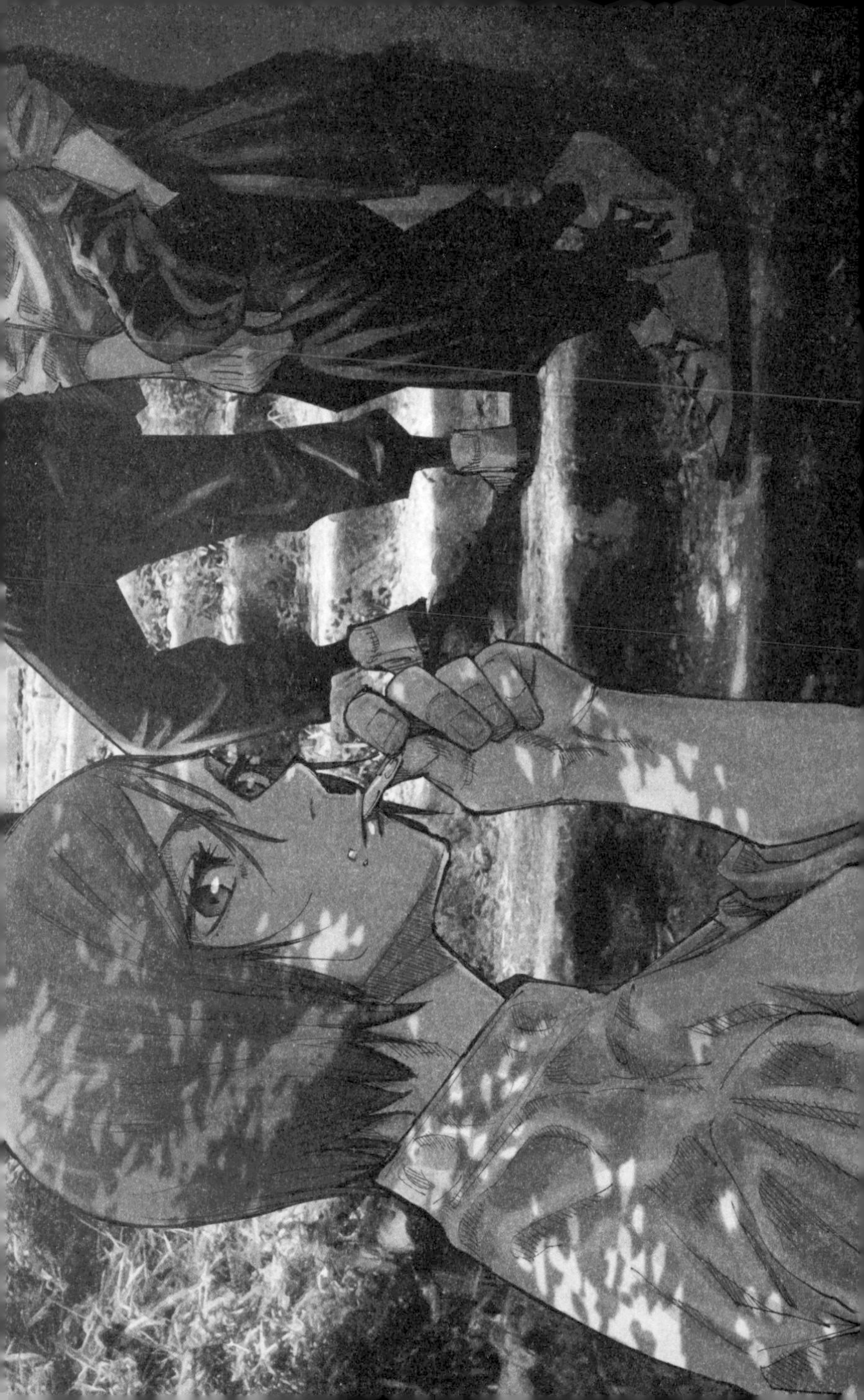

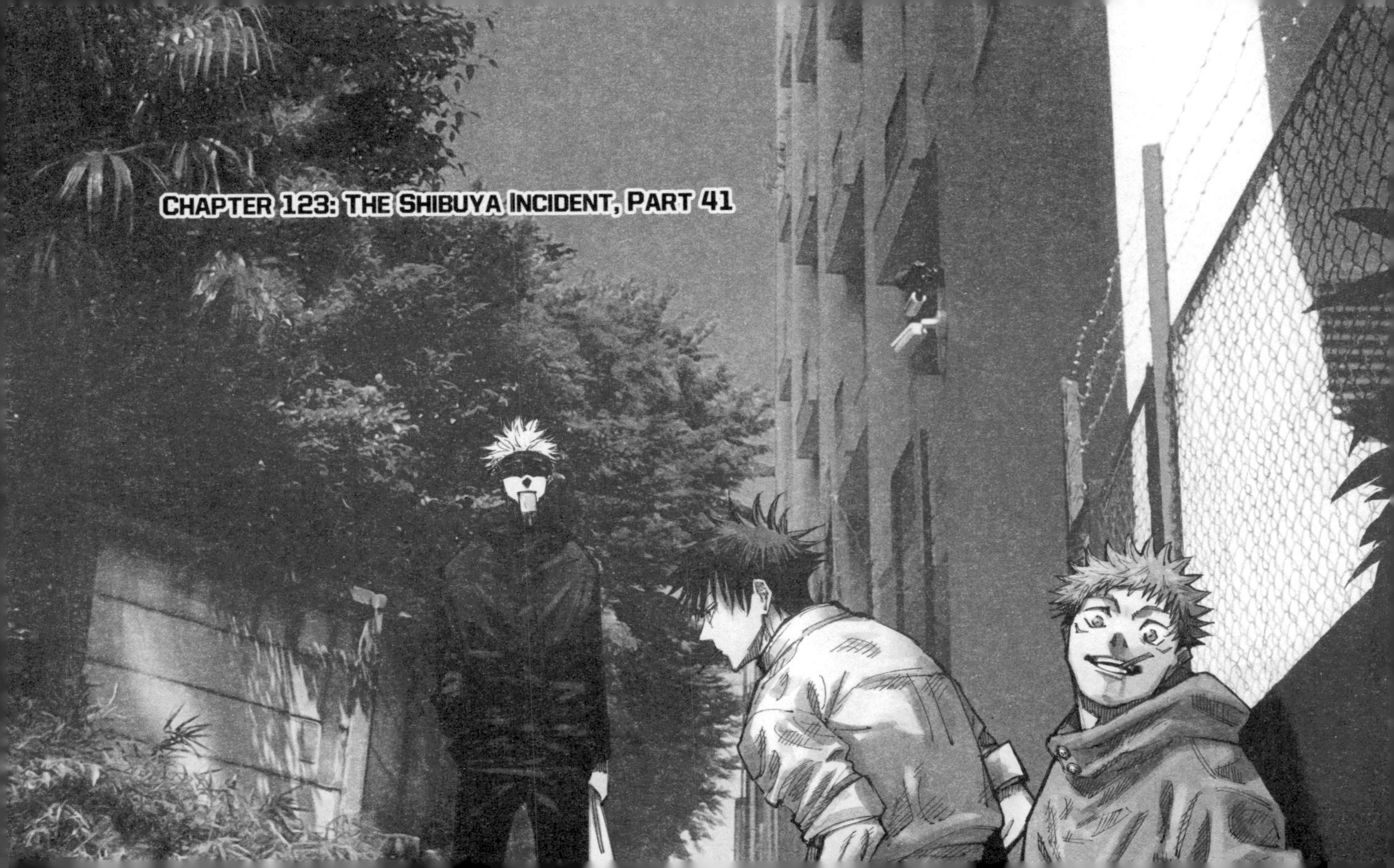
CHAPTER 123: THE SHIBUYA INCIDENT, PART 41

JUJUTSU KAISEN

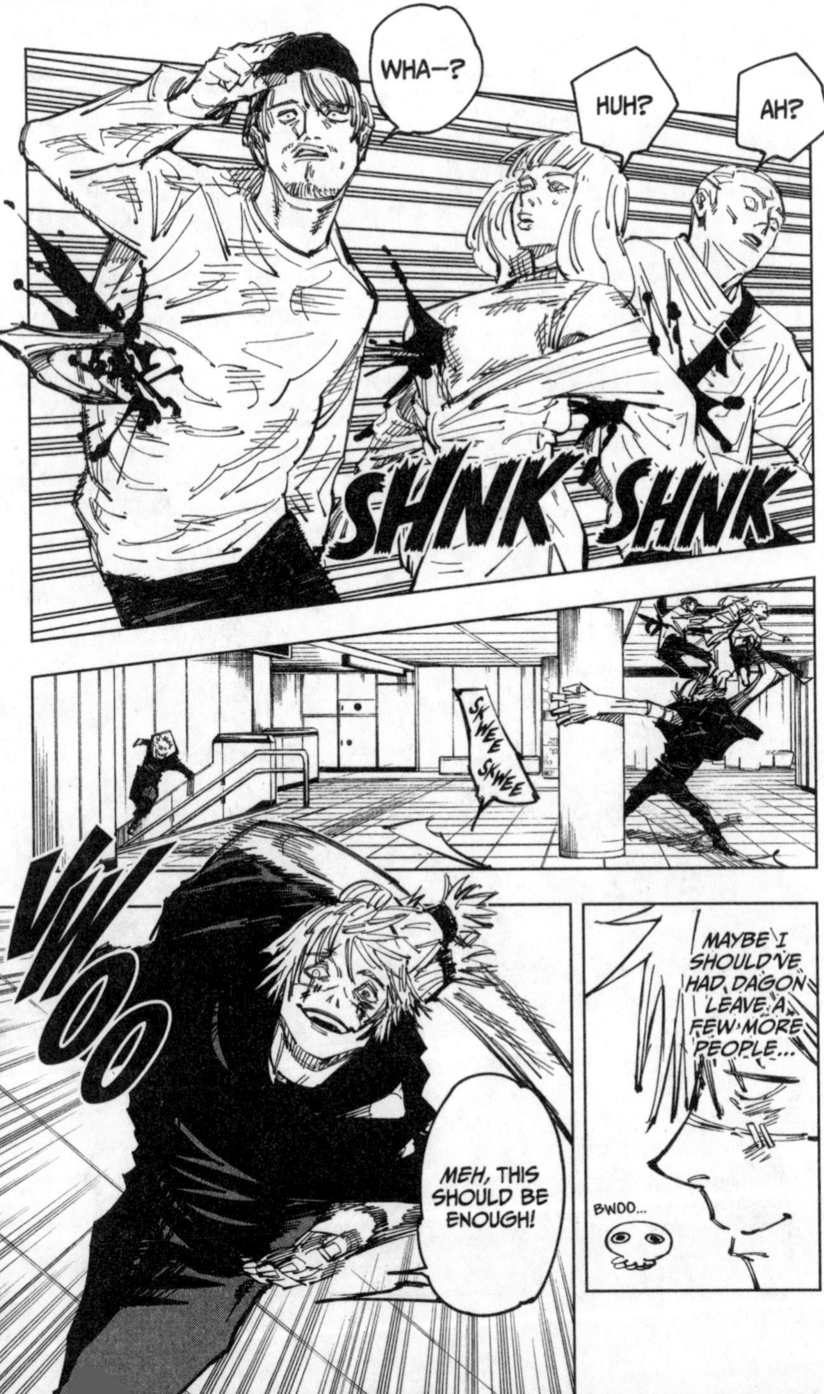
AH?
HUH?
WHA—?
SHNK SHNK
SKWEE SKWEE
MAYBE I SHOULD'VE HAD DAGON LEAVE A FEW MORE PEOPLE...
BWOO...
VWOO
MEH, THIS SHOULD BE ENOUGH!

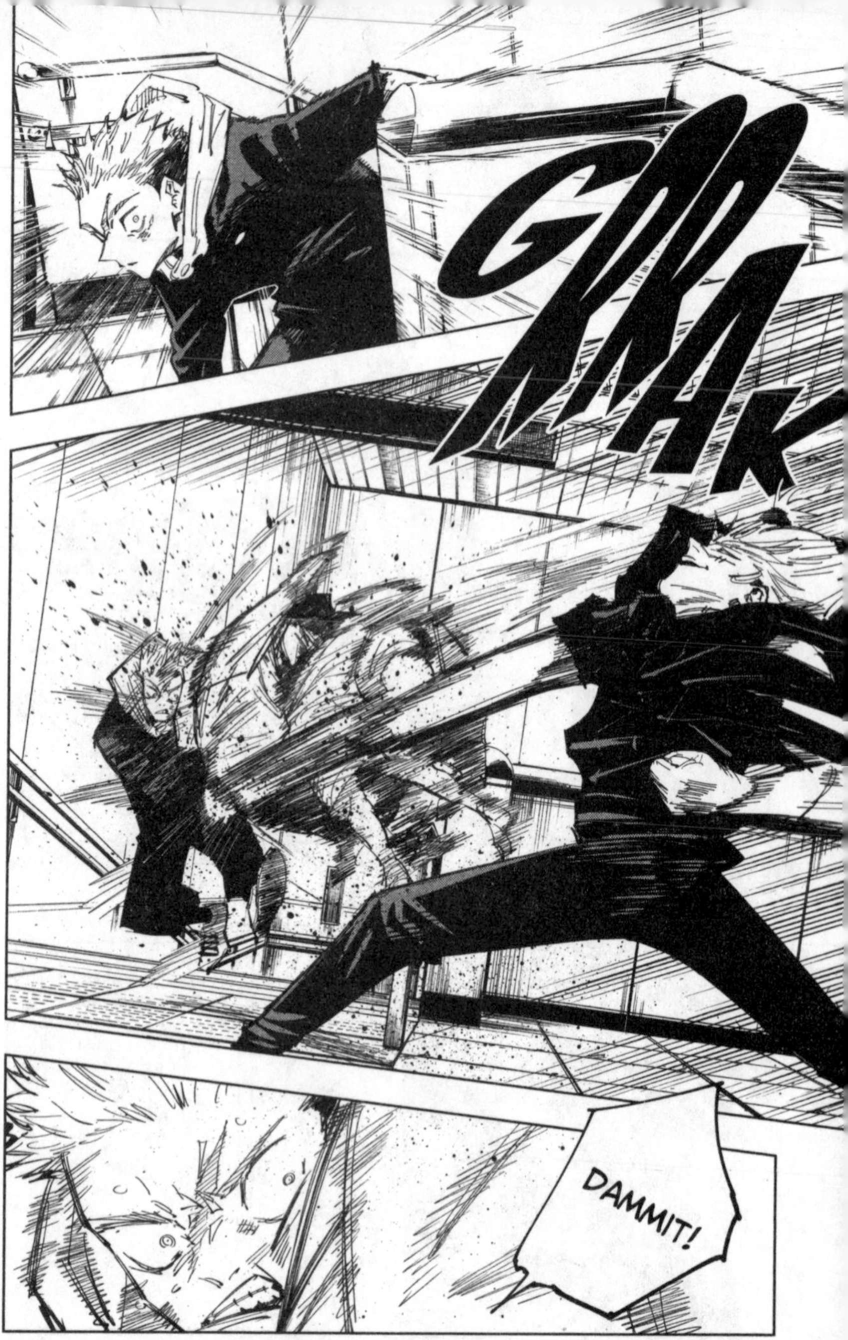
GWAK
DAMMIT!

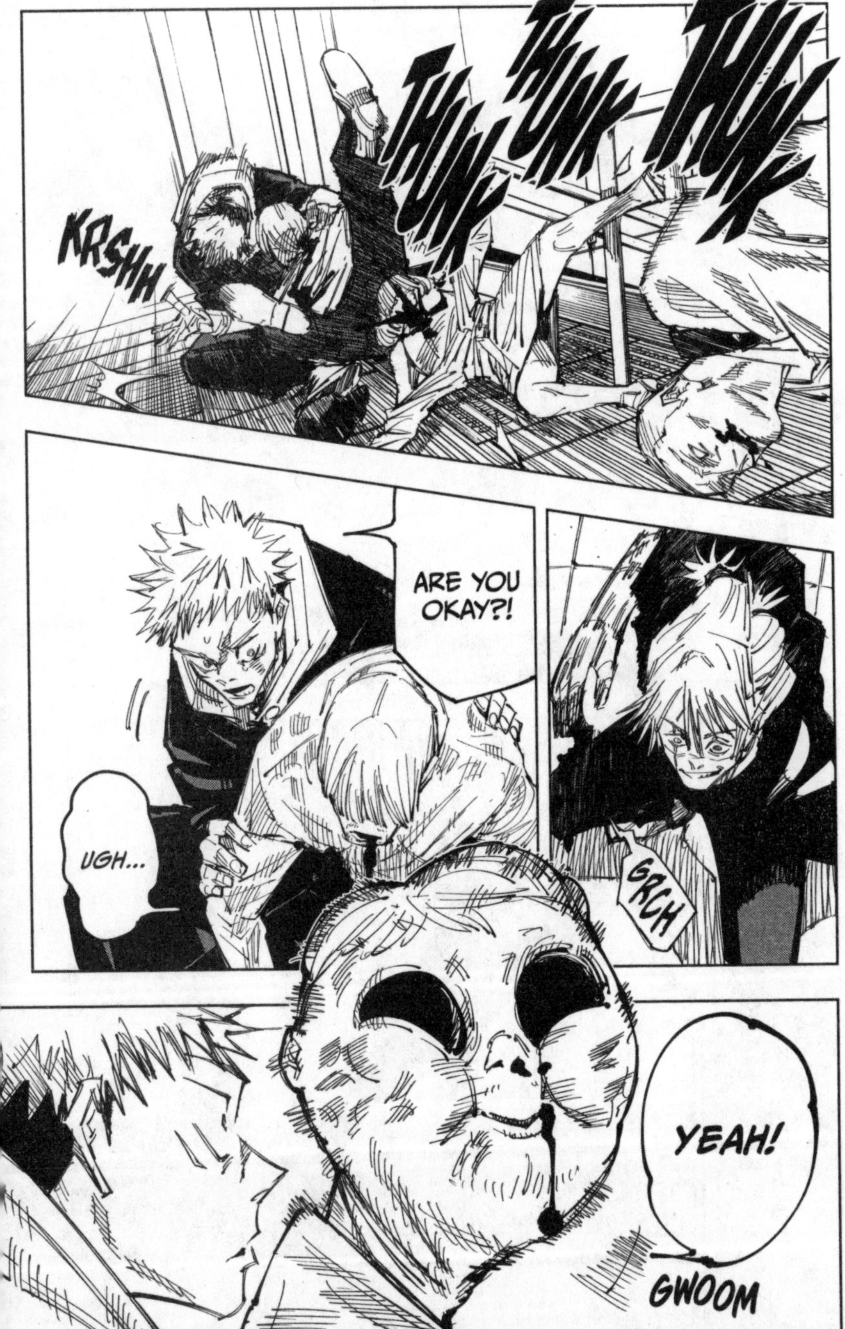
THUNK
THUNK
THUNK
KRSHH
GRCH
ARE YOU OKAY?!
UGH...
YEAH!
GWOOM

POP

SPLAT
SPLAT

CRAP, I—

I CAN CHANGE MY FORM LIKE THE ORIGINAL, BUT...

...I CAN'T MANIPULATE TRANSFIGURED HUMANS OR OTHER SOULS.

BWOOM

BUT THANKS FOR WEARING YOUR-SELF DOWN...

...FOR ME!

I'M NOT FIGHTING ITADORI. I CAN MANIPULATE MY FORM AS MUCH AS I WANT WITHOUT INCURRING RISKS.

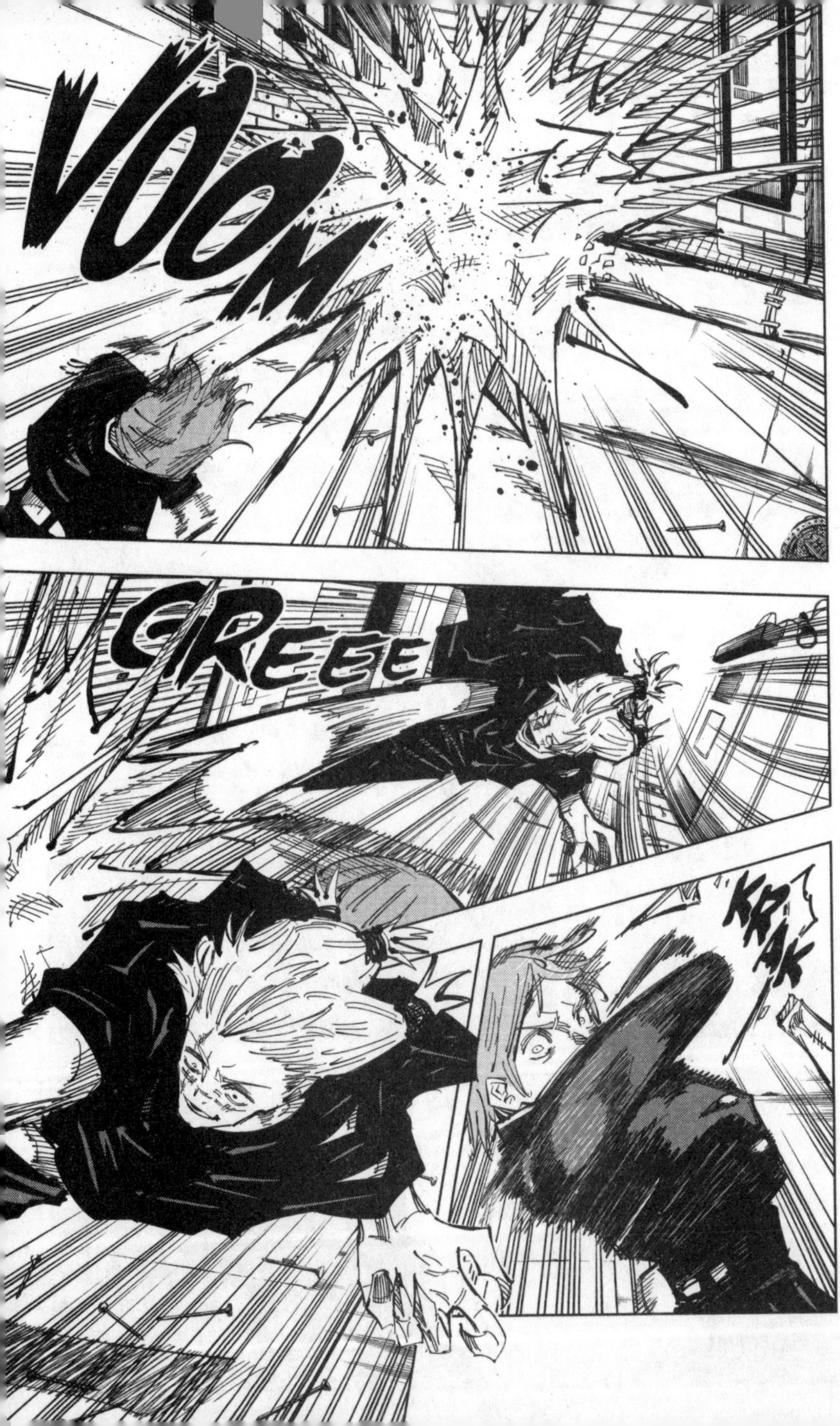
VOOM
CREEEE
KRAK

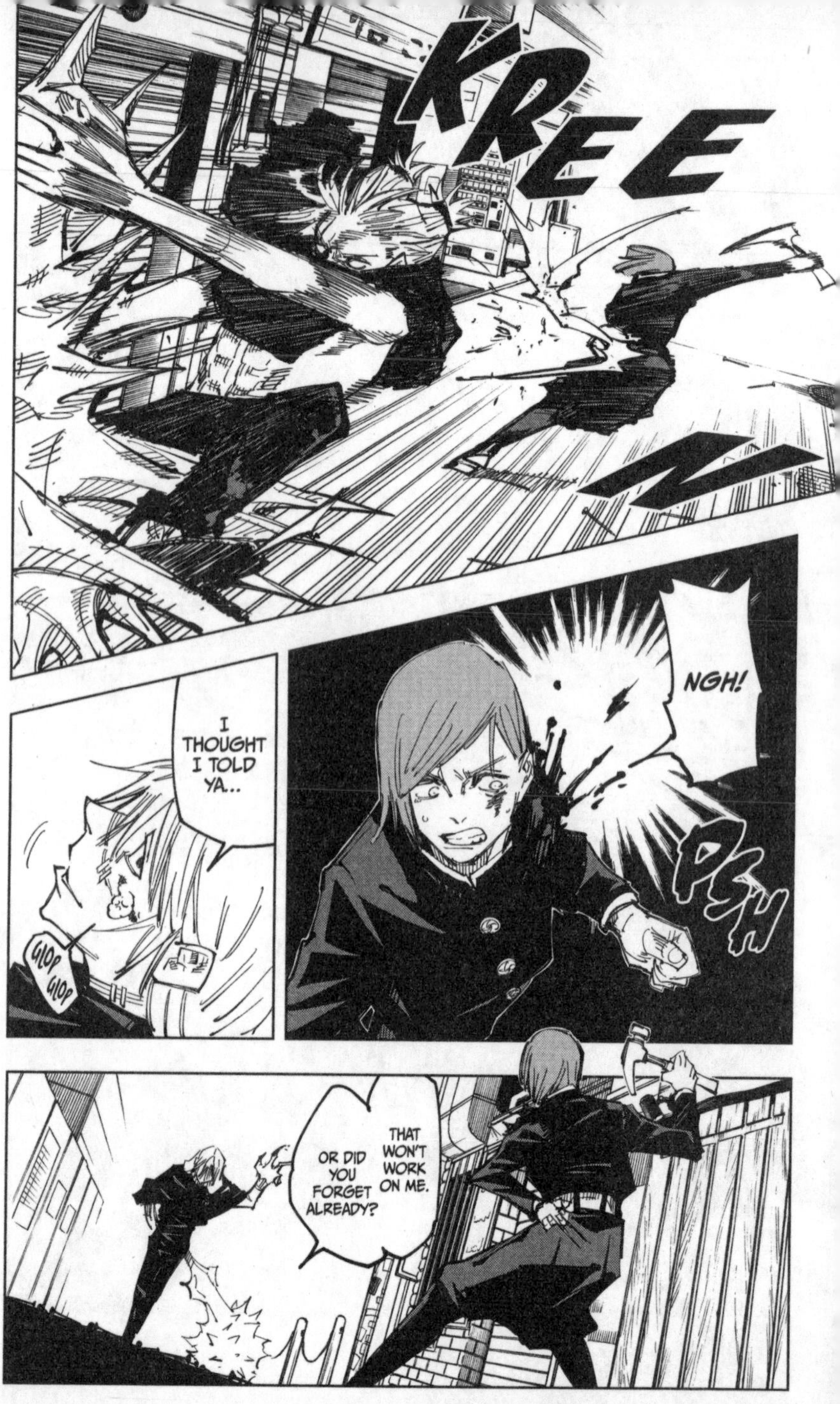
KREE
NGH!
DSH
I THOUGHT I TOLD YA...
GLOP GLOP
THAT WON'T WORK ON ME.
OR DID YOU FORGET ALREADY?

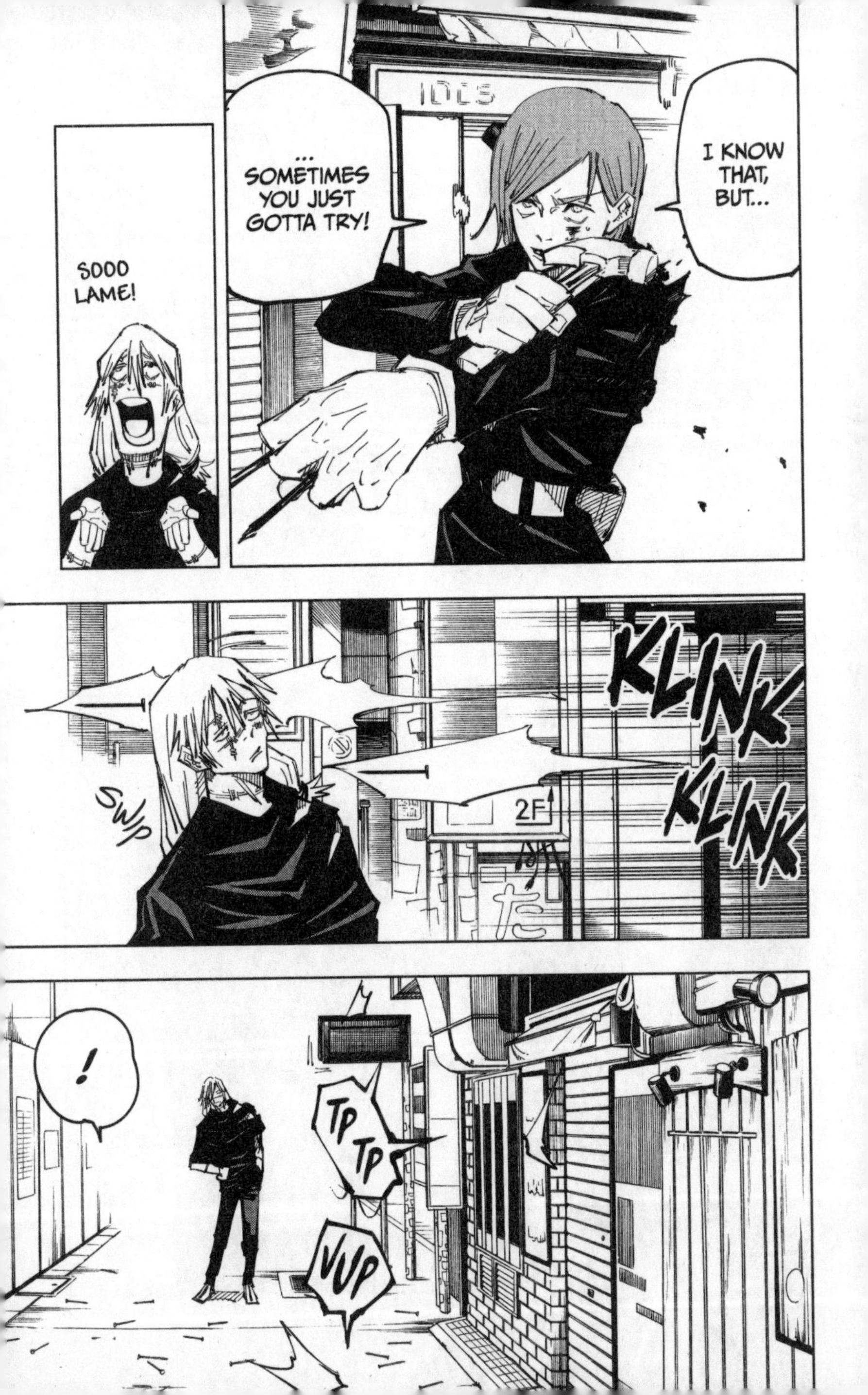
I KNOW THAT, BUT...
... SOMETIMES YOU JUST GOTTA TRY!
SOOO LAME!
KLINK KLINK
SWIP
2F
!
TP TP
VUP

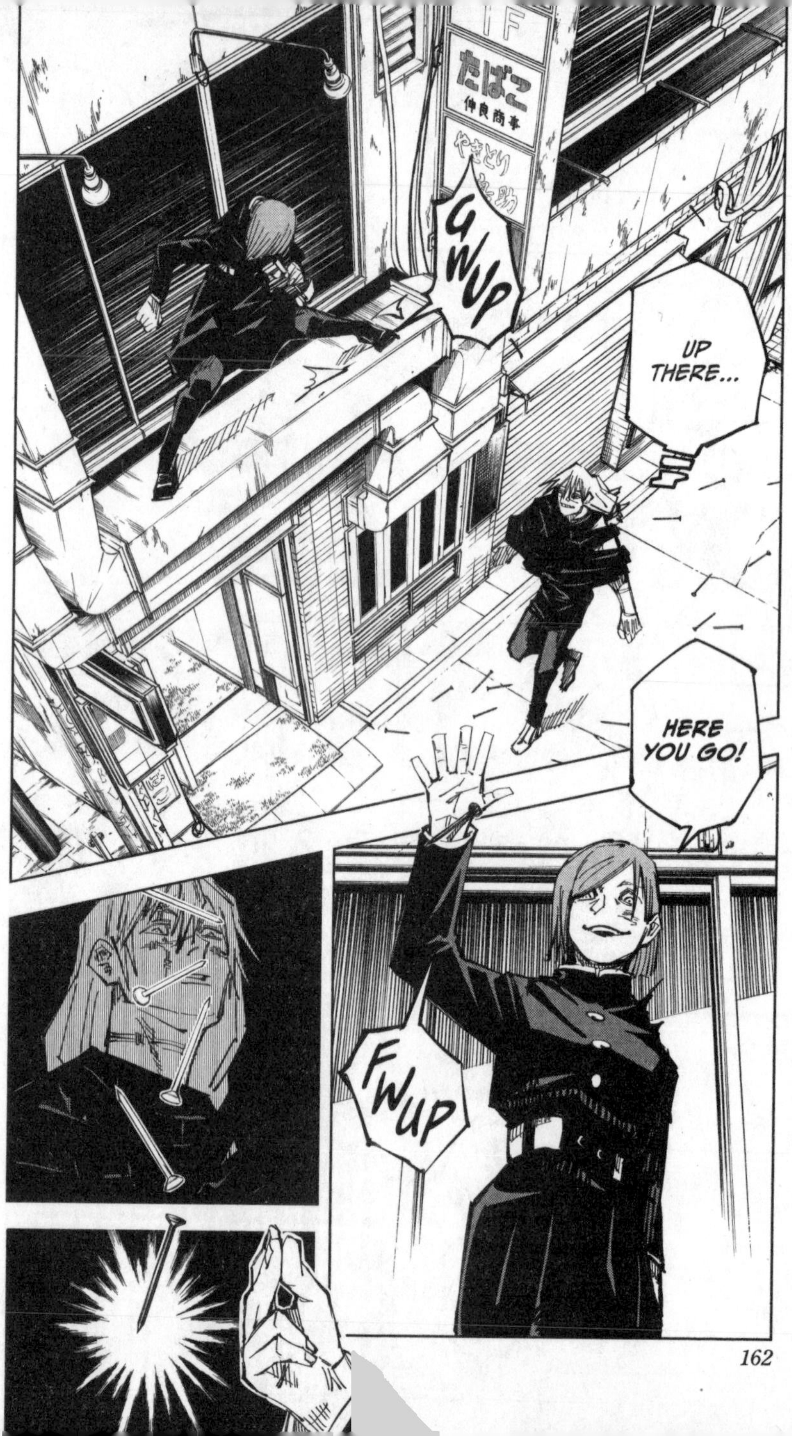
たばこ
仲良商事
やきとり
GWUP
UP THERE...
HERE YOU GO!
FWUP

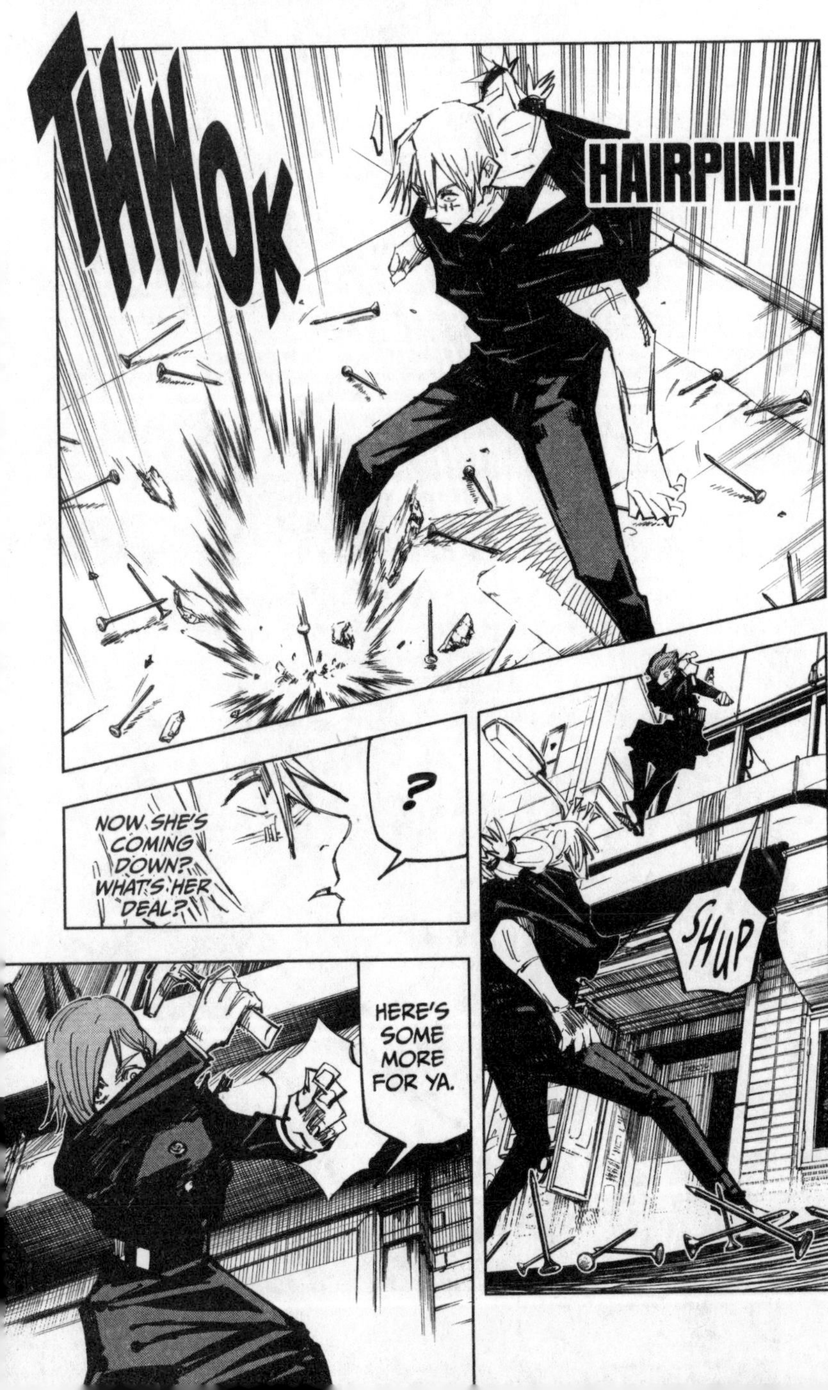
THWOK
HAIRPIN!!
SHUP
?
NOW SHE'S COMING DOWN? WHAT'S HER DEAL?
HERE'S SOME MORE FOR YA.

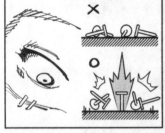

THE FIRST ONE RATTLED THE NAILS TO MAKE THEM POINT UPRIGHT!

!!

THOK THOK THOK THOK

HAIR-PIN!!

...

I'VE BEEN THINKING ABOUT IT.

BUT WHAT DOES THAT MATTER?

EVER SINCE I WAS TOLD ABOUT YOUR CURSED TECHNIQUE, I'VE THOUGHT...

...THIS...

...WOULD BE EFFECTIVE AGAINST YOU.

!!

SHE WAS BLUFFING TO MAKE IT SEEM LIKE SHE DIDN'T HAVE A PLAN!

BEFORE...

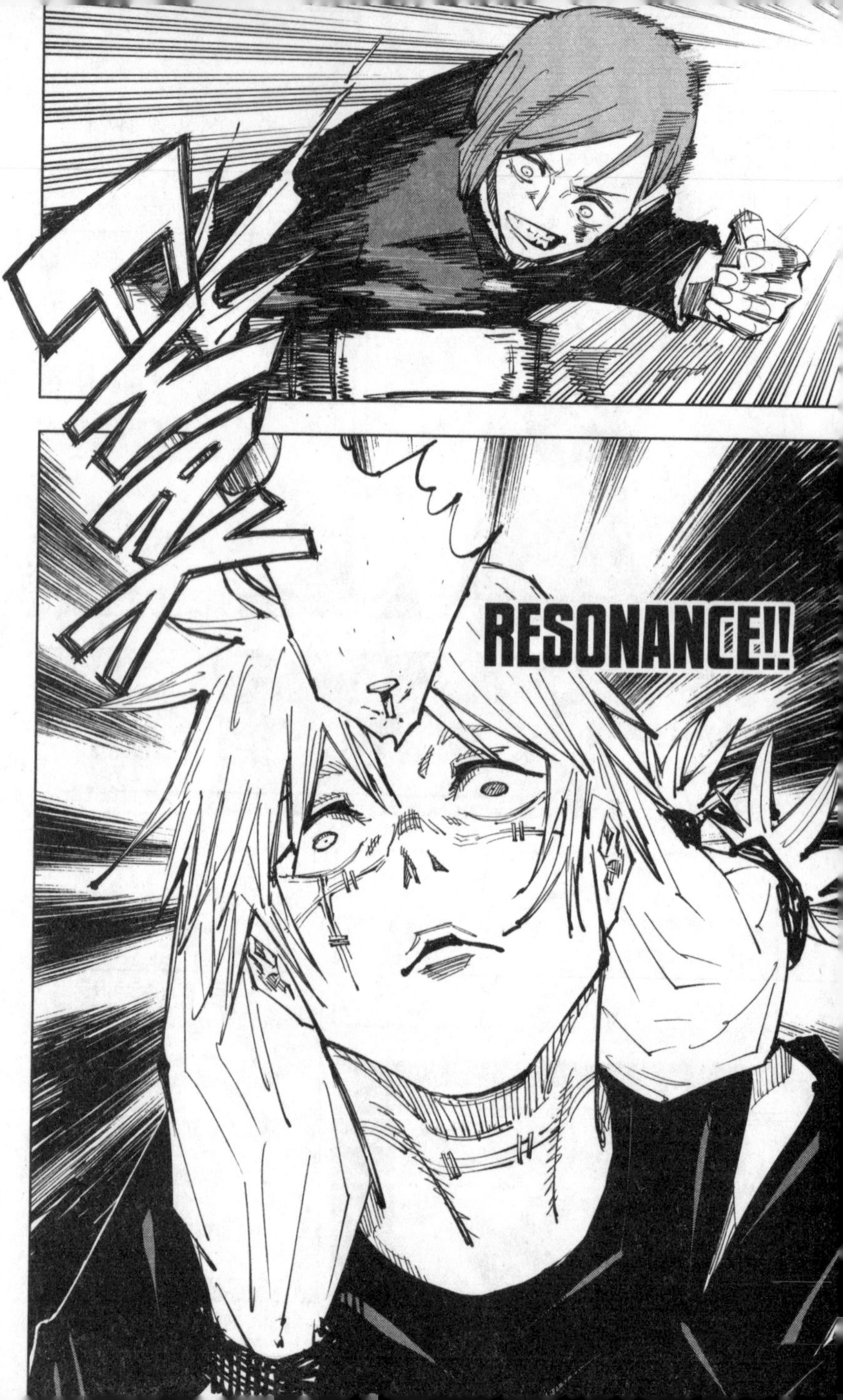
RESONANCE!!

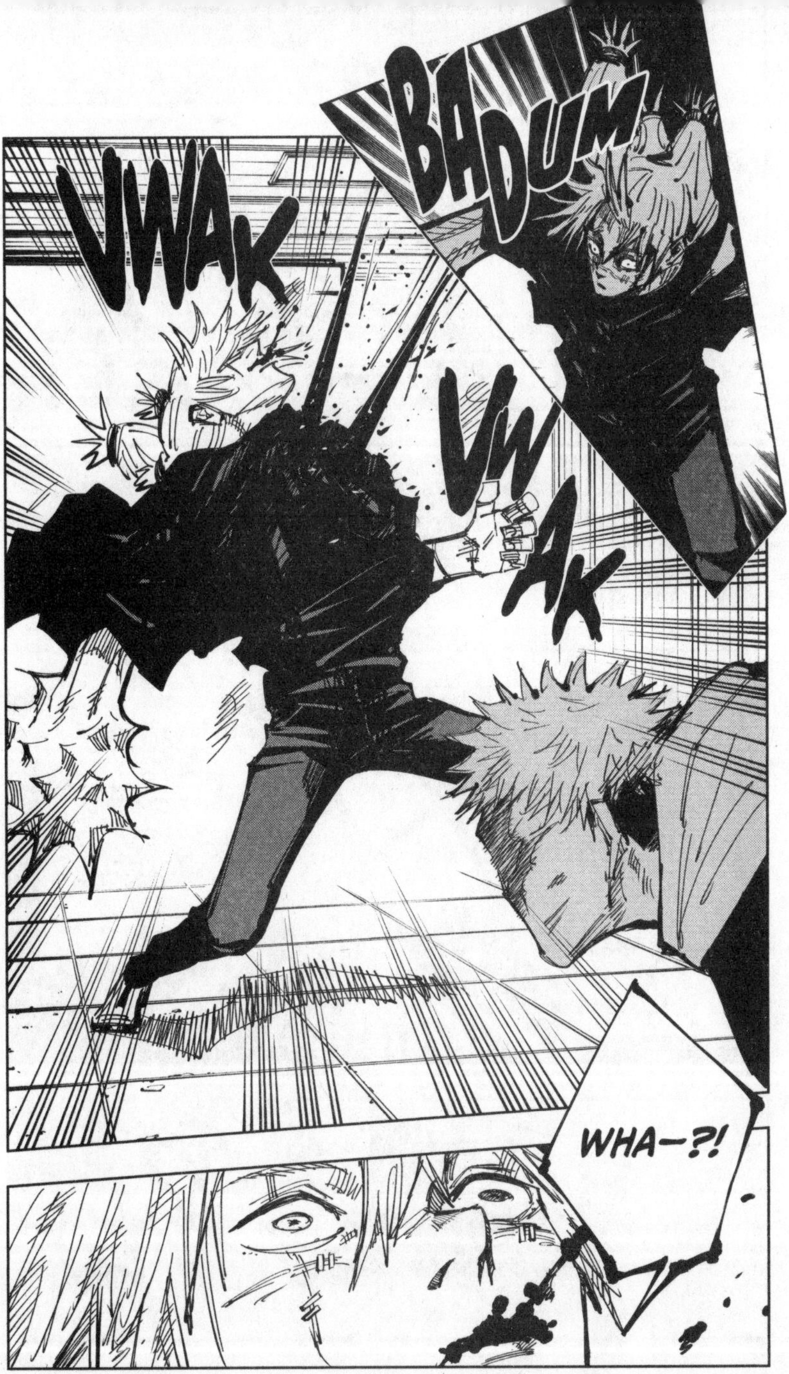
BADUM
VWAK
VWAK
WHA—?!

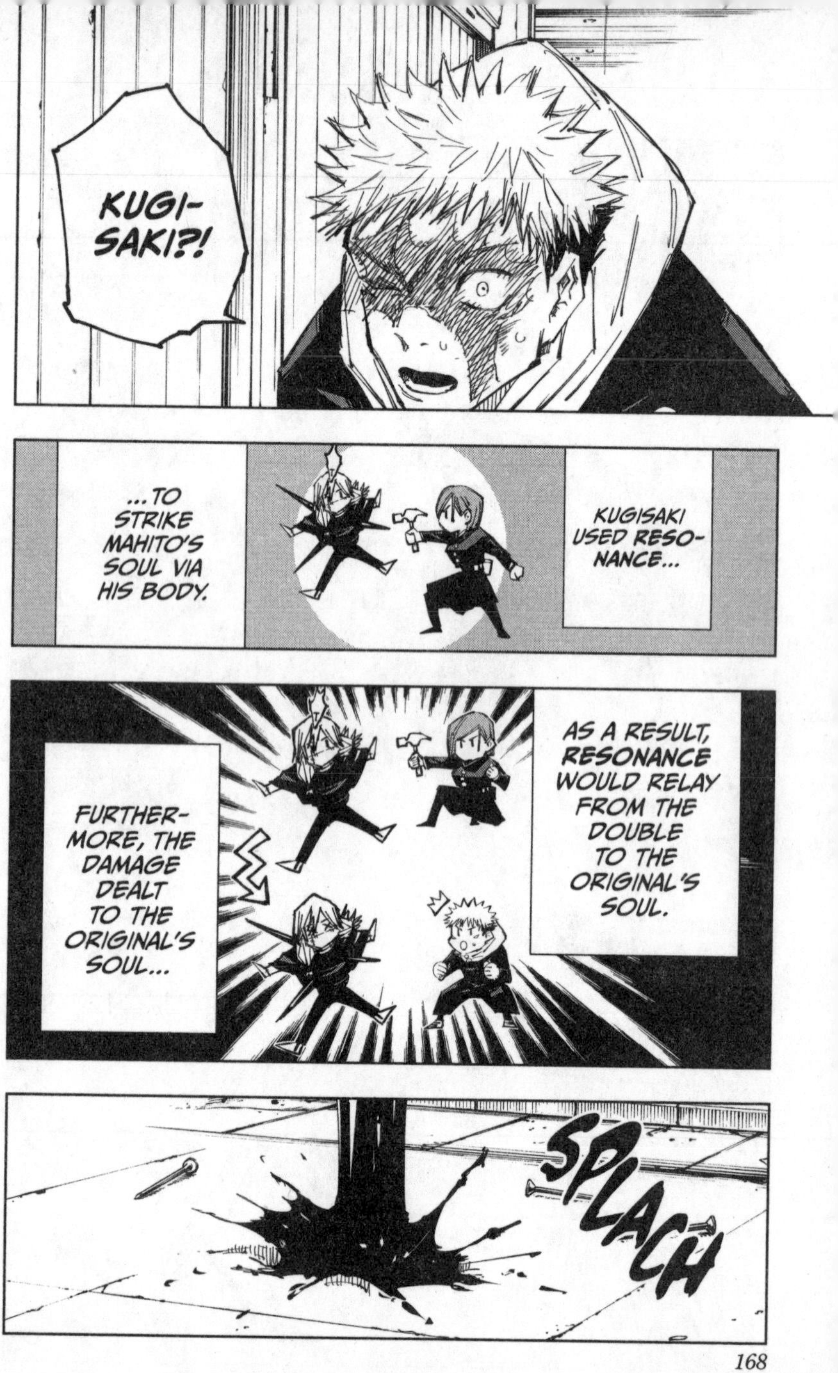
KUGI-SAKI?!
KUGISAKI USED RESO-NANCE...
...TO STRIKE MAHITO'S SOUL VIA HIS BODY.
AS A RESULT, RESONANCE WOULD RELAY FROM THE DOUBLE TO THE ORIGINAL'S SOUL.
FURTHER-MORE, THE DAMAGE DEALT TO THE ORIGINAL'S SOUL...
SPLACH

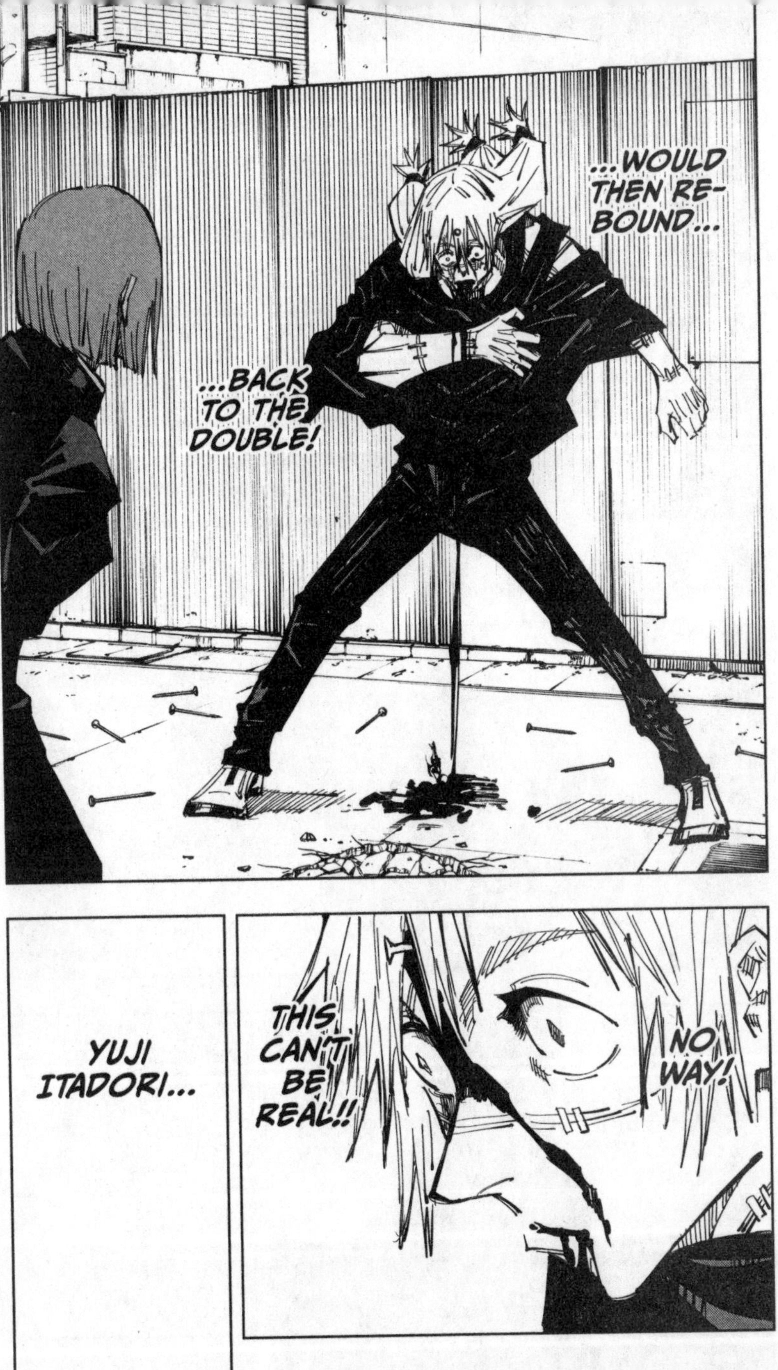
...WOULD THEN RE-BOUND...
...BACK TO THE DOUBLE!
NO WAY!
THIS CAN'T BE REAL!!
YUJI ITADORI...

...ISN'T MY ONLY...

...NATURAL ENEMY!

...DETONATE SOMEWHERE ELSE NEARBY.

I JUST FELT MY CURSED ENERGY...

HM... THAT'S WEIRD.

...YOU COULD'VE JUST GRABBED ME.

AND BACK THEN...

KREE

YOUR CURSED ENERGY ISN'T REALLY ALL THAT STRONG.

HOW DO I PUT THIS...

...SO YOU CAN'T USE YOUR CURSED TECHNIQUE, AM I RIGHT?!

YOU'RE LIKE A DOUBLE OR SOMETHING...

GRCHK

CORRECT...

A Nice Story

• Hiramatsu-san drew this design
of a young Kugisaki for the anime,
and I used it in the manga too.
• When Hiramatsu-san draws
Kugisaki, she's actually cute.

KUGI-
SAKI...?!

174

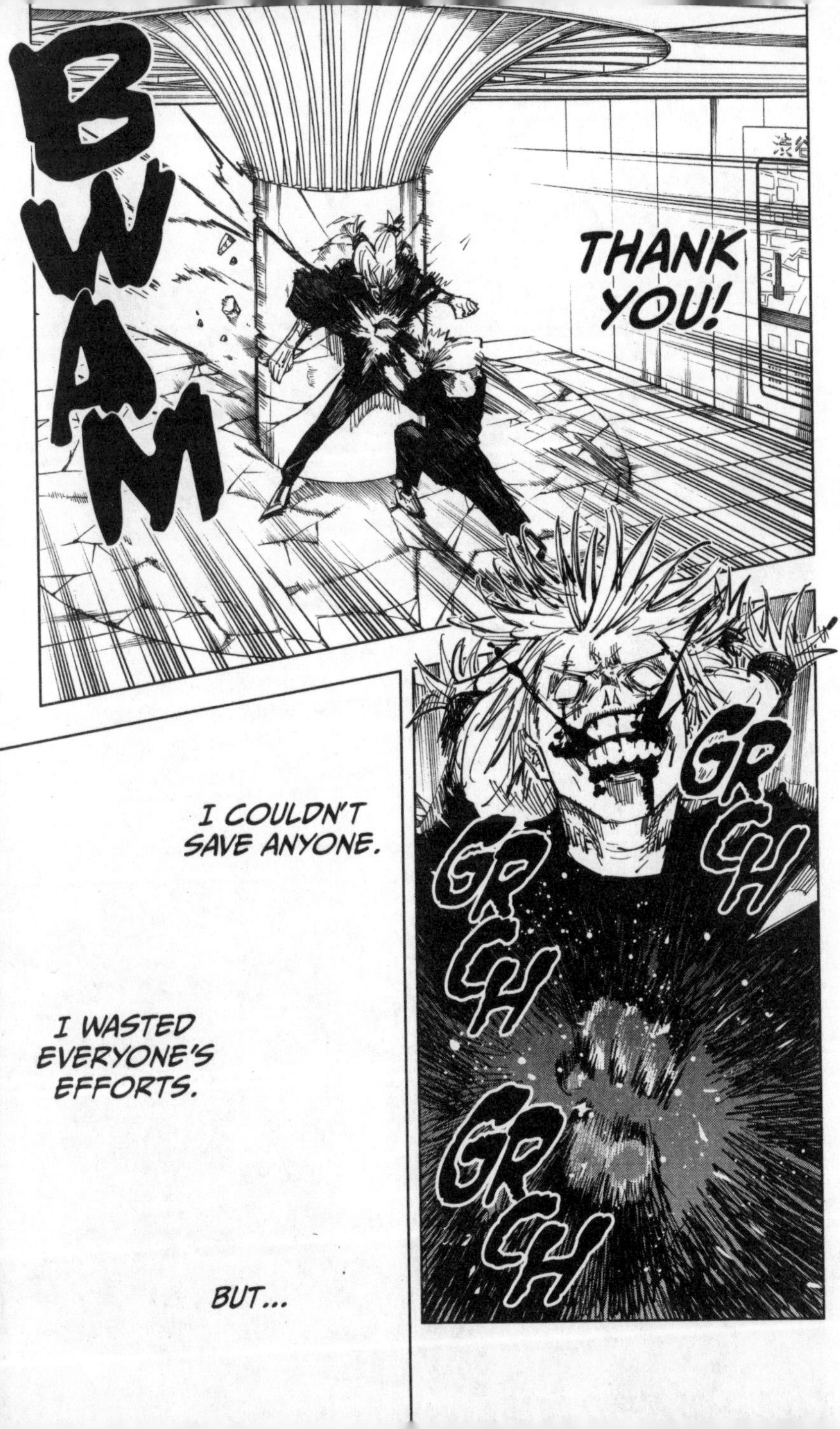
THANK YOU!
BWAM
GRCH GRCH
GRCH GRCH
I COULDN'T SAVE ANYONE.
I WASTED EVERYONE'S EFFORTS.
BUT...

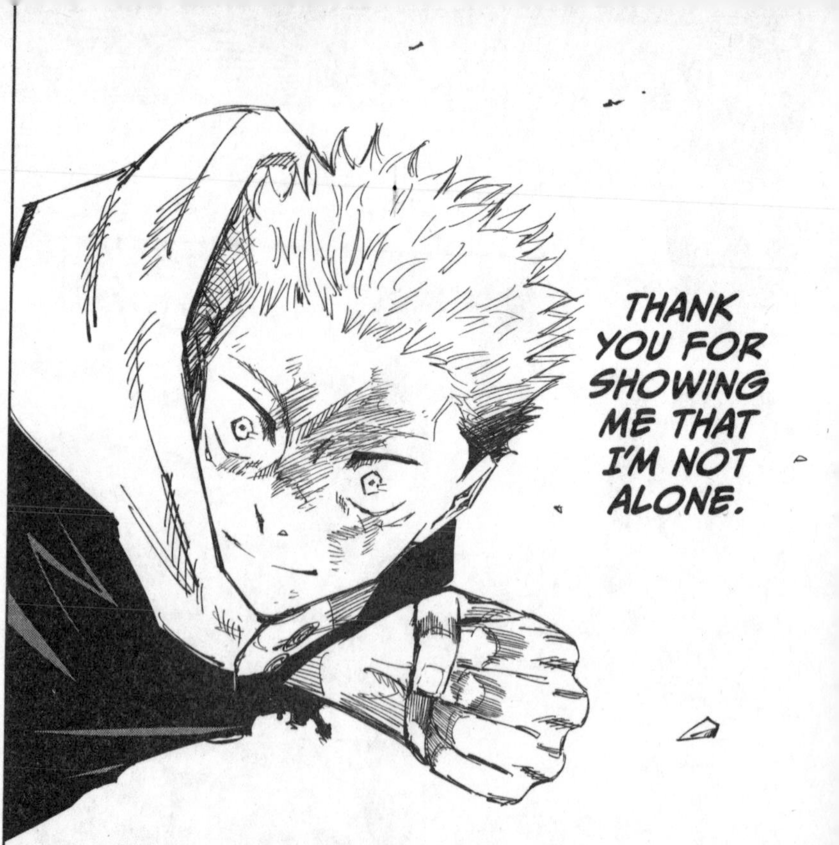
THANK YOU FOR SHOWING ME THAT I'M NOT ALONE.
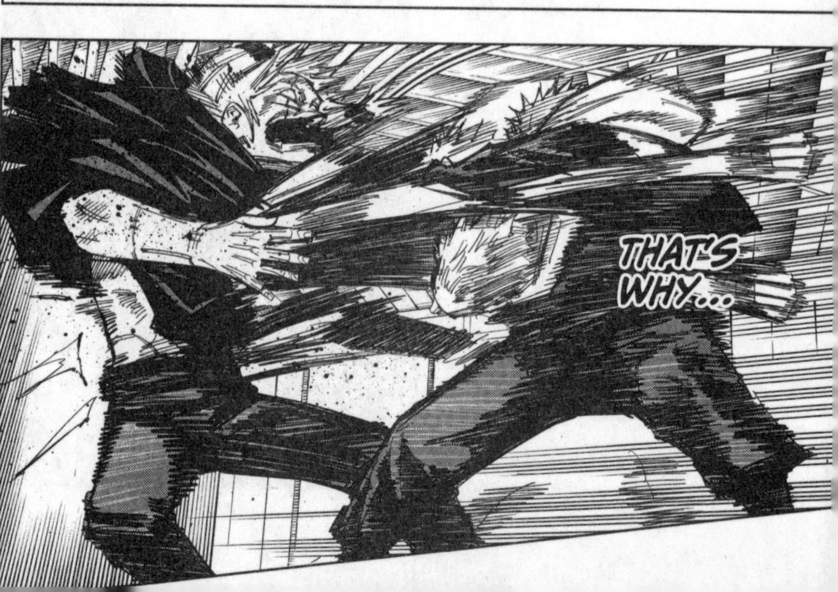
THAT'S WHY...

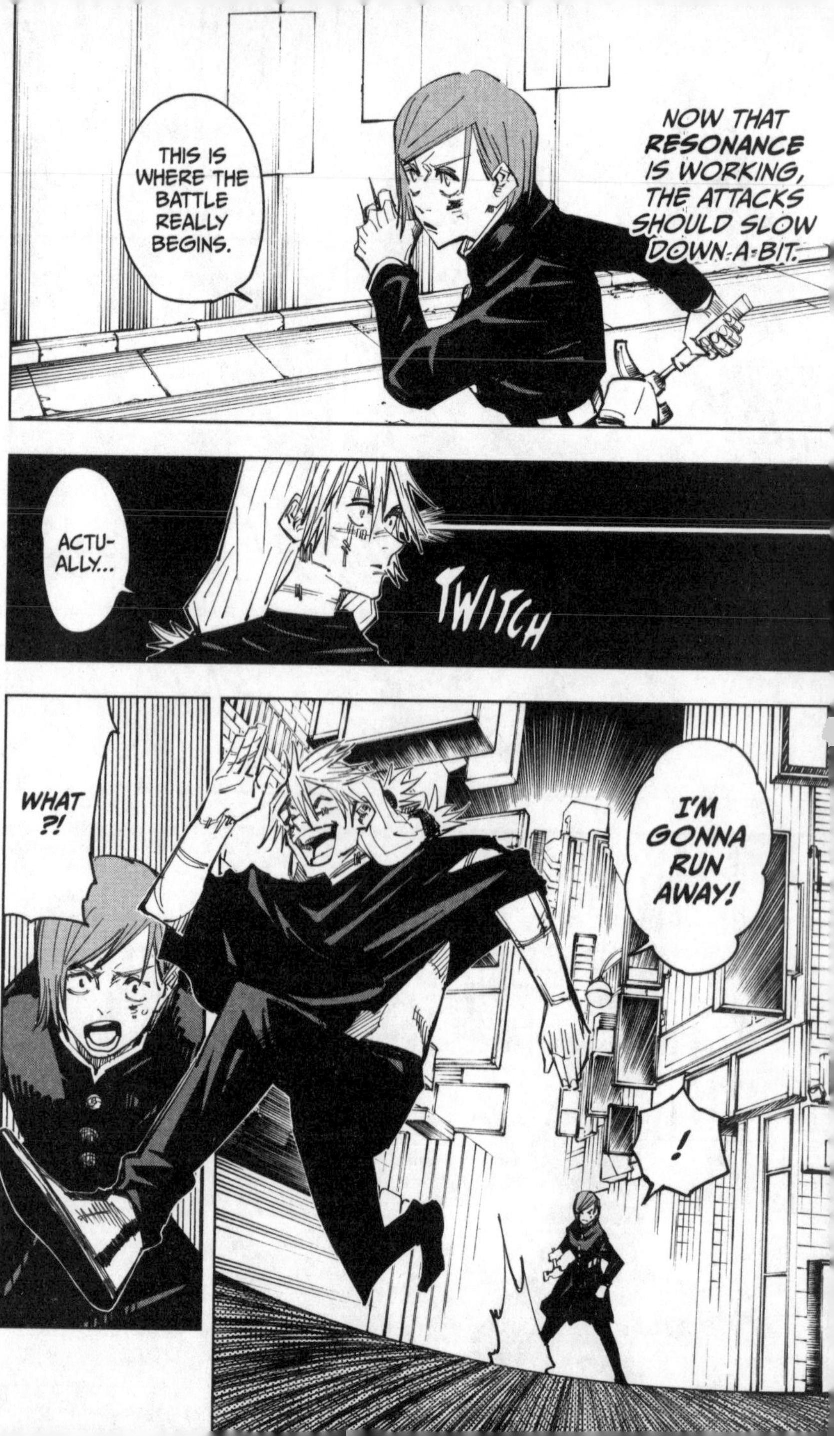
NOW THAT RESONANCE IS WORKING, THE ATTACKS SHOULD SLOW DOWN A BIT.
THIS IS WHERE THE BATTLE REALLY BEGINS.
ACTU-ALLY...
TWITCH
I'M GONNA RUN AWAY!
!
WHAT?!

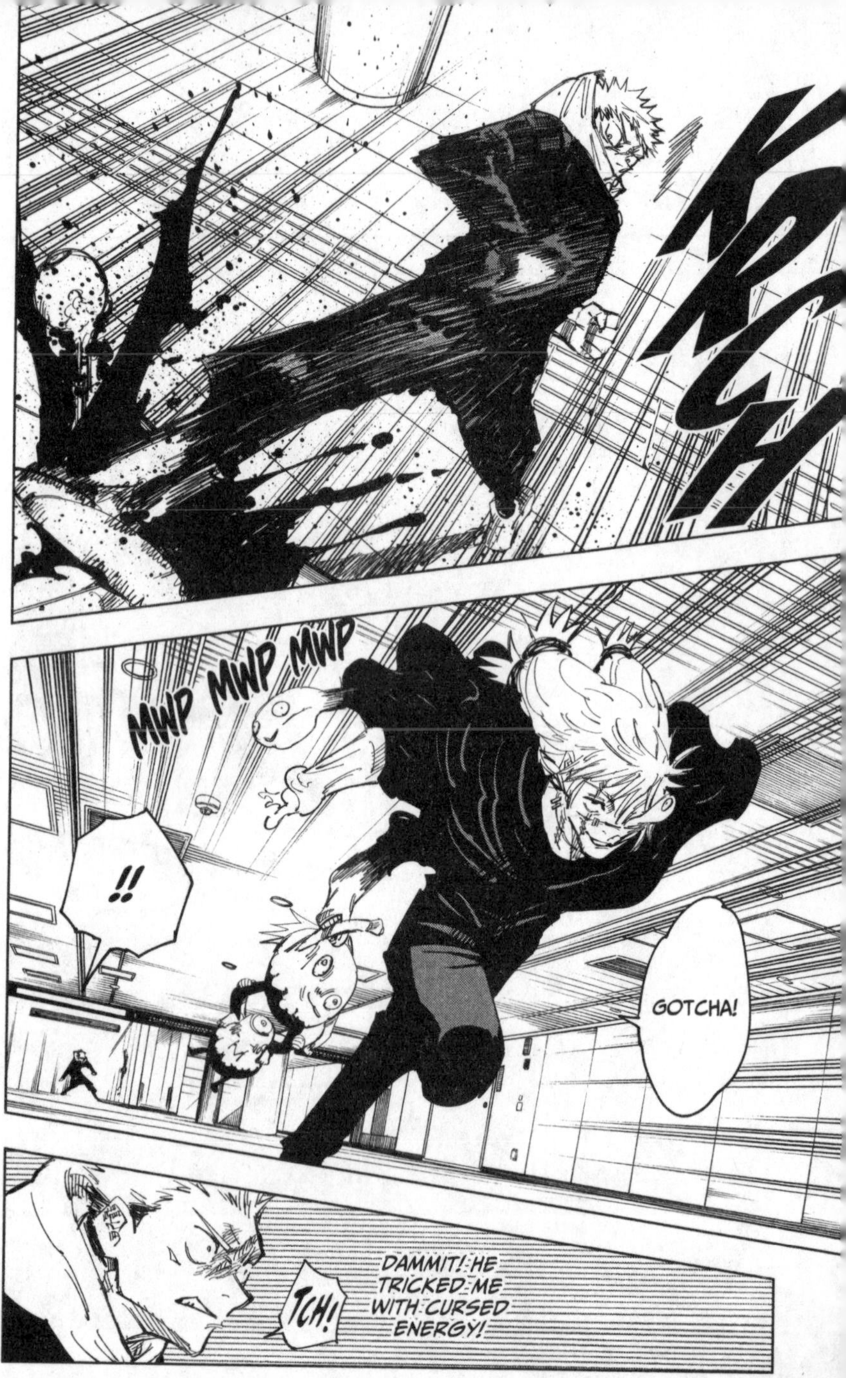
MWP MWP MWP
!!
GOTCHA!
DAMMIT! HE TRICKED ME WITH CURSED ENERGY!
TCH!

TP

TOMP

TWO MAHITOS?!

DUN DUN DUN DUN DUN

IS HE TRYING TO FUSE BACK TOGETHER TO HEAL?!

WAS THAT DOUBLE SOMEWHERE ELSE BEFORE?!

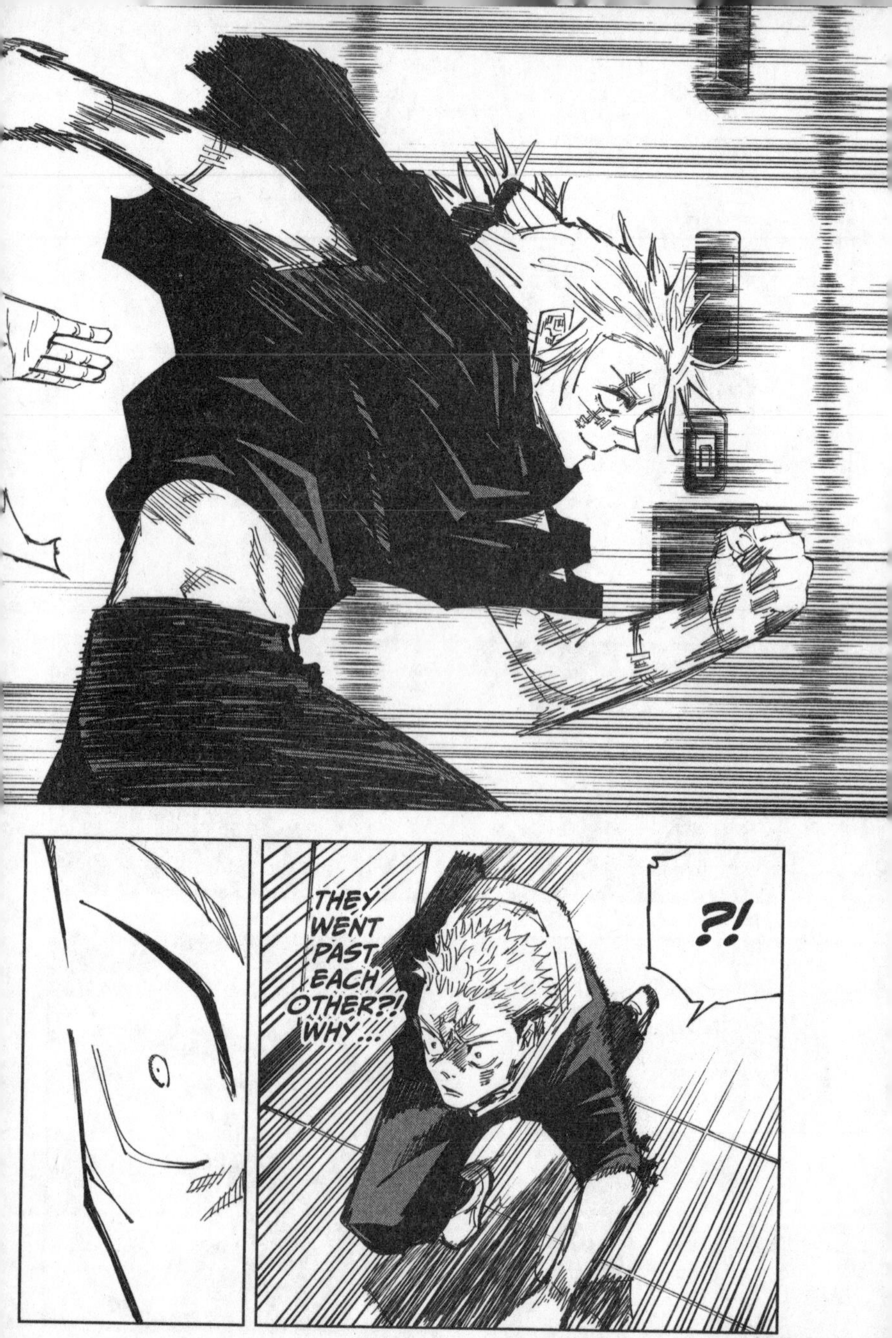
?!
THEY WENT PAST EACH OTHER?! WHY...

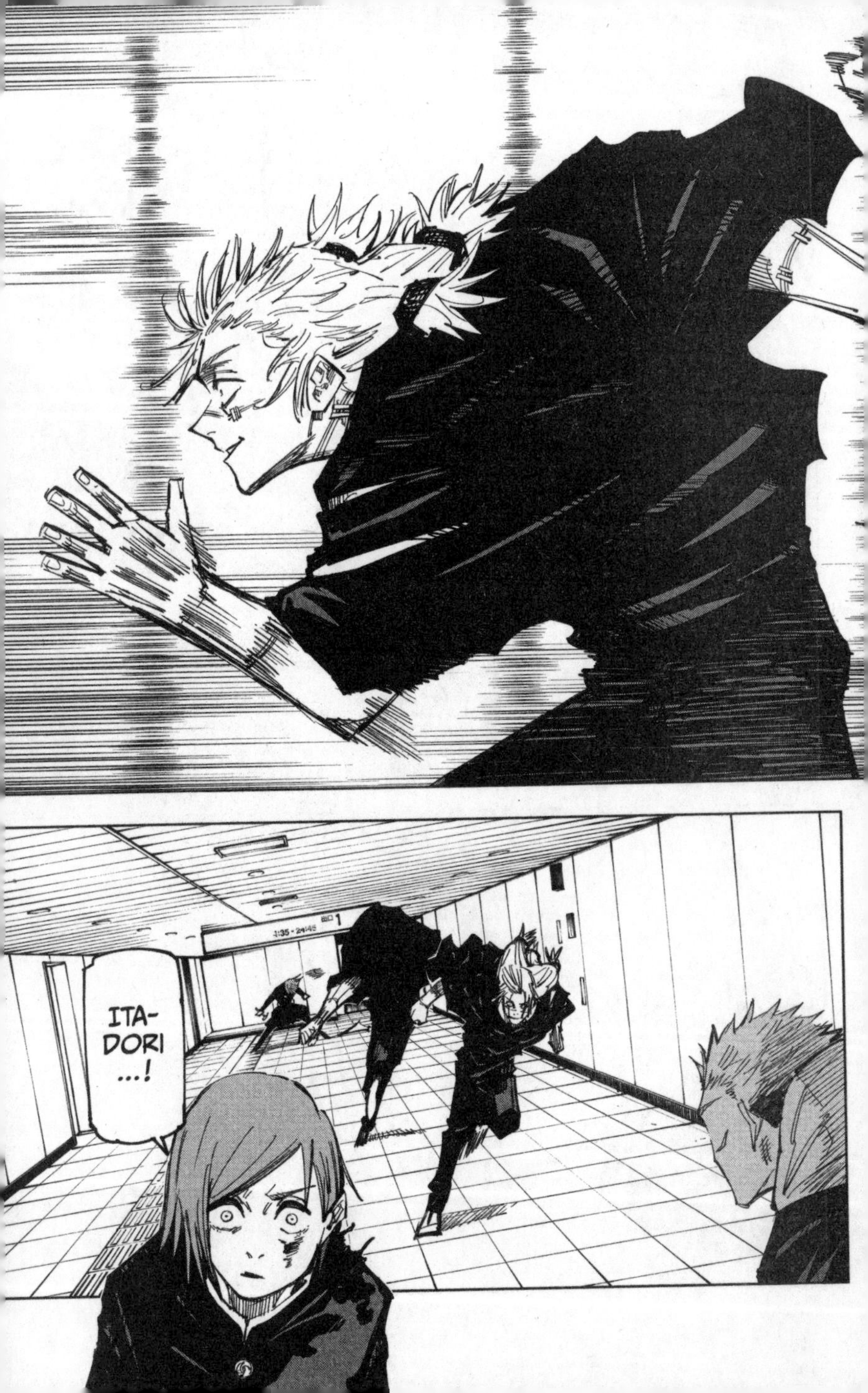
ITA-DORI …!

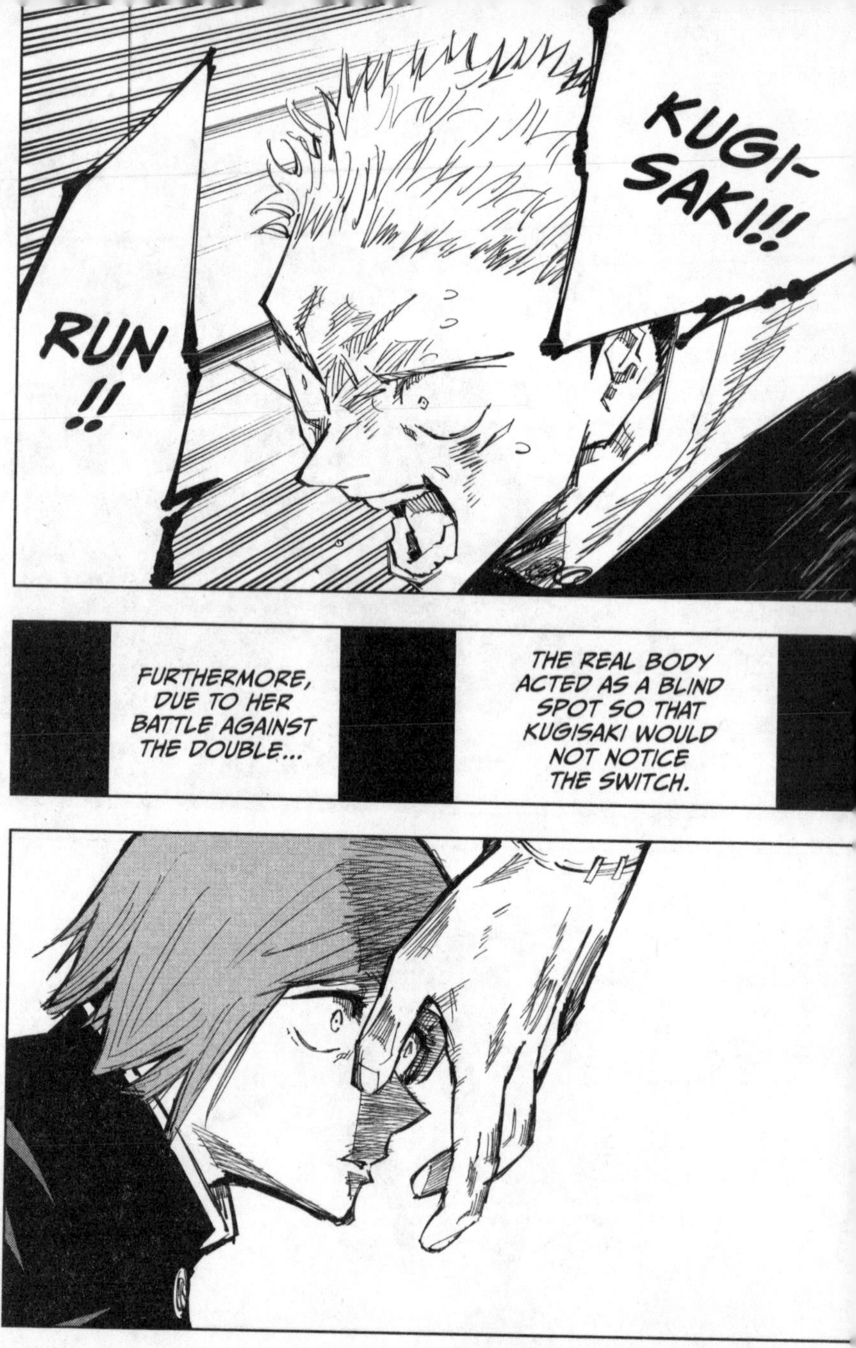
RUN !!
KUGI-SAKI!!!
FURTHERMORE, DUE TO HER BATTLE AGAINST THE DOUBLE...
THE REAL BODY ACTED AS A BLIND SPOT SO THAT KUGISAKI WOULD NOT NOTICE THE SWITCH.

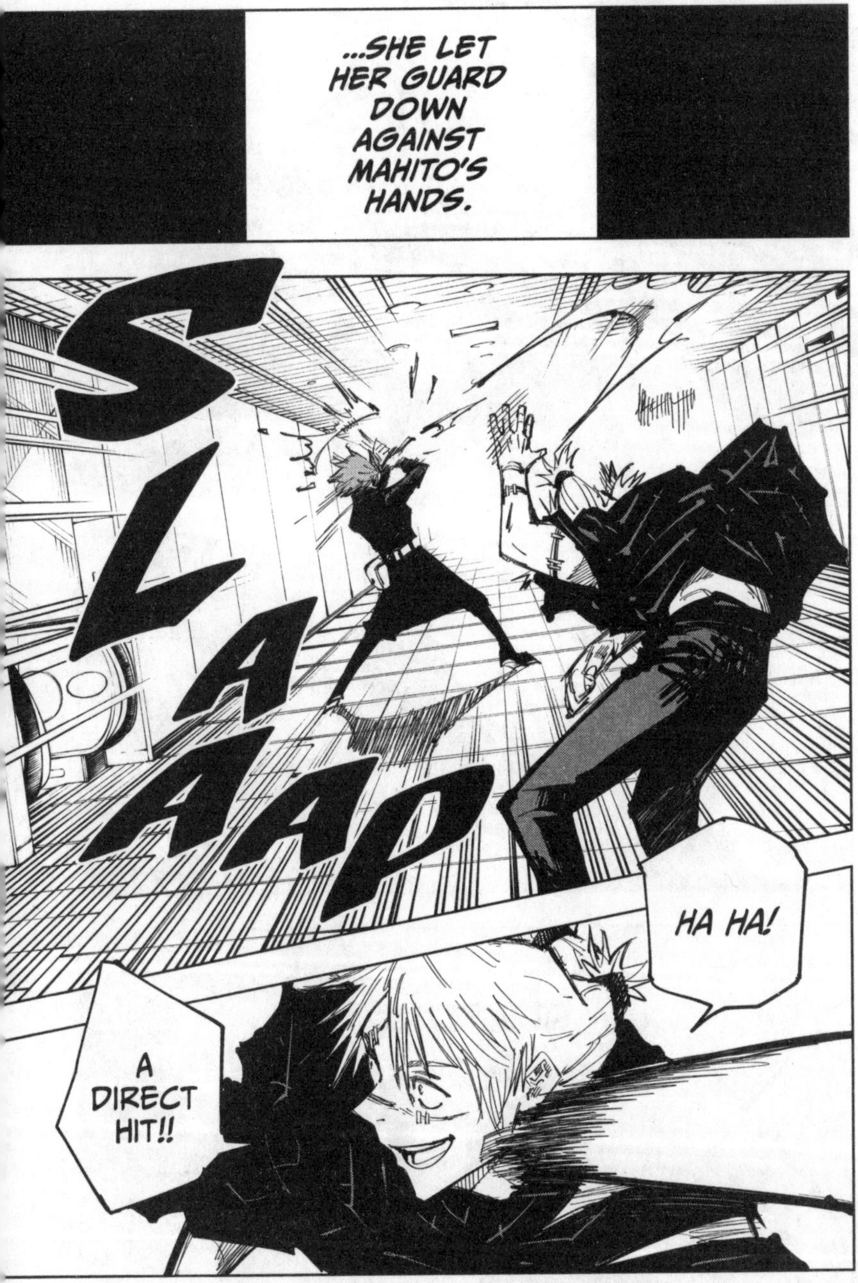
...SHE LET HER GUARD DOWN AGAINST MAHITO'S HANDS.
SLAAAP
HA HA!
A DIRECT HIT!!

GRIIIINCH

YOU'RE IN MY WAY!

NOW THEN...

KUGI-SAKI!!!

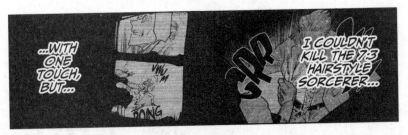

...WITH ONE TOUCH, BUT...

I COULDN'T KILL THE 7:3 HAIRSTYLE SORCERER...

...HOW ABOUT YOU?

2009...

TO BE CONTINUED

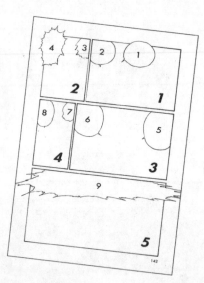

JUJUTSU KAISEN
reads from right to left, starting in the upper-right corner. Japanese is read from right to left, meaning that action, sound effects, and word-balloon order are completely reversed from English order.